Of Suffocated Hearts and Tortured Souls

Of Suffocated Hearts and Tortured Souls

Seeking Subjecthood through Madness in Francophone Women's Writing of Africa and the Caribbean

Valérie Orlando

LEXINGTON BOOKS
Lanham • Boulder • New York • Oxford

LEXINGTON BOOKS

Published in the United States of America
by Lexington Books
A Member of the Rowman & Littlefield Publishing Group
4720 Boston Way, Lanham, Maryland 20706

PO Box 317
Oxford
OX2 9RU, UK

British Library Cataloguing in Publication Information Available

Library of Congress Cataloging-in-Publication Data
Orlando, Valérie Key, 1963–
  Of suffocated hearts and tortured souls : seeking subjecthood through madness in
francophone women's writing of Africa and the Caribbean / Valérie Orlando.
    p. cm
Includes bibliographical references and index.
  ISBN 0-7391-0562-0 (cloth : alk. paper) – ISBN 0-7391-0563-9 (pbk. : alk. paper)
  1. African literature (French)—Women authors—History and criticism. 2.
Caribbean literature (French)—Women authors—History and criticism. 3. Mental
illness in literature. I. Title
PQ3980.5 .O74 2003
840.9'353—dc21   2002012542

Printed in the United States of America

∞™ The paper used in this publication meets the minimum requirements of
American National Standard for Information Sciences—Permanence of Paper
for Printed Library Materials, ANSI/NISO Z39.48-1992.

For Zahia and her sisters

Contents

Preface

Une pression dans la poitrine. Un vide trop grand ou un écrasement? Inintelligible cauchemar. Le souffle s'accélère. Les yeux s'écarquillent. Elle court, traverse le pont, grimpe sur le balcon avant, se jette dans la mer. . . . L'épuisement la calme peu à peu.

[A pressure in the chest. A void too big or a crushing? Unintelligible, nightmare. Breathing that accelerates. Eyes that stare wide-open. She runs, crosses the bridge, climbs up to the balcony before throwing herself in the sea. . . . Exhaustion, calm, little by little.]

—Malika Mokeddem, *N'Zid* (2001)

My sickness came on rather late—at fifteen—(you say I must tell you all) and I had much pain with it. When I was eighteen I had a hard winter, practicing at the piano, dancing, studying. In the spring I began to have pains in the back, and at times frightful headaches. . . . I at last had a regular attack of what the doctors called nervous prostration or spinal irritation. . . . I lay in bed for many months and suffered as women do—from backaches and headaches, and pains boring into the base of my brain.

—Anonymous author, "The Confessions of a Nervous Woman" (1896)

The words of this second epigraph written by an anonymous woman author at the end of the nineteenth century for the *Post-Graduate Journal*, an American academic journal devoted to studying women's "nervous depression," reverberate across the years and are echoed by heroines today in francophone women's writing of Africa and the Caribbean. Fear, oppression, isolation, and physical ailments are common subjects in francophone feminine works by authors from Algeria, Cameroon, Guadeloupe, Haiti, Martinique, Morocco,

Senegal, and Tunisia. These nervous depressions and physical sufferings are symptoms that manifest when women are pushed to the edge, marginalized in the outside realms of what is considered "normal" by their respective societies. They become foreign, alien beings who challenge the status quo. *Étrangeté*—foreignness—forces the heroines of the novels analyzed in this book to endure emotional instability and bodily deprivation.

My study draws on the psychoanalytical, philosophical, and literary domains of contemporary theory to formulate an innovative discursive framework in which to study the francophone author's thematic use of madness. The links that I draw between these three vast disciplines will, I hope, explain the historical as well as cultural reasons for madness as a prevalent theme in the francophone novel. The need to decipher the interplay between facets of the psyche and the self as well as identity and agency is necessary when dismantling what often seems like insurmountable hurdles encountered by women everyday within their respective societies. I believe that by formulating a cogent discourse between these facets, the realm of madness as explored by these women authors will become less opaque. Through exploration of the socioeconomical as well as the cultural and historical parameters that have shaped women writers' works, I hope to delve deeper into francophone women's views on living, working, motherhood, and liberation in our contemporary world.

Since the 1970s, Maghrebian and sub-Saharan African research in mental health has shed some light on the abject effects of traditionalism, postcolonial politics, and economic hardship that have influenced women's mental health. In her seminal study *Une Psychiatrie moderne pour le Maghreb* [*Modern Psychology for the Maghreb*] (1994), Moroccan psychiatrist and researcher Ghita El Khayat carefully traces the development of psychiatric treatment throughout the Arab world, beginning with the first insane asylum founded in 765 A.D. in Bagdad. Her goal is to objectively view madness as a clinician trained both in Western-European and Arabic medicine as well as to point out that, long before the West, the Arabs had developed guidelines for psychological study based on the first *Traité de la mélancolie* [*Treatise on Melancholy*] written by Isaac Ibn Omrane in the tenth century. More importantly, El Khayat studies the history of mental illness and its effects on family health with regard to the holistic well-being of Moroccan society.

Other groundbreaking works such as *Enthnopsychiatrie maghrébine: Représentations et thérapies traditionnelles de la maladie mentale au Maroc* [*Maghrebian Ethnopsychiatry: Traditional Representations of Mental Patients in Morocco*] (1993) by Ali Aouattah, *L'Homme Maghrébin dans la littérature psychiatrique* [*The Maghrebian Man in Psychiatric Literature*] (1994) by Robert Berthelier, and Nadia Mohia-Navet's *Les Thérapies traditionnelles dans la société kabyle* [*Traditional Therapies in Kabyle Society*] (1993) have contributed to research that studies mental illness as a component of traditional cultural beliefs as well as considers links that can be forged between indigenous traditional and modern western treatments used to cure dementia, schizophrenia, depression, and melancholy in North Africa. In sub-Saharan Africa, Daniel Schurmans's *Le Diable et le bon sens: Psychiatrie anthropologique de l'Afrique Noire à l'Europe* [*The Devil and Good Sense: From Anthropological Psychiatry of Black Africa to Europe*] (1994), Ibrâhîm Alfâ Sow's *Les Structures anthropologiques de la folie en Afrique Noire* [*Anthropological Structures of Madness in Black Africa*] (1980), as well as Bougoul Badji's *La Folie en Afrique: Une rivalité pathologique* [*Madness in Africa: A Pathological Rivalry*] (1993) (which studies cases of madness particularly in Senegal) have provided new frameworks in which to conceptualize madness in terms of modernization and its effects on African peoples. As Sow contends, the rejection of the mentally ill by African communities has become "more common and more emphatic as the environment becomes more urbanized." The recent plethora of theoretical works on mental illness in the African diaspora in the last fifteen years demonstrates that the clash between modern and traditional spheres and the ensuing consequences are increasingly felt in traditional societies. The mental stability of men and women as rendered in literature is following suit, becoming a prevalent theme in contemporary African literary discourse.[1]

The subject of women's madness in the latter part of the twentieth century has been a popular theme of choice in literary, clinical, and scientific studies. Phyllis Chesler's *Women and Madness* (1972), Sandra Gilbert and Susan Gubar's *The Madwoman in the Attic* (1979), Shoshana Felman's *Writing and Madness* (1985), Jill Astbury's *Crazy for You: The Making of Women's Madness* (1996), and Rebecca Shannonhouse's *Out of Her Mind: Women Writing on Madness* (2000) are but a few of the critical studies over the course of almost thirty years that weave a path from the clinical to the literary realms of (primarily white-anglophone) women's expression on, and about, mental health in Western European and American societies.

As I come to my own conclusions about madness depicted in African and Caribbean francophone women's novels, I draw upon not only African studies but also European studies done by psychoanalytical theorists such as Sigmund Freud and Jacques Lacan to form my hypotheses. Philosophical works by Gilles Deleuze, Félix Guattari, and Michel Foucault also are prominent reference points in this book. While perhaps one could find fault with my reliance on the masculine purveyance of Western European thought to form my arguments, I also seek to point out the shortcomings of the hypotheses of these *grands hommes et philosophes* who so diligently sought to shape ideals about women's identity and sexuality in the past century. White European and American anglophone women have learned a great deal from the various philosophical-psychoanalytical dogmas these men contrived for feminine being and identity within Western society. Indeed, many contemporary female scholars and philosophers (Elizabeth Grosz, Rosi Braidotti, Juliette Flower Maccannell) have drawn on these earlier male discourses to formulate new feminist platforms, dismantling the masculine fetters that psycho-analytic thought forged to bind women. Many of these male tomes currently serve as texts against which women write and form their own rules to analyze their psyche and identity. These feminist discourses are new *becomings* that, as philosopher Juliette Flower Maccannell suggests, situate a *free* female subject who develops a feminine ethic and "a woman's way" counter to the psycho-sociological and historic boundaries men have construed for women.[2] This feminine ethic is based on a new set of standards with which women carve out original modes of identity and discourse that pertain to them. Feminine essence is the product of a desire that is spurred on by the need to develop free agency—authority—in a productive *outside* world. According to women, this world is liberated from traditional mores, debilitating stereotypes, and oppressive masculine prerogatives.

Liberation and the discovery of their own feminine essence (power), as Mariama Bâ's heroine Mireille of *Un chant écarlate* discovers, mean women no longer must live by the phallocentric rules men have contrived for them. However, as this heroine eventually realizes, living outside, on the marginal fringes, can also present women with the flip side of liberty—madness. Mireille, a white, French woman abandoned by her Senegalese husband for a Senegalese woman and barred by his traditional society from ever totally being accepted, wonders "[à] quel moment la férocité de son tourment fit-elle basculer sa raison?" [(at) what moment did the ferociousness of her torment push her to lose her sanity?].[3]

My study explores the conjuncture of otherness, exile, and marginalization and how these states of being contribute to madness. Additionally, I seek to explore how madness is rendered thematically in the feminine francophone works of African and Caribbean novelists. The relationship these women authors have to their respective countries, tribes, cultures, and histories (colonial and postcolonial) is multifaceted. I have also found that the representation of madness in the novels of francophone African and Caribbean women is multilayered with regard to severity. Some heroines succumb to madness, while others survive and learn to live within the parameters of marginalization and exile. Others still are able to construct *another* place where they reconcile their marginalization and turn it into a productive space of agency.

Although I have chosen to study madness as a reoccurring theme in the francophone novel, I by no means wish to negatively stereotype African and Caribbean women's mental health. Madness has been (and continues to be) a dominant theme in Western, white Anglo-European women's discourse as well. Terminology plays an important role in this discourse, as white Anglo-European feminists, authors, and philosophers have discovered over the years. For women of the Afro-Caribbean diaspora, seeking to find new manners in which to articulate their feminine condition, terminology also becomes a central topic of immense importance. Some of the most problematic words for women writing from the Afro-Caribbean diaspora are the terms *West* and *Western*. It must be emphasized that, in this book, when I use the term *West*, I am using it to denote Western-European and Anglo-American, white spheres. Like the authors who figure prominently in my work, I am aware that contentious issues associated with these terms abound for non-whites living in Europe and America and must be addressed. Conflicts arise, for instance, when contemplating what belonging to the *West* means, certainly for authors from the Caribbean. The term is often used to define Western Europe and America (United States) as compared to the *East* (Near or Far, connoting Arab or Asian peoples), and encourages (particularly within the media) stereotyping differences between "us" and "them." Stereotypes conceived in the West to define these "other" places occur on many levels: religious (Muslim), skin tone (black or brown), and "foreign" traditions and practices. Further, geographically speaking, the idea of "West" or "Western" is contentious for those living in the "West Indies" who are considered part of the West regionally, yet, do not share Anglo-European values and traditions. Guadeloupe and Martinique are exceptional examples when discussing geographical allegiances to the idea of "west" because they are considered part of France. For the authors writing from these islands, reaping the benefits of being from the "West" is all but elusive as Lacrosil and Warner-Vieyra demonstrate through their heroines, Cajou and Juletane. Women's discourse from the Afro-Caribbean diaspora continues to be shaped and framed by the phallocentric Anglo-European (white) terms that have been construed for it. In light of these issues, it is time to rethink the validity of constructs such as *West*, and *East*, *developing world* and *first world* when discussing literature written in our postcolonial era.

Throughout this work I often refer to "postcolonial" structures, theory, and practice. I must admit that my use of the term *postcolonial*, like *West* and *Western*, is primarily due to lack of a better word. The term *postcolonial* has been a topic of wide debate in literary circles in recent years. Postcolonial scholars tend to agree that literature written in the first few years of the postcolonial era (considered by most to be the post-1960s, although other literary pundits have stated that "the postcolonial" encompasses literature written after World War II) is different from the themes of contemporary authors writing from the former colonial diaspora. Where militant nationalism shaped early works by Frantz Fanon and Albert Memmi, contemporary themes have encompassed more sociocultural subjects important to authors in formerly colonized countries. For some literary theorists, the question of whether or not we are "in" a postcolonial era has come to the forefront of discussion. Ella Shohat and Robert Stam stress in their pivotal work *Unthinking Eurocentrism* that "postcolonial theory has failed to address the politics of location of the term 'postcolonial' itself." It has also generated ambiguity because "post" usually connotes some sort of closure of a historical epoch, "a movement beyond obsolete discourses."[4] This fact is evident, for example, in the works of Northern Irish authors, who proclaim they have not enjoyed a postcolonial environment, and as mentioned earlier, writers from the French islands of Guadeloupe and Martinique, who maintain that, although embracing the fruits of movements such as Négritude, there is nothing postcolonial about the milieu from which they write. The "coloniality" for these groups is still a determining factor for how they are perceived and how they view their own existence in the world community. The globalized use of the term *postcolonial* has grouped together emerging anglophone and francophone literatures of African countries as well as those of Asia, Australia, Bangladesh, India, the South Pacific, Malta, Pakistan, and Canada. The only commonality between these countries' literatures is that they "emerged in their present form out of the experience of colonization and asserted themselves by foregrounding the tension with the imperial power."[5] Such effacement of "spatiotemporal lines" as well as the individuality of each country's colonial and after-colonial experience "blurs the assignment of perspectives."[6] As Shohat and Stam explain, the postcolonial experience is being shared by numerous subjects all from different angles of their encounters with colonialism, generating ambiguity in the meaning of the term:

> Given that the colonial experience is shared, albeit asymmetrically, by (ex-) colonizer and (ex-)colonized, does the "post" indicate the perspective of the ex-colonized (Algerian, for example), the ex-colonizer (in this case French), the ex-colonial settler (*pieds noir*), or the displaced immigrant in the métropole (Algerian in France)? Since most of the world is now living in the aftermath of colonialism, the "post" neutralizes salient differences between France and Algeria, Britain and Iraq, the US and Brazil.[7]

The term *postcolonial* is particularly problematic for women who saw few of the rights they championed during the decolonizing, independent movements of the 1960s bear fruit once independence was achieved. Subsequent postcolonial governments in Algeria, Senegal, and Cameroon shuffled women to the sidelines and told them to wait their turn in the face of the immediacy of building new, independent nations.

Current themes in francophone literature of Africa and the Caribbean by women espouse a plethora of issues that are crucial in the development of women's identity and ever changing social roles. Some of these issues are postcolonial in nature, while others reflect the socioeconomic conflicts of our contemporary times. Certainly, as women carve out a new *feminine ethic* for themselves, new terms must also be developed to explain what and whom they are about. For the sake of situating the literature analyzed in this critical study, I will continue to use the term *postcolonial* since it is familiar to those who draw on this work as a resource in the field. Yet as we consider the novels of francophone women, let us keep forever in the back of our minds the certainty that new sites of history are being built, and with them, more original terminology will, most assuredly, follow suit.

NOTES

1. Ibrâbîm Sow, *Anthropological Structures of Madness in Black Africa* (New York: International Universities Press, 1980), 30.

2. Juliette Flower Maccannell, *The Hysteric's Guide to the Future Female Subject* (Minneapolis: University of Minnesota Press, 2000), xv.

3. Mariama Bâ, *Un Chant écarlate* (Dakar: Les nouvelles éditions africaines, 1981), 243.

4. Ella Shohat and Robert Stam, *Unthinking Eurocentrism: Multiculturalism and the Media* (New York: Routledge: 1994), 38.

5. Bill Ashcroft, Gareth Griffiths, and Helen Tiffin, *The Empire Writes Back: Theory and Practice in Post-Colonial Literatures* (New York: Routledge, 1989), 2. Also see my book, *Nomadic Voices of Exile: Feminine Identity in Francophone Literature of the Maghreb* (Athens: Ohio University Press, 1999) for further discussion of the pitfalls of the term *postcolonial* in relation to francophone literature.

6. Shohat and Stam, *Unthinking*, 39.

7. Shohat and Stam, *Unthinking*, 39.

Acknowledgments

There are many people who contributed to my sanity and well-being as I wrote about a very tumultuous world filled with many tortured women. In particular, I would like to thank my friends and colleagues in the Modern and Classical Languages and Literatures Department as well as from other disciplines at Illinois Wesleyan University. Marina Balina who has been a mentor, friend, and colleague; Joy Calico who has listened to my long diatribes about academic life; and Rebecca Gearhart who has offered so much anthropological insight on my very literary interpretations of African cultures, thank you all for your support of my work and research. Zahia Drici friend, colleague, and confidant—thanks so much for your continued interest in my long, unending theories on Algerian women and politics. Thanks to my colleague Scott Sheridan who has provided numerous words of encouragement; and to Anne Magnan Park who has edited my work written in French. Special thanks to Robyn and Mack Brothers who lent me their house in Villepreux, France, in the summer of 2001, allowing me to draft two chapters in their peaceful French garden. Warmest thanks to my aunt Marie Girmens and my cousin Isabelle Girmens who invited me to the Pyrénées mountains to enjoy the quiet of their village, write, and reflect on my work in the summer of 2002.

I am particularly grateful to Tracy Denean Sharpley-Whiting who has generously offered helpful comments and suggestions on the manuscript and, over the years, has provided her adamant support as a scholar and a friend of my work. Special thanks to my colleague Robert Bray who graciously took time out of his summer vacation to read, edit, and offer his valuable advice on the final version of the manuscript.

In addition, special recognition should go to Illinois Wesleyan University's Mellon Center for the financial support it provided during the last three years for my research and travel to Morocco, Tunisia, and Madagascar. Special thanks to the committee members of Illinois Wesleyan University's Artistic and Scholarly Grant program which awarded me with two grants in the Spring of 2000 and 2002 to conduct research at the Archives d'Outre-mer in Aix, France.

Of equal importance is my gratitude to the committee members of the Illinois Wesleyan Faculty Development Committee who awarded me with a Junior Faculty Leave in the Spring of 2002 during which I was able to finish the manuscript and send it off to my editor in a timely fashion.

Thanks to my editor Serena Krombach at Lexington Books who has been so supportive and helpful, believing in the completion of the book before it was even halfway done.

A warm-hearted thanks to Haitian artist Joseph Cantave who provided the photo of one of his beautiful paintings, *Rainbow Woman*, to grace the cover of this book, visually granting us insight into a woman's colorful soul.

To my family: my mom, Carolyn; my dad, Andrew; my mother-in-law, Thérèse; Ann; Brandon; and Sonja thanks for your love and support; and last, but not least, I owe so much to my husband, Philippe, who has edited my French translations, kept me sane when I thought I wasn't, and put life into perspective for me.

The author and publisher are grateful for permission to reproduce the following copyrighted material:

A version of my article *"Writing New H(er)stories for Francophone Women of Africa and the Caribbean,"* in *World Literature Today* 75, no. 1 (winter 2001): 40–50, reproduced with the kind permission of the editors of *World Literature Today.*

A version of my study of Hajer Djilani's work which first appeared under the title: "Deterritorializing New Roles for Women in Hajer Djilani's *Et pourtant le ciel était bleu . . ."* in my book *Nomadic Voices of Exile: Feminine Identity in Francophone Literature of the Maghreb* (Athens: Ohio University Press, 1999) reproduced with the kind permission of the editors at Ohio University Press.

The author wishes to thank Joseph Cantave for granting permission to reprint his beautiful work *Rainbow Woman* on the cover.

Introduction

Writing New H(er)stories for Francophone Women of Africa and the Caribbean

> Self-sacrifice—as the major ethic of the female culture—has been one of the most effective psychological blocks to women's open rebellion and demand for self-determination. It has also been a major tool of male manipulation of females.
>
> —Phyllis Chesler, *Women and Madness* (1972)

> At an initial stage, there was a pure and simple adoption of the well-known formula, "Let's win over the women and the rest will follow."
>
> —Frantz Fanon, *A Dying Colonialism* (1959)

> [N]ationalism and feminism have never mixed very well. Women were used in national liberation struggles—in Algeria, Iran, Palestine, to name only a few—only to be sent back to their kitchens after "independence" had been gained.
>
> —Evelyn Accad, *Sexuality and War* (1990)

> Every woman is engaged in a process of adaptation to a complex situation where new and old attitudes towards life and self are interrelated.
>
> —Marnia Lazreg, *Algerian Women in Question* (1994)

At the beginning of a new millennium, the work of contemporary francophone women authors is situated at the crossroads of both western and Afro-Caribbean history and philosophy. On the historical level, women's writing in Africa and the Caribbean was rarely referenced for the first half of the past century. Women have usually had their histories written for them

1

by men, interjecting rarely to alter masculine depictions. Both colonial and, even to some extent, postcolonial historical perspectives have left women with little voice and presence on the page.[1] Philosophically, literary movements such as Négritude,[2] while promoting the revitalization (and, as some would say, the reinvention) of African thought, have left women out of the literary loop, circumscribing their selfhood within the larger—according to V. Y. Mudimbé—African *gnosis*.[3] How do African and Caribbean women writing in French, then, situate themselves with respect to these historical-philosophical junctures? Most notably by creating their own unique feminine space wherein they foster new trajectories toward new feminine *becomings*. Female subjecthood as defined by current African and Caribbean francophone women authors is formed not only from new ideals of the mind but also from the conceptualization of an original body politics; a corporeal reality that promotes a sexually differentiated structure of the speaking subject. Such a new speaking subject is no longer understood as an ahistorical object, but rather is viewed as a body linked to, and interwoven with, a plurality of systems: political, cultural, economic, and historical. The new feminine subject is a site of contestation where sociocultural and political struggles play themselves out, are heard by all, refashioned and retransmitted on a woman's own terms. As Moroccan sociologist Fatima Mernissi contends, "It is [with] access to public space, employment, and education that women's lives have undergone the most fundamental changes. Space, employment and education seem to be the areas where the struggles which agitate society (especially the class struggle) show up in the lives of women with the greatest clarity."[4] Postcolonial theorist Gayatri Spivak also explains that the public sphere is characterized by all that represents culture and politics, as well as the social, professional, economic, and intellectual areas of daily life. Women who step into the public sphere as agents planning their destinies are essentially stepping into an environment of marginality and of exile where their numbers are few.[5] Engaging this marginalized environment allows women to historically construct new knowledge of women's selfhood as defined by women. "History of the self . . . is the self we find in ourselves," Allen Thiher explains, and this fact is crucial to building a genealogy of knowledge about the self and one's identity: "If the self exists as articulated by various language games that have unfolded historically, then the self exists as a historical project within which we can expect to find both continuities and ruptures, circularities and recurrences, in terms of its historical development."[6]

Women authors of francophone Africa and the Caribbean define a separate space in which history and philosophy become something *other* for women. This space may be thought of as a *vel*, a place where the overlap of male history and philosophy takes place, deferring to a *woman's way*.[7] The *vel* is psychoanalyst Jacques Lacan's *Möbius strip* where philosophy and history twist around to form a third, uncharted space. Philosopher and feminist Elizabeth Grosz explains the image of the *Möbius strip* as "the torsion or pivot around which the subject is generated. The [torsion causes] a kind of interface of the inside and the outside, the pivotal point at which inside will become separated from outside and active will be converted into passive."[8] Within this pivotal point women find their voice and engage new processes of selfhood. The outside twists to meet the inside forming a fold which Deleuze and Guattari suggest is a place of speech and "expressive matter, with different scales, speeds and different vectors." Speech is "expression, a *Gestaltung"* where the inside and the outside "[move] between matter and soul."[9] Writing within the interface of this fold is both liberating and terrifying because it is uncharted and unknown. It is a place where women define their feminine ethic, where the self is in process and in metamorphosis. This self can be violent, hysterical, and even self-destructive, as evidenced in novels such as Myriam Warner-Vieyra's *Juletane*.[10] Or, as Aminata Sow Fall's *Douceurs du bercail*[11] demonstrates, the feminine self may be a seeker of tranquility, peace, paradise, and fulfillment through human contact and the writing of a new, feminine history.

As francophone women writers write *in* this new space, their works engage a variety of issues, the most important of which is feminine emancipation, both in legal and social spheres. At the present time, women authors of the Maghreb, francophone sub-Saharan Africa, and the Caribbean are undertaking feminine research that exposes how religious values, law, society, and culture all influence women's lives. Women's emancipation requires first and foremost the breaking away from (and of) traditional phallocratic/centric roles that have hemmed them in the confines of traditional sociocultural spaces. In contemporary francophone literature, women take flight and step out of sociocultural boundaries to explore identity. These women authors are *deterritorializing* to build new social projects where the historical, the cultural, and the economic all come into play. As Gilles Deleuze and Félix Guattari state, deterritorialization is a "signifying rupture" that always assures the subject a break with the past: past life histories, past destinies, and past traditions.[12] Such a rupture promotes the re-creation of the subject, forcing her to adopt to new frontiers and fields of reference. Within the *vel*—this tantalizing new public space of agency—a feminine speech is fashioned.

"Access to a human self and to its world is largely a matter of language."[13] Finding the words to explore the self has been crucial for women. In order to study the environments in which women live, the traumas and conflicts that their societies cause for them, as well as the dementia to which they often succumb, a purely feminine language—*une écriture féminine*, to use Hélène Cixous's concept—must be developed and nurtured. Yet, access to the pen and to the language that ensues from it has been problematic for francophone African and Caribbean women. Irène Assiba d'Almeida aptly states in her book *Francophone African Women Writers: Destroying the Emptiness of Silence* that "the dynamics of speech and silence are far from being simple and clear-cut [in francophone Africa]."[14] Speech (or lack thereof) has been a central theme used by western literary critics to define African and Caribbean feminine writing within a postcolonial context. For authors such as Assia Djebar and Aminata Sow Fall, the importance of women's voices used to rectify history and establish a place in it has been the core theme of their work. As we study the literary production of women authors from the regions discussed here, it becomes apparent that their speech takes many forms. In sub-Saharan francophone Africa, not only colonialism but also traditional mores shaped women's roles within their tribes. Cultural constraints determined how women literarily contributed to their respective societies. In Senegal and Cameroon, women were (and continue to be) the keepers and transmitters of oral traditions. As *griottes*, women storytellers passed down countless generations of oral lore.

Although modern literature written in French by African men took root in Africa in the 1930s, francophone women from the three regions discussed in this study did not begin to write at the same time. Women in the Maghreb, particularly Algeria, began writing in the 1940s, while colonial occupation was still in force over the region.[15] The most notable works among these early women authors are Berber Marie-Louise Taos Amrouche's autobiography *Jacinthe noire* (1947) and Djamila Debèche's *Leïla, une fille algérienne* (1947) and *Aziza* (1955). Assia Djebar's first novel, *La Soif* (1957) and her second novel, *Les Impatients* (1958), are superb, though both were misunderstood by Algerian critics at the time.[16]

In Morocco, women's writing has not been as prevalent as in Algeria. Elissa Chimenti wrote *Au coeur du harem* in 1958, however, it was not until the 1970s that another renowned literary contribution by a woman was noted in Moroccan francophone literary circles. Saïda Menebhi's *Poèmes, lettres et écrits de prison*, published in 1978, offers commentary on the political repression of postcolonial, Moroccan society. Fatima Mernissi has noted that women's illiteracy rates in Morocco have significantly hindered their contributions to literature, certainly in French. However, works such as Fatima Alaoui's *L'Arbre sans racines ou je ne suis que journaliste* (1982) and poet Fatema Chahid Abaroudi's *Imago* (1983) have achieved notoriety.[17]

Tunisian women's writing, like that of men, has been most prolific in the area of poetry. Yet, it is well noted that Sophie el Goulli's 1966 study entitled *La Tunisie dans la littérature occidentale* provided one of the first comparative studies of Maghrebian and Western literature. Hajer Djilani, author of *Et pourtant le ciel était bleu . . .* (1994) and of *Hamza* (1996), is one of the most recent Tunisian novelists writing in French and significantly contributing to contemporary francophone literature.[18]

It was not until the 1970s that women in sub-Saharan Africa (particularly from Senegal and Cameroon) began writing, much later than their North African colleagues. As African scholars point out, although women from this region have been speaking for centuries, their speech has been contained within tribal and/or family boundaries. Public oral milieus destined for women were usually viewed as marginalized segments of society. Here *griottes* reigned but often were thought to be possessed by demons.[19] In the 1970s women authors from sub-Saharan Africa did begin to take up the pen. *Femme d'Afrique: La Vie d'Aoua Kéita racontée par elle-même* offered one of the first autobiographies by an African woman.[20] In 1976 Aminata Sow Fall helped break the gender barrier in Senegal by publishing the first major novel in French written by a Senegalese woman.[21] Her novel *Le Revenant* was the first representation of the condition of women in Senegal.[22] Sow Fall has continued to write for over two decades, contributing to the Senegalese canon with works such as *L'Ex-père de la nation* (1987). Her novel *Douceurs du bercail* (1998) explores the situation of African women with respect to a variety of sociocultural issues, the most important of which are the economic difficulties faced by Senegalese people (particularly women), immigration, and racism.[23]

Cameroon author, poet, and playwright Werewere Liking has contributed *On ne raisonne pas le venin* (1977), *Du Rituel à la scène chez les Bassa du Cameroun* (1979), *Une Vision de Kaydara* (1984) and *Orphée-Dafric* (1982). Her most well-known novel, *Elle sera de jaspe et de corail* (1984), promotes her most radical views on the re-creation of speech, particularly for and by women. Calixthe Beyala, who divides her time between Cameroon and France, has added her literary voice to women's writing of the African diaspora with works such as *C'est le soleil qui m'a brûlée* (1987), *Le Petit Prince de Belleville* (1992), and *Mama a un amant* (1993).[24]

In the Caribbean, Martinican Suzanne Césaire and Paulette, Jane, and Andrée Nardal wrote for revues and journals of the 1930s and 1940s published by the poets of the Négritude movement. Recognition of Martinican Mayotte Capécia's controversial novel *Je suis martiniquaise* (1941) (with which Frantz Fanon takes issue in his 1952 work *Black Skin, White Masks*) should also be considered as an important cornerstone for women's writing from the Antilles. Women's literary voice in the Antilles became significantly developed in the 1950s and 1960s with works by authors such as Haitian Marie Chauvet (*Fille d'Haïti,* 1954; *Amour, colère, et folie,* 1968), and Guadeloupian Michèle Lacrosil's *Sapotille et le Serin d'argil* (1960) and *Cajou* (1961). Their groundbreaking work led the way for later authors such as Guadeloupian Maryse Condé's *Ségou* (1984), *Hérémakhonon* (1976), *Une Saison à Rihata* (1981), *Moi Tituba, sorcière . . . Noire de Salem* (1986), *La Vie scélérate* (1987), *Traversée de la mangrove* (1989), *Les Derniers rois mages* (1992), and *La Colonie du nouveau monde* (1993) as well as Simone Schwarz-Bart's

Un Plat de porc aux bananes vertes (1967) and *Pluie et vent sur Telumée Miracle* (1972). This second generation of feminine writing from the Antilles particularly draws attention to the feminine condition in terms of tradition, modernity, and conflicts of class in the Caribbean.[25]

Women from Africa and the Caribbean have traversed the Négritude movement (often writing against it) and scrutinized literary ideologies such as *Antillanité* and *Créolité* in order to express at last an original feminism in their works. Yet, it is still clear that these authors are searching to find new paths to original modes of discourse that will be applicable for expressing their needs and desires in the twenty-first century. These female authors do agree that when a woman steps outside the confinement of village and home to speak in her own words she becomes automatically politically engaged and compelled to become an active agent for herself and other women within her society.

Women as active agents, challenging the prerogatives of male public space, place themselves on equal footing with men. Certainly women's writing in Algeria in the postcolonial years has been nothing but a political act of defiance. The development of women's associations within the emergence of numerous political parties after Algerian independence in 1962 led women to write. Writing seemed to be the only way to "understand the relationship between gender and nationalism" and the about-face the Front de la Libération Nationale party perfected with regard to women's rights once its promoters were in power.[26]

From feminine authors, researchers, and academics of immense notoriety, such as Algerian Assia Djebar and Moroccan Fatima Mernissi, to those recently entering the arena of the contemporary francophone literary field, women of Algeria, Cameroon, Morocco, Guadeloupe, Haiti, Martinique, Senegal, and Tunisia are striving to gain an active presence in society and culture in order to shape new roles for women in politics, literature, and history. Francophone authors from the Maghreb and sub-Saharan Africa, such as Malika Mokeddem and Aminata Sow Fall, cultivate a deterritorialized space—a milieu detached from sociocultural purviews—that does two things: first, it allows women to break the traditional feminine interior area of ultra-traditional circles; and second, it fosters the building of a new platform of agency in public *exterior* areas (such as those of politics, law, and cultural activism, therefore recontextualizing previous representations of women) in African literature.

In Malika Mokeddem's *L'Interdite*[27] the heroine realizes that it is only after confronting, and subsequently persevering over, violent political conflicts, exile, feelings of solitude, and marginalization that she is able to reach a place of true self-knowledge. Unfortunately neither author nor heroine is able to right any of the political, social, cultural, or economic wrongs of her country single-handedly. The freedom granted to Sultana, lead protagonist of *L'Interdite*, does not come without a price to pay. Deterritorialization from her family and tribe as well as a life of nomadism condemns her to a destiny of wandering and of *étrangeté*—foreignness. This foreignness often throws feminine characters into a new reality that is marginalized, exiled, and full of despair. Julia Kristeva underscores the fact that "liberty" as well as "solitude" fashion a double-edged sword that comes from writing in the margins of established norms.[28] *Étrangeté* is a means of resistance, a price that has been paid for crossing over boundaries to foster communication in a public space of active agency. "In crossing a border the *étranger*," Kristeva notes, "has changed [her] discomforts into a base of resistance, a citadel of life. . . . Without a home, [she] disseminates . . . : multiplying masks and false-selves."[29] The world of *étrangeté* generates feelings of duality, of "being split apart," as Malika Mokeddem's heroine, Sultana, acknowledges at the end of her story.[30] It is often in a shattered world that the francophone author is able to find the secrets to her selfhood. In order to confront these feelings of multiplicity and duality so often expressed by feminine authors, Malika Mokeddem places her female characters in spaces of negotiation. These spaces exist outside the normal boundaries within which they are expected (by family, fathers, husbands, culture, and society) to operate.[31] In *L'Interdite* Mokeddem's principal protagonist, Sultana, enters a space of agency that leads her not only to a unique type of freedom, but also to solitude and self-doubt.

HYSTERICALLY SPEAKING

In his *Second Discourse* (1755) Philippe Pinel, Europe's first psychiatrist repeatedly referred to madness as a product of modernized civilization. He came to this conclusion as he documented the dementia and mental illness of great thinkers such as Jean Jacques Rousseau. Allen Thiher points out that Rouseau himself professed that "disease is increased by progress, hence by history."[32] From the mid-1700s (considered the debut of the modern period) forward, the schism that had been described by Descartes and perceived by Rousseau between psyche and self (mind and body) led to more frequent study of these two spheres as separate entities. Exploration of the psyche became a means by which the author could delve further into the unreachable and, I might add, unexplainable realms of the self. In France as the age of the *Lumières* waned, literature became a focal point through which to assess the world of the psyche and, thus, madness:

> Literary texts propose[d] that within the mad there is a principle, a self, or a form of consciousness, that can listen to its own madness . . . there is within the mad an inner distance between madness and some vital center that allows the mad to speak reflexively about their madness.[33]

Representation of madness in the francophone feminine novel has been shaped historically, certainly by the evident factor of colonialism and, later, by revolution. Psychiatrist Frantz Fanon, born in Martinique and schooled in France, discussed the psychological effects of colonialism and colonial repression by the French in Algeria in his seminal work *Les Damnés de la terre* (*The Wretched of the Earth*).[34] Although he did not directly address the influence of colonialism on the mental health of Algerian women, Fanon did dedicate a significant portion of his book to drawing a link between the colonial war and mental illness among Algerian men. He condemned the colonial system, exposing it as "a systematic negation of the other person and a furious determination to deny the other person all attributes of humanity." This system of negation repeatedly forced the colonized to question "Qui suis-je en réalité?" [In reality, who am I?]. Colonialism disoriented and cut off the colonized from any sense of place, selfhood, and identity.[35] Scholar Tracy Sharpley-Whiting points out in her groundbreaking work *Frantz Fanon: Conflicts and Feminisms* that lack of direct contact with Algerian women made it almost impossible for Fanon to conduct any case analyses of their mental health. Most of his patients were either colonial white women and men or Algerian Muslim men. Fanon's observations as noted in *Les Damnés de la terre* are based on his time as a psychiatrist at the hospital in Blida, Algeria.[36] Fanon does discuss women's mental and physical well-being in less clinical terms in his 1959 study *L'An Cinq, de la Révolution algérienne* (*A Dying Colonialism*). In this work he closely scrutinizes the roles of Algerian women in the domestic, as well as revolutionary, spheres, stating emphatically that the war could not be won without their participation. In *A Dying Colonialism*, the psychiatrist underscores the fact that "revolutionary war is not a war of [only] men."[37] As the struggle to eradicate French oppression became acute in the late 1950s, and more and more women were called upon to participate in the revolution, the Algerian freedom fighters realized that nationhood could not be achieved solely by the efforts of male rebels. Algerian men could not deny the contributions to the independence movement women had been repeatedly making.[38] From 1956 forward, Algerian women increasing participated in the revolutionary movement. Perceived by the French to be unassuming, passive, docile, and harmless, these veiled women were perfect for passing bombs, ammunition, and supplies to the rebel fighters of the Front de la Libération Nationale (FLN). Under their long *haïks* (traditional Algerian dress), Algerian women hid the armory of an entire revolution. It is true that, without their aid, independence would have been more difficult to achieve. Fanon delineates women's contributions to the war, pointing out the important significance, ideologically, women's roles played in the revolutionary process. Women hoped that these roles, transformed by revolution, would guarantee their eventual emancipation from the cultural bonds of Muslim traditionalism. Through revolution, they became possessors of their own bodies, wills, and spirits. The revolution had a cathartic effect and gave women access to the *outside*—a site beyond the veil, the interior walls of home, and the submission they had endured under colonialism and the phallocratic mores of their own culture. Through the psycho-cultural upheaval of tradition, which the war inevitably caused, Algerian women were granted a venue to a new identity. As Fanon explains, "she" in times of revolution "learns both her role as a woman alone in the street and her revolutionary mission instinctively."[39] Discovery of their revolutionary mission led Algerian women to subvert the patriarchal organization of labor, culture, and society to which they had grown accustomed over the centuries, allowing them to embrace a new identity. Revolution became a focal point for change because it offered Algerian women a window through which to see *what could be*. It set into motion the possibility of a new social order, while granting women the opportunity to form a new platform on which to build an ideology of contest.[40]

Algerian women thought that by breaking with tradition a new social order would develop, generating a new consciousness more favorable to them. Such a new social order would replace women's former identity with one that was independent and active. Algerian women's postcolonial identity would no longer be construed in white, European, orientalist, seductive terms, or cowed as passive and manipulated females for Algerian men.[41] Unfortunately in the years after independence, the new social consciousness that women had hoped for slowly was effaced. In the end the "language of revolution that extolled the woman fighter who became 'free' the moment she joined the movement gave way to the language of immutable gender inequality."[42] Algerian women found themselves abruptly silenced. Commenting on the continued perseverance of the masculine "social superego," Marnia Lazreg denounces the overbearing masculine authority that has ruled women with an iron hand since the end of the revolution in Algeria. This heavy-handed authority has driven women often to madness.[43]

Algerian Assia Djebar's novels are significant literary contributions that span more than forty years. Her works best exemplify the changes in how women were perceived within the Algerian nationalist psyche both pre- and postindependence and, later, how they were systematically victimized by the overwhelming religious fundamentalist politics that engulfed the country in the early 1980s. One of her first full-length novels *Les Enfants du nouveau monde*, published in 1962, documents the hopes, dreams, and sorrows of women caught up in the revolution in Algeria and their immediate social concerns thereafter. *Les Enfants du nouveau monde* is particularly useful when synthesizing the place of women in postrevolutionary Algeria. Her novel is significant for its critical analysis of and about the roles of women in Algeria during and after the war and has drawn attention to the importance of francophone literature in shaping women's rights across the postcolonial world. *Les Enfants du nouveau monde* explores the historical legacy of colonialism and militancy in Algeria, while incorporating themes that encompass other issues important to women and the newly independent nation. As early as 1961 Djebar sought to rectify the lack of attention addressed to women by the male militant government of Algeria. She anticipated that women's participation in the revolution would force Algerian legislation to subsequently acknowledge the importance of political-economic feminine roles in the newly liberated country. Her novel ends on a somewhat positive note. In the last scene of *Les Enfants du nouveau monde*, a lone freedom fighter walks toward a rebel mountain hideout. He sees a little girl and asks: "Tu as eu peur?" [Were you frightened?]. She responds negatively and runs off toward the sun "pour s'amuser avec ses chèvres" [to play with her goats].[44] The images of youth and freedom abound as the rebel fighter stands alone on the hillside, watching the little girl laughing carefree as she runs away. Although there is emphasis placed on the hope of Algeria's youth within these last pages, Djebar leaves the future of Algeria to be determined by others. Her message is clear: 1961 was too early to tell what impact postcolonial politics would have on women.

Djebar's 1997 work, *Oran, Langue morte*, paints a different picture of women's lives in Algeria. A collection of scenes, short stories, and incidents depicting women as victims of violence at the hands of the Front Islamique du Salut (FIS) (the ultra-fundamentalist movement that has targeted female teachers, journalists, and authors as infidels) makes the novel less a work of literature than a treatise for political action. Her novel is a forum that exposes the horrors of the Algerian civil war of the 1990s that impeded democracy and upheld totalitarianism. Djebar's collection of stories are heart-wrenching and filled with despair and once again draw readers' attention to the phallocratic, socio-traditional structures that do not support women in Algeria:

> Récit après récit. . . . Des femmes victimes pour leur savoir, leur métier ou pour leur solidarité—morsures de l'inquiétude! Le récit continuera; il se poursuivra de halte en halte, d'épreuves en affliction, en déceptions, en sursauts réprimés ou en offenses avalées. . . . Le récit, non le silence, ni la soumission tourbe noire; les paroles, en dépit de tout, posent jalon, avec la rage, la peine amère, et la goutte de lumière à recueillir dans l'encre de l'effroi. Par instants, la mort dévoile sa face: son rictus se déchire d'un coup. . . . Qu'attendent là-bas tant de femmes—jeunes et vieilles, elles vont au travail: à l'école, à l'hôpital, au bureau ou simplement au marché pour s'approvisionner. Elles vont le coeur noué . . . bravant la menace. Moi qui aurais voulu esquisser ici leurs silhouettes, pérenniser leur marche, les maintenir dehors, au besoin malgré un soleil noirci, moi, je rêve pour elles, je me remémore "en" elles.
>
> [Story after story . . . women, victims for their knowledge, their profession or their solidarity; bites of anxiety! The story will continue; it goes on from break to break, from tests to affliction, to deceptions, to suppressed bursts or to swallowed offenses. . . . The story, not the silence, nor suffocating submission; the

words, despite all, lay the groundwork, with rage, bitter pain, and the drop of light collected in the ink of terror. At times, death unmasks its face: its cruel grin tears in one stroke. . . . What do so many women wait for over there—young and old, they go to work, to school, to the hospital, to the office, or simply to the market to buy their food. They go with knotted hearts . . . braving the menace. Me, who would have wanted to trace their silhouettes here, perpetuate their step, keep them outside, out of need despite a blackened sun, me, I dream for them, I remember myself "through" them.][45]

From her early writing to the present, the concern Djebar raises in her novels for women's welfare and well-being within the confines of a violent hyper-phallocentric society is shared also by her Maghrebian, sub-Saharan African, and Caribbean feminine contemporaries. Historically, women speaking out from these geographical locations also meant (and still does in some regions) total ostracism. In her study of the status of women in Africa, Senegalese Awa Thiam points out in her 1978 book *La parole aux négresses* that "in countries where religious and family tradition are implacable, to revolt is equivalent to social suicide. To refuse [such traditional practices as] female excision or infibulation . . . would mean to accept being shunned by society, to renounce marriage."[46] Coupled with the overbearing pressure to conform to traditional tribal mores, sub-Saharan African women have also succumbed to what Carole Boyce Davies contends is African "women's obsession for the Europeanization of themselves . . . [which] causes irreversible and sometimes tragic alienation."[47] This validation of European ways as the pinnacles of perfection has been prevalent certainly since the last vestiges of colonialism disappeared from Africa in the 1960s. Women have often been manipulated by postindependence corruption and greed which have, unfortunately, plagued postcolonial African societies since the end of the 1960s. Much of this greed is due to African governments' adaption and subsequent implementation of some of the same old colonial infrastructures used by the former occupier. The ideology espoused by African governments promoting the misconceived need to Westernize has led countries such as Senegal and Cameroon to open the floodgates of capitalist schemes that succeed, more often than not, in hurting the people they profess to deliver from poverty and backwardness. With capitalism comes images of Western consumption and mass media, catching women up in unrealistic paradigms where they lose sight of their true selves. Within the context of the Antilles, Guadeloupian Maryse Condé reiterates the severity of capitalist Western seduction with respect to women in her critical study *La Parole des Femmes* in which she states that in "a contradictory fashion [society] demands of [a woman] to remain the keeper of traditional values and to [act as a] wall against the anguishing rise of modernism, while the whole society is engaged in the course of progress. When she gives into overwhelming vertigo, which is frequent, they condemn her."[48]

African women corrupted by European ideals of beauty and wealth has been a common theme in African and Caribbean literature and film. Senegalese Sembène Ousmane's 1973 novel and film, *Xala*, and Moussa Sene Absa's 1997 film, *Tableau Ferraille*, are excellent examples of artistic media that encourage Senegalese women to denounce European ideals in favor of finding an African woman's feminism that will work within the system to change society for the better. This new place/role must be defined on African women's own terms. In the past, as African women have pointed out, their roles in literature have been limited to wife and mother, idealized for their maternal *centeredness* in traditional settings. "A whole body of literature exalts childbirth, nursing, magnifying the attachment of a mother to her child," Condé exclaims.[49] Even Sembène Ousmane, who has championed women's rights in Senegal, often succumbs to idealizing women in traditional roles in his films and novels. Although, in some instances, women in his novels are able to temporarily break free of traditional structures, as evidenced in his seminal work *Les bouts de bois de Dieu* (1960), they more often than not are forced back into sociocultural established norms once the conflict for which they lent a hand to men is over. Moussa Sene Absa's film *Tableau Ferraille* leaves his newly emancipated heroine Gagnesiri's destiny ill-defined once she defies tradition and abandons her husband, taking nothing except the clothes on her back. As she sails out to sea in a boat pushing off the coast of a Senegalese fishing village, majestic and alone with only men sailors to paddle her away, the audience is left to ponder her fate. Absa's question seems to be "what now?" with respect to the future of those Senegalese women who choose independence and atypical principles by which to live. Is the price of their emancipation marginalization from family and clan? As scholar Karen Wallace points out, "[when] forced to struggle with social, political, philosophical or sentimental problems, the Black female character often [finds] herself cut off from the past, and trapped within the confines of a system of alienation."[50] Even if freed of their sociocultural traditional duties as Ousmane and Absa depict them, African women still feel isolated, once liberated from their domestic bonds. "The refusal of maternity," writes Condé, "may also be understood as the conscious or unconscious rejection of traditional and dominant images"; thus men feel threatened and overcompensate in order to "persevere [against] certain attitudes."[51] Even in Sembène's works, where his Marxist views and ideals concerning women as equal participants in society and as masters of their own destiny are evident, his hypotheses on the future of African women are often grounded in overzealous optimism.[52] He offers no sure predictions of how women will be perceived by the cultural milieus they have forsaken. Women disengage themselves from the demands of traditional societies in order to follow new paths of feminine engagement, but their future, certainly as Absa's film demonstrates, is still immensely unclear. We therefore must ask whether this optimism is purely due to a masculine glossing over of the adversities present in women's everyday lives? Or is it simply because Sembène and Absa, like many other authors and filmmakers (particularly male), are unsure what the *new* African woman's destiny will be and where her place in modern society lies?

Out on the borders of tradition, within the often hostile area of the *vel*, women authors writing from the francophone diaspora discover the intricacies not only of public agency but also of their psyche. "It is debilitating to be any woman in a society where women are warned that if they do not behave like angels they must be monsters," writes Sandra M. Gilbert and Susan Gubar.[53] So often the socialization of women in patriarchal societies has led to hysteria and sickness, creating women-mutants out of pain and stifled access to subjectivity. "The despair of the monster-woman" becomes something "real, undeniable, and infectious" as she tries to grasp something in the way of normalcy.[54]

For centuries, western, white, anglophone women authors have navigated in the literary realm between the "fundamental extremes of angel and monster" to criticize the oppression of the "male text's 'imposition' upon women."[55] The francophone feminine author, like her white anglophone counterpart, not only condemns patriarchal discourse as hindering feminine agency within the African diaspora, she also blames the patriarchal sociocultural systems that continue to bear down upon her, maintaining an oppressive status quo even in our postcolonial era. Shoshana Felman writes that "madness is the impasse confronting those whom cultural conditioning has deprived of the very means of protest or self-affirmation." This madness has characterized the "very status of womanhood" and must be contested on all levels.[56] Often, writing is the only means to thwart the loss of subjectivity for women who, on a daily basis, confront imminent psychological damage caused by oppressive sociocultural barriers (consider the condition of women in formerly Taliban-ruled Afghanistan as an extreme example of the results of masculine oppression and misinterpretation of cultural traditions at women's expense). Certainly since the dawn of the postcolonial era, writing has afforded women authors of the formerly colonized diaspora the means to strike back and reclaim their agency. Hélène Cixous exclaims that "woman must write woman" because it is only through their own writing that "women will confirm women in a place other than that which is reserved in and by [men]."[57]

The different representations of madness in the francophone novels considered in this study are the results of many factors. Insanity is often caused by the heroine's exile, isolation, and/or marginalization—either forced by masculine power or self-imposed—as she seeks to challenge age-old traditions in her culture. In some instances hysteria is a positive catalyst toward a truer knowledge of the self and acts as a force that empowers and allows her to overcome debilitating obstacles. Perhaps the voice of the hysteric is, as Cameroonian author Werewere Liking suggests, the result of our modern age where "a lunatic language must be born to allow lunatics to express themselves in the face of an age of lunacy."[58]

Madness in the feminine novel is not a new subject, as Gilbert and Gubar suggest. Since the dawn of civilization women have *literarily* fought men to gain a voice in society and culture as well as to acquire access to the pen. Describing women's psychological duress, Elisabeth Mudimbé-Boyi appropriately insists that insanity often "functions . . . as a metaphor of the female social condition and alienation."[59] Defining insanity within the realm of the fictional text becomes a means to say what cannot be said. The "unsaid, the unsayable" then "attempts to find an outlet by disguising itself in illness or in madness."[60] For many francophone feminine authors, expressing madness through the act of writing becomes therapeutic. The pen represents one of the few viable tools women have had to *right/write themselves in/to/* history. It offers a means to "say" on the written page, in black and white, something about themselves and their roles. "Precisely because a woman is denied the autonomy—the subjectivity—that the pen represents, she is not only excluded from culture (whose emblem might well be the pen) but she also becomes herself an embodiment of just those extremes of mysterious and intransigent otherness which culture confronts with worship or fear, love or loathing."[61] The pen, in metaphorical terms for Gilbert and Gubar, is the maleness, the physical power, of subjecthood. Without the pen, women have little agency and access to sociopolitical and cultural domains. Access to this instrument of power puts women on equal footing with men. Writing is the key to self-inscription into an economy of *being*. Women who write of themselves are fostering new terms of subjectivity, creating autobiographies that have never been told. As Paul de Man stipulates, "autobiographical discourse [is] a discourse of self-restoration."[62] The female novelist becomes *génétrice* of her own progeny and mistress of her own destiny. She becomes a matriarch who has a chance to challenge patriarchy. Yet, women francophone novelists of Africa and the Caribbean have discovered, like their western-European anglophone counterparts, that confronting patriarchy and dominant male sociopolitical systems inevitably causes harm to their own well-being. Often there is a price to pay, and frequently voicing feminine issues has the potential to destroy subjecthood, sending the author's heroine into an abyss of insanity from which she cannot extract herself. Women have learned that they must confront and fight, with possible personal risk, or fold up on themselves, close their minds, and succumb to the oppressive system. Speaking from exile, Assia Djebar attests that her very existence depends on her writing and that she must always write as if tomorrow were her last day: "When I write, I write always as if I am going to die tomorrow. Each time I finish I ask myself if this is really what one expected of me, because the murders continue. I wonder what [writing] is good for. If not to clench teeth so as not to cry."[63]

TOWARD A WOMAN'S PSYCHOANALYTIC-POLITICAL
PHILOSOPHY OF SELFHOOD

Drawing on the works of Sigmund Freud to explain identity and, certainly, how women's hysteria is represented in literary terms is controversial at best. Repeatedly, feminist authors, scholars, and philosophers have taken issue with Freud's faulty clinical and societal hypotheses pertaining to women. In her work, Jill Astbury dismantles Freud's hypotheses on women and hysteria. She systematically exposes the detrimental influences Freud's ideology has had on female psychological diagnoses and how his hypotheses "have all pervaded our cultural consciousness" and continue to haunt women's psychological treatment to this day.[64] Astbury effectively outlines how Freud was responsible for jettisoning women to the abyss of science as he developed his theories on women and neurosis:

> Freud's conventional notions of women's nature and proper position in society extended far beyond his own domestic arrangements. His writings on women show how readily he accepted prevailing "scientific" views on women and how thoroughly they informed the explanatory framework of his theorizing.[65]

As Asbury contends, this theorizing, based on popular scientific speculation of the day (particularly Darwin's work), led to Freud's investment and "belief in recapitulation theory." According to the psychoanalyst, "each individual somehow recapitulated in an abbreviated form the entire development of the human race." These abbreviated forms were placed on a scale, known as the *phyletic scale*. Women and the "lower races" were fixed at the bottom rungs according to evolutionary "theories" based on their "weak nature." Since women and people of non-European (non-white) origins were thought to be lower on the scale and, thus, less emotionally developed, it was up to the white, educated man to oversee their psychological well-being. Women were barred from any strenuous activities and forbidden to take part in the sociocultural production and economy of their society. A woman's place, according to Freud, was in the home, where domestic duties were her prerogative.[66]

Freud's work on psychology and feminine neurosis certainly retarded women's access to public agency. It also contributed to the harmful misogynic rhetoric of the late nineteenth century that was used politically to curtail women's civil rights. This rhetoric, based on an entire science developed by and for men, would take women years to dismantle. Within current feminist theses stressing contemporary modern women as being multi-embodied subjects who develop identity through active sociocultural associations, looking back on several hypotheses set forth by Freud seems almost irrelevant. Yet, as we female scholars, philosophers, and authors continue to undo the adverse ideologies that have hindered our emancipation, it is important to review Freud and others who have shaped erroneous hypotheses that have dictated how women carry out their lives. As we continually redefine our identity and selfhood with regard to sociocultural power constructions, we must redefine our self-affirmation through channels in society that are active and public.

Women philosophers and psychiatrists have been able to turn the tables on phallocentric ideologies to further their own purposes. Particularly Freud's explanation of "surface consciousness" as put forth in his 1923 paper "*The Ego and the Id*" does contain some relevant points that could be useful for women as they construct new discourses for themselves.[67] The psychoanalyst used his hypothesis about surface consciousness to further explore theories on the conscious and unconscious. His underlying premise that surface consciousness is an integral part of a "psychical map which later becomes the site of the ego" is important in understanding how women's bodies and minds are inscribed upon by society and culture.[68] According to Freud, the outside of human consciousness is the body and the skin, and it is in these locations where the primary sites of sensations and feelings are created. It is this outside surface, the Ego, that acts like a web between internal and external perceptions. French philosophers Gilles Deleuze and Félix Guattari would later call these *percepts* and *affects*. These external and internal perceptions are inscribed on the self, leaving behind *residues* on the subject's surface. Residues are important for thought processes and for the development of the Id. From the depths of the Id emerges the Ego. "It is easy to see that the ego is that part of the id which has been modified by the direct influence of the external world. . . . The ego represents what may be called reason and common sense, in contrast to the id, which contains the passions."[69] For a being to enjoy full development of the Id, and in turn the Ego, both external and internal flows of perceptions must be ensured. "The conscious ego . . . is first and foremost a body-ego."[70]

Building on the idea of inward and outward flows, French philosopher Maurice Merleau-Ponty later discusses the primacy of external perception as a crucial link in the development of the body. For this twentieth-century philosopher, a subject's existence is brought to life only when "the subject is thrown open to the world . . . [to] the presence of nature."[71] This connection with other environments external to the subject's own is later explored by Michel Foucault who stipulated in his writings the importance of a subject's historic genealogy in shaping itself and its body with respect to the world environment (in historical, philosophical, and ideological terms). In Foucauldian philosophy, the subject is a subject only through historical linkages. The founding of a being's historical genealogy, as Elizabeth Grosz points out in her summary of Foucault's work, unsettles "established models of knowledge and epistemological presumptions involved in the production of history, philosophy, and morality."[72] Study of historical genealogy allows us to see how history has affected bodies and shaped identities and how these identities, in turn, have been "investment for power's operations." The body that has the power rules the writing of history and the development of philosophies. It is therefore important for women to understand this power in order to find a way to divert its original male sources and, subsequently, wield it for their own gains. "Power and knowledge are mutually conditioning."[73]

For women, this psychoanalytic-phenomenological construction of the ego is extremely important when considering madness, loss of subjectivity, and women's domination by phallocentric, oppressive structures. While falling short of promoting women's agency individually, at least, when taken as a whole, the hypothesis provides a positive building block for explaining why women need to rethink, reconstruct, and rewrite history for and about women, on their own terms. If the development of the ego and, thus, identity relies on *inscription* of the persona, or the surface of the being, then the primacy of the *outside*—active agency in the visible circles of culture: the street, the workplace, the outside spaces of cultural production—is imperative for women. Often, this outside is marginal and even mad. Although dementia is, for all intents and purposes, debilitating, as Phyllis Chesler remarks in her 1972 seminal study on women and madness, many contemporary feminists argue that the realm of madness can serve the woman author well to fight the "male logos that excludes the truly feminine voice from the information system that determines what counts as culture and rationality."[74] If women continue to draw on masculine logoi that have ruled their language and destroyed any hope of creating an original identity for themselves, then perhaps madness as a location outside of the norm, on the liminal edges of society and culture, could offer a means to discover the "affirmative of a self beyond sanity determined by masculine rationality."[75] Writing from the realm of madness is perhaps a way to establish a new set of communicative signifiers that escape male codes. Perhaps writing in this space means finding and/or discovering other systems that will bring women into their own logos. "Madness or illness is the space that makes possible the constitution of [a woman's] text" and, as Elisabeth Mudimbé-Boyi remarks, "illness is the place from which [feminine] discourse emerges."[76]

Affirmation of this potentially empowered outside *self* is something for which women authors strive. However, embracing madness as a catalyst for true knowledge of the self is like walking on thin ice. It is certainly a subject that has generated heated debate for western-European and American feminists since the 1970s. Claims to alterity have been championed by French feminists such as Luce Irigary and Hélène Cixous for years. Yet, do we really want to condemn women to the hysteric spaces of the marginalized in order to explore the feminine condition in hopes of eventually establishing a feminine logos? I argue that we should take that risk. If madness is used by women to embrace a truer sense of self, then perhaps it will empower them. Through the actions and the dementia of their heroines, the authors studied in this book, although they themselves are not mad, explore a deeper sense of the feminine self and selfhood as well as the injustices and constraints that their societies and men have placed on them. It is this extradiegetic madness—a state created by the writer to study the female condition within the realm of fiction—that perhaps will offer women authors the power to re-create a *woman's way*, a new set of ethics for and about women.

A feminine form of communication with others (male and female), even in traditional sociocultural environments, promotes the idea of a new "universality" that is "understood as the inclusion of all concerned." Within this universality there is "the reciprocity of equal recognition of the claims of each participant [in the community] by all others."[77] When women engage speech they are automatically destroying the private, hermetically sealed world that has been contrived for them by male sociocultural and political structures (disguised in many forms: nationalist, colonialist, Orientalist, religious-fundamentalist). Gayatri Spivak claims that active, public discourse deconstructs "the opposition between the private and the public."[78] Spivak insists that outside, public space characterizes all that represents culture: politics, professional life, society, power, economics, and intellectual production. Contrastingly, the interior, private domain associated with women represents all that is passive, emotional, domestic, and sexual. When women breach these socioculturally defined lines and enter the public sphere, they become menacing, transformed into seductive monsters who threaten the phallocratic order. What lies before these Medusas, as Sandra Gilbert and Susan Gubar define women who go against the norm to defy cultural barriers?[79] Are exile and marginality the only results that are probable? In more extreme cases, madness and death await the woman who dares to exist on the *outside*. Yet, even these risks become minimal for women who view public agency as the only means of access to the one thing they have been denied: the right to a voice and to negotiate their identity on their own terms. Jürgen Habermas contends that the outside space of cultural production is where there is "a circular process in which the actor is two things in one: an *initiator* who masters situations through actions of which he[/she] is accountable and a *product* of the traditions surrounding him[/her], of groups whose cohesion is based on solidarity to which he[/she] belongs, and of processes of socialization in which he[/she] is reared."[80] Overstepping boundaries into this realm of public agency in turn frees up women's ability to reinscribe or *write* their identity. Such an establishment of identity, or what Habermas defines as *sign*, involves a new body of ethics that results in a change of attitude favoring new modes of feminine discourse.

Understanding and having access to the realm of the public is important for all women. Establishing public agency, although different in certain aspects depending on the society and culture, marks a new beginning, or a new *becoming*, for women.[81] For women in the postcolonial world, obtaining a voice in public space is more problematic than it was for white European or American women a generation ago. However, women of the African diaspora still embrace many of the same processes in order to achieve their objectives. All women, whether white or of color, must step into the public realm in order to establish agency and make their voices heard. As the novels analyzed in this book demonstrate, this public sphere often means exile and marginalization for the heroine as she is pushed to the peripheries of traditional feminine roles. Unlike men (whose entrance into sociocultural production is a preordained privilege), for women, society and public constructions outside family and home are, often only symbolic. Juliette Flower Maccannell explains that "society says, 'You are a woman' as it situates you as daughter, sister, wife, mother. Your unconscious, responding to the tone in which this assignment is made, says: 'I am not!' Or, 'Yes, indeed!' Or, 'Am I?'"[82] A woman doubts her place with regard to the public sphere from the beginning, even deep down in her subconscious. Once out on the liminal edges of her society, she either fights for, agrees with, or questions her role within the sociocultural boundaries of her community. In sum, women, unlike men, must choose how they position themselves in the sociopolitical economy of the culture in which they live. This position will forever determine how they are judged by others.

For Sultana in Malika Mokeddem's novel *L'Interdite*, the streets and public areas of her village home on the edge of the Sahara are daunting locations filled with hostility. Opposition to her free movement by the phallocentric powers ruling there becomes too overpowering, compelling her to renounce her cause as a woman doctor helping the women of her native village. She finally is forced to leave. Although she fails to exercise her freedom as an active contributor to village society, she does persevere in realms of her own self-discovery and finally overcomes her childhood nightmares surrounding the murder of her mother by her father. Facing former fears, she refashions her identity and returns to France in exile, but with her sanity. At the end of the novel she realizes that, although she must live in exile in France, she is able to construct a sphere of agency independent of the sociocultural constraints that rule the lives of the women she leaves behind in her native village. Contrastingly, however, she must live with the disappointment she feels of not being able to combat the religious fundamentalist forces that have engulfed her village and oppress women on a daily basis. Forced to flee Algeria, Sultana feels she has somehow failed by not having been able to liberate the women of Aïn-Nekla from the ultra-religious dogma of the Front Islamique du Salut (FIS) as well as oppressive cultural traditions that leave them with few choices.

In contrast to Sultana, Juletane, principal heroine of Myriam Warner-Vieyra's book *Juletane*, tells a different story. Living in exile in Paris, the

young protagonist feels isolated and alone as she ekes out a living in her immigrant neighborhood. Her life is full of despair as she tries to cope with
a foreign world to which she feels no attachment. Her homeland is but a
dream, since she has never really known the Antilles Islands firsthand. Opportunity for a better life seems to present itself when she meets Mamadou,
her future Senegalese husband. Subsequently, her hopes are dashed, once
she realizes that she is bound up in a polygamous marriage and has traded
her Parisian prison of solitude for a Senegalese traditional life where women
are restricted to domestic circles, enjoying little say or power in the village
community. There are no alternatives for Juletane. She is barred from engaging with others (particularly men) in public space, disenfranchised from
the social, political, and cultural spheres of the Senegalese village because
she is foreign and doesn't speak her husband's language. She chooses self-
imposed exile from Mamadou's world, the result of which leads to her madness and death.

Hysteria and madness do not, however, always mean the end to subjectivity for women, as Cameroonian Calixthe Beyala's novel *Tu t'appelleras Tanga* suggests. "The hysterical fantasy [can lead] toward the future" Maccannell proclaims as she draws on the writings of Lacan who
explains that the hysteric state can "witness the birth of true speech . . .
becoming [a] . . . regathering of revolutionary potentiality."[83] In Beyala's
novel, Tanga's body dies but her hysteria transfers her soul and psyche
into the body of Anna-Claude. Anna-Claude *becomes* the Other; she is
Tanga at the end of the novel. Although Beyala's work explores the fantasy world of two women caught up in a hysterical mode of psychological
transference, it is also politically charged. Tanga defies the phallocentric
constructions of a violent culture that threw her into prison because she
tried to survive in a society that offered few choices to women with no
family ties. Although madness leads to death, Tanga's spirit is transferred
to another who lives and retells her story. Anna-Claude "knows that Tanga
was waiting for her in order to die—open, offering herself, so she could
give her words to speak before crossing the borders and lying down full
length as a still-life."[84] Anna-Claude listens and then tells the dying
woman, "Continue your story. It will guide me; it is what you must be-
queath to me."[85] The hysteric state becomes a generating machine—a Desiring Machine—that picks up force through the voice of Tanga, spurring
on a *becoming-other*. Deleuze and Guattari explain in their work *Anti-
Oedipus: Capitalism and Schizophrenia* that the schizophrenic is truly
connected to the inside and outside of the conscious. Tanga, who merges
with Anna-Claude, produces "the one within the other"; they become "the
outside and the inside" assuring that these diametrically opposed poles
"no longer have any meaning whatsoever."[86] It is through the hysteric
mode that the inside of Tanga merges with the outside of Anna-Claude.

"What the schizophrenic experiences, both as an individual and as a member of the human species, is not at all any one specific aspect of nature, but nature as a process of production," and through this process, human beings become united with "everything that is production."[87] Madness in this instance does not become reductive, effacing subjecthood; rather, it takes on positive aspects, acting as a catalyst for the continuation of feminine essence. Tanga passes on to an active state of being through Anna-Claude. Women's subjectivity is not conquered by the male phallocratic order that put the two women in prison and attempted to annihilate their very being. Faced with the inevitability of death, women's spirit persevered and feminine essence was not extinguished. Tanga, through dementia, has established another relationship beyond sacrifice and death with the outside world where her history is continued.

These "francophemmes,"[88] women of Africa and the Caribbean who write in French, those who are exiled and those who live clandestinely fighting for human rights in their own countries, are conceptualizing new ways to study their past as well as to plot new plans for their future through literature. They are *becoming* a new identity, fashioned in the *vel*; which is a beyond where all preconceived notions, whether historically, phallocratically, or traditionally ordained, are taken to task, questioned, and then reconstructed. Their discourse posits a multiple feminine subject that reflects a panoply of connections, crisscrossed by many cultures, languages, nationalities, and ways of looking at the world. Instead of essentializing the feminine ideal, African and Caribbean women authors are transgressing boundaries between their bodies and their minds while using their pens to gain access to areas once forbidden to them as they write *their* stories.

In this book, the novels of twelve authors—Mariama Bâ, Calixthe Beyala, Nina Bouraoui, Marie Chauvet, Hajer Djilani, Aminata Sow Fall, Leïla Houari, Suzanne Lacascade, Michèle Lacrosil, Yamina Mechakra, Simone Schwarz-Bart, and Myriam Warner-Vieyra—are grouped by what I define as three *states* of being, which manifest through the psyche. These states are described within thematic parameters that explore the various degrees of women's emotions and mental stability as they confront immense hurdles that are often socioculturally, politically, and economically determined.

The preface of my analysis explores the space from which women are writing in/of/about Africa and the Caribbean. Within the francophone novel, women authors define a separate space in which history and philosophy become something *other* (in both positive and negative terms) for women. This space may be thought of as a *vel*, a place where the torsion of male history and philosophy takes place, making room for a *woman's way*. This feminine way of being, as Juliette Flower Maccannell astutely defines it in her work *The Hysteric's Guide to the Future Female Subject*, is the product of negotiating in a space in between traditionalism and modernism and, in many instances, between the realms of sanity and madness. It is a Third Space through which women discover agency and the power to exert the right to selfhood and identity freed of masculine domination.[89] Feminine manners of communication influenced by marginalization and exile within this space are negotiated and rethought. Within the Third Space lies the possibility of madness and/or the liberating lucidity that comes from self-discovery. As a woman writes within this generating space of selfhood, the pen becomes her weapon of subjectivity. She wields it to "legitimize her own rebellious endeavors."[90] The pen is the vehicle with which women mete out the "isolation that [feels] like illness, [the] alienation that [feels] like madness, [and] the obscurity that [feels] like paralysis."[91]

The chapters of this book are organized by what I define as three psychological states. In State I, "Mediating Identity in Foreign Spaces," *étrangeté— le vide*—between the heroine and the culture in which she must live is explored on numerous levels in the novels *Claire-Solange, âme africaine* by Suzanne Lacascade and *Zeida de nulle part* by Leïla Houari. The estrangement from their respective societies that these heroines experience is caused by exile from family, social group, and/or home country. The works considered in this section exemplify situations wherein the protagonists are caught up in lives of duality as they are forced to live and function in two conflicting worlds. Although it is difficult to negotiate the isolation they feel, the women in these novels come to terms with living in a space in which they are *split* in two. These heroines are destined to endure an existence divided by two languages, two cultures, and often two continents.

Suzanne Lacascade and Leïla Houari bring to light their heroines' feelings about both liberty and solitude, the results of having to live in between these everyday divisions in their lives. Etrangeté is a double-edged sword. "In crossing a border the *étranger*," Julia Kristeva remarks, "has changed [her] discomforts into a base of resistance, a citadel of life" without a home "[she] disseminates, multiplying masks and false-selves."[92] Etrangeté is the space situated in between tradition and modernism as well as the heroine's country of origin and the European milieu she is forced to adopt.

State II, "Writing in Madness," defines situations that leave the heroines in these novels ultimately without any choices. These women are not able to overcome the psychological demands that exile and/or marginalization have caused them. They slip into utter madness, lose their self-control and, more often than not, take their own lives or die from despair. Novels by Mariama Bâ (*Un chant écarlate*), Calixthe Beyala (*Tu t'appelleras Tanga*), Nina Bouraoui (*La Voyeuse interdite*), Marie Chauvet (*Amour, Colère, Folie*), Michèle Lacrosil (*Cajou*), and Myriam Warner-Vieyra (*Juletane*) are grouped here to demonstrate the insurmountable influences of exile, marginalization, fundamentalist religion, phallocratic politics, and sociocultural oppression on the heroines. As these authors attest, the abject factors present in their environments ultimately lead their heroines to madness. Unlike Lacascade and Houari's protagonists who, in the end, are able to find peace and establish some semblance of equilibrium in their lives (even while living in a foreign environment), the women in the novels analyzed in State II all succumb to madness. These are female characters who cannot escape the prison of dementia. Isolation, oppression by men and governments, and the violence of war and sociocultural upheaval are not quelled and play roles in the final demise of each author's ill-fated woman. In the words of Michel Foucault, "insanity only leads to heartbreak, and, from there, to death."[93] Confinement is a principal factor in each heroine's demise. Sociocultural constraints and male power over them also contribute to these women's degenerated physical being.

State III, "Reconciliation: Feminine Utopias," defines the lives of heroines who have succeeded in surviving (both mentally and physically) personal as well as sociocultural traumatic events. Although women are obliged to negotiate many negative aspects present in their lives, they triumph in combating patriarchal systems and the adverse effects of marginalization and alienation that have pushed so many women to insanity. In contrast to the group of protagonists in State II, this group of heroines creates their own utopias. The anonymous heroine in Yamina Mechakra's *La Grotte éclatée*, Hajer Djilani's Chems in *Et pourtant le ciel était bleu*, Télumée of Simone Schwarz-Bart's *Pluie et vent sur Télumée Miracle*, and Asta, principal protagonist of Aminata Sow Fall's novel *Douceurs du bercail*, even after pain and suffering (and bouts of momentary madness) caused by war, racism, and death, succeed in creating their own space freed of all preordained rules and regulations defined by masculine prerogatives and oppression. The unfettered spaces described in the novels considered in this section are utopias, fostering a universalist dialogue that can be shared and understood by women of all cultures and backgrounds. In State III, reconciliation with home, country, and community, after having surmounted and survived overpowering moments of insanity, allows these women to constructively continue their lives. The protagonists realize an environment that nurtures their own well-being as well as that of others in their communities. The heroines also find inner peace and a sense of purpose living in the utopias that they have created. In particular, Sow Fall's novel *Douceurs du bercail* depicts how the humiliation of one woman can be overcome and turned into positive social change not only for herself but for her community as well. The author draws on a philosophy of life that celebrates Pan-Africanism to promote her message that women are at the forefront of change in their societies. Women also can be the only viable negotiators of their own new, modern roles. Sow Fall's Pan-African project, promoting universal civil rights, expands beyond the literary to incorporate not only feminist, but humanist messages as well.

I have chosen a comparative framework through which to study these authors who represent five African francophone countries and three Caribbean islands. As one would suppose, such a comparative framework might lead to generalities, something that I have strived to avoid. It is my wish to draw conclusions about the representations of madness in these novels by traversing contemporary Western and Afro-Caribbean postcolonial and francophone literary theory. I hope that my own conclusions will expose readers to the incredible richness of the francophone feminine author's novel. The crux of my analysis lies in formulating hypotheses on, and critiques of, how the francophone feminine author has situated herself at the crossroads of history and philosophy. On a historical level, women's writing in Africa and the Caribbean was rarely referenced for the first half of the past century. Women have usually had their histories written for them by men, intervening rarely to alter masculine depictions of themselves. Philosophically, literary movements such as the Négritude movement, although promoting a new Afro-Caribbean consciousness, left little room for women's participation in literature produced in these regions before 1970.[94]

Today African and Caribbean women construct identity as positive agents who seek to explore their undocumented history as well as the roles they play in changing contemporary societies. Their discourse posits a multiple-feminine subject that reflects many connections crisscrossed by a variety of cultures, languages, nationalities, and ways of looking at the world. Instead of essentializing the feminine ideal (body and subjectivity), contemporary African and Caribbean women writers are transgressing boundaries that were once forbidden, often fighting the insanity that lurks ready to engulf them, in order to write themselves into history as never before.

NOTES

A version of this chapter was first published in *World Literature Today* 75, no. 1 (winter 2001): 40–50.

1. According to Christopher Miller, the first book written by an African francophone author was a 1920 school textbook entitled *Les Trois Volontés de Malic* by Ahmadou Mapaté Diagne, a Senegalese man educated in the French colonial school system. (See Christopher Miller, *Theories of Africans* [Chicago: University of Chicago Press, 1990], 249). Jean Déjeux estimates the date of the first text written in French in Algeria by a nonnative Frenchman to be 1891. He credits the first novella, *La vengeance du cheikh*, to Algerian author M'Hamed Ben Rahal. The novella was published in *Revue algérienne et tunisienne, littéraire et artistique* (see Jean Déjeux, *Maghreb: Littératures de langue française* [Paris: Aracantère, 1993], 31).

2. Négritude, a literary movement begun in the early 1930s by Aimé Césaire, Etienne Léro, Jules Monnerot, Léon-Gontran Damas, and Jacques Romain (among others) sought to "determine a strategy for promoting the individuality of African culture." Négritude soon blossomed into the radical "affirmation of African political thought" and solidified the anticolonial rhetoric of African independence movements

in the 1960s. (V. Y. Mudimbé, *The Invention of Africa: Gnosis, Philosophy, and the Order of Knowledge* [Bloomington: Indiana University Press, 1988], 86–87). The literary-political movement, however, has been widely criticized by African feminists for its exclusion of women's issues. Only a few women, such as Paulette and Andrée Nardal and Suzanne Césaire, wrote in the Négritude venue during the early 1930s and 1940s.

3. V. Y. Mudimbé distinguishes *gnosis* as a term to "extend the notion of philosophy to African traditional systems of thought, considering them as dynamic processes in which concrete experiences are integrated into an order of concepts and discourses . . . . Etymologically, *gnosis* is related to *gnosko*, which in the ancient Greek means 'to know.' Specifically, *gnosis* means seeking to know, inquiry, methods of knowing, investigation, and even acquaintance with someone" (*Invention of Africa*, ix).

4. Fatima Mernissi, *Doing Daily Battle: Interviews with Moroccan Women* (New Brunswick, N.J.: Rutgers University Press, 1989), 3.

5. Gayatri Spivak, *In Other Worlds* (New York: Routledge, 1988), 207. See also my book, *Nomadic Voices of Exile: Feminine Identity in Francophone Literature of the Maghreb* (Athens: Ohio University Press, 1999) for further reading on the link between franco-phone women authors, agency, and public space.

6. Allen Thiher, *Revels in Madness: Insanity in Medicine and Literature* (Ann Arbor: University of Michigan Press: 1999), 10.

7. See Juliette Flower Maccannell, *The Hysteric's Guide to the Future Female Subject* (Minneapolis: University of Minnesota Press, 2000), xv.

8. Elizabeth Grosz, *Volatile Bodies: Toward a Corporeal Feminism* (Bloomington: Indiana University Press, 1994), 36.

9. Gilles Deleuze and Félix Guattari, *The Fold: Leibniz and the Baroque*, translated by Tom Conley, (Minneapolis: University of Minnesota Press, 1993), 34–35.

10. Myriam Warner-Vieyra, *Juletane* (Dakar: Présence Africaine, 1982).

11. Aminata Sow Fall, *Douceurs du bercail* (Abidjan: NEI, 1998).

12. See Gilles Deleuze and Félix Guattari, *Mille Plateaux* (Paris: Editions Minuit, 1980); translation, *A Thousand Plateaus* (Minneapolis: University of Minnesota Press, 1987).

13. Thiher, *Revels in Madness*, 4.

14. Irène Assiba d'Almeida, *Francophone African Women Writers: Destroying the Emptiness of Silence* (Gainesville: University Press of Florida, 1994), 2.

15. Several French women considered Franco-Algerian have been included in Algerian francophone women's bibliographies, notably, Anna Colnat who wrote the novel *Virginie Duparc, terrienne d'Algérie* published in Philippeville, Algeria, in 1936.

16. *La Soif* was written when the author was only twenty and focuses on women's emancipation. *Les Impatients* was criticized for its focus on a bourgeois family, alienated from tradition (see Belinda Jack, *Francophone Literatures* [Oxford: Oxford University Press, 1996], 180). Additional works by Algerian women authors include Zohra Drif's *La Mort de mes frères*, published in 1960, which offers a woman's point of view of the carnage of the Algerian war. Other Algerian women authors writing in the years following independence in 1962 include Aïcha Lemsine (*La Chrysalide: chroniques algériennes*, 1976) and Yamina Mechakra (*La Grotte Éclatée*, 1976). More recently, Leïla Marouane's *La Fille de la Casbah* (1996), Latifa Ben Mansour's *La Prière de la peur* (1997), Sabrina Kherbich's *Nawal et Leïla* (1997), and Rachida Titah's *Un Ciel trop bleu* (1997) have been published. In theater, Algerian women

continue to make contributions with works by playwrights such as Myriam Ben's *Leïla, suivi de Les Enfants du Mendiant* (1998).

17. Additional works by Moroccan women include: Farida El Hany Mourad's *La Fille aux pieds nus* (1985), Badia Hadj Nasser's *Le Voile mis à nu* (1985), Noufissa Sbaï's *L'Enfant endormi* (1987), Antoinette Ben Kerroum-Covlet's *Gardien du seuil* (1988), Selma El Melhi's *Vie trahie* (1988) and *A l'ombre du papyrus* (1990), Farida Hani Moura's *Faites parler le cadavre* (1990), Fatiha Boucetta's *Anissa captive* (1991), and Leïla Chellabi's *D'une citoyenne: Reflexion sur le, la, les politique*(s), a political essay published in 1994. They all have been hailed as invaluable additions to women's world writing. In theater, contributions by Moroccan women include Amina Lhassani's *Nour ou l'appel de Dieu: Pièce en trois actes* (1994) and, in poetry, Aicha Rachad's *Havre de paix* (1996) and Aicha Amara's *Mogador, fille d'Aylal* (1997) complement recent literary contributions made by Moroccan women.

18. Tunisian women, like men, have made significant contributions in poetry. Poetic works include Jacqueline Daoud's *Traduit de l'abstrait* (1968), Malika Golcem Ben Redjeb's *Graines d'espérance* (1970), Nicole Gdalia's *Racines* (1975), *Les chemins du nom* (1984), *Il dit* (1987), and *Monodie* (1990), Amina Saïd's *Paysages, nuit friable: Poèmes* (1980), *Sables funambules: Demeures, traces et méditations* (1988), *Feu d'oiseaux* (1989), and *L'Une et l'autre Nuit* (1993), Béhija Galloul's *Le Lac en flammes* (1982), and Souad Hedri's *Une Larme sur un poème* (1997). Tunisian women's prose consists of many prominent novels such as Jalila Hafsia's *Cendre à l'aube* (1975), Souad Hedri's *Vie et agonie* (1978), Frida Hachemi's *Ahlem* (1981), and Hélé Beji's *L'Oeil du jour* (1985).

19. Miller, *Theories of Africans*, 164.

20. Madame Diallo Aoua Kéita retells the story of her life as midwife and former Deputy of the Republic of Mali. Comprehensive and incredibly detailed, this large tome meticulously recounts the traditions and customs of the peoples who live in this region. Kéita also offers a glimpse into the early years of feminist activism in Mali from 1931 to 1960, during which "with other women she helped shape the political orientation of her country on the eve of independence" (See D'Almeida, *Francophone Women Writers*, 189, note 21).

21. Two other women of notable importance writing in the 1970s were Aoua Kéita (*Femme d'Afrique: La Vie d'Aoua Kéita racontée par elle-même* [Paris: Présence Africaine, 1975]) and Nafissatou Diallo (*De Tilène au plateau: Une Enfance dakaroise* [Dakar: Nouvelles Editions Africaines, 1975]). Their works were more autobiographical in scope. (See Miller, *Theories of Africans*, 250).

22. Miller, *Theories of Africans*, 250.

23. Additional works by Senegalese women include Lydie Dooh-Bunya's *La Brise du jour* (1977), Awa Thiam's *La Parole aux négresses* (1978), Mariama Bâ's *Une Lettre écarlate* (1986), Nafissatou Dialo's *De Tilé au plateau: Une enfance dakaroise* (1975), Andrée Blouin's *My Country, Africa: Autobiography of the Black Pasionaria* (1983), Ken Bugul's *Le Baobab fou* (1983), and Catherine N'Diaye's *Gens de sable* (1984). From the Côte d'Ivoire and Gabon, authors such as Véronique Tadjo (*A Vol d'oiseau*, 1986) and Angèle Rawiri (*Fureurs et cris de femmes*, 1989) have made considerable contributions to francophone literature.

24. The list of authors mentioned in this section is by no means exhaustive. For comprehensive lists and discussions of and about many more women francophone authors

(particularly of the Maghreb), readers are encouraged to consult the *Banque de Données Limage* (http://www.limage.com). For in-depth discussion of sub-Saharan African works by women see Irène Assiba D'Almeida's work, *Francophone African Women Writers: Destroying the Emptiness of Silence* (Gainesville: University Press of Florida, 1994) and Belinda Jack's *Francophone Literatures: An Introductory Survey* (New York: Oxford University Press, 1996).

25. See Christiane P. Makward's article, *"Cherchez La Franco-Femme"* in *Postcolonial Subjects: Francophone Women Writers*, ed. Mary Jean Green et al. (Minneapolis: University of Minnesota Press, 1996), 118.

26. Marnia Lazreg, *The Eloquence of Silence: Algerian Women in Question* (New York: Routledge, 1994), 195. Lazreg, as well as other historical chroniclers of the Algerian war, such as Frantz Fanon, has pointed out that, without the aid of women, the FLN would have assuredly lost their struggle against the French military during the 1954–62 war.

27. Malika Mokeddem, *L'Interdite* (Paris: Grasset, 1993).

28. Kristeva, *Strangers to Ourselves*, 23.

29. Kristeva, *Strangers to Ourselves*, 8.

30. Mokeddem, *L'Interdite*, 191.

31. Placing Algerian women in roles in which they are not normally permitted to play in Algerian traditional society is a theme in all of Mokeddem's works. See her novels: *Le Siècle des sauterelles* (Paris: Ramsay, 1992), *Les Hommes qui marchent* (Paris: Grasset, 1997), *Des rêves et des assassins* (Paris: Grasset, 1995), and *La Nuit de la lézarde* (Paris: Grasset, 1998), as well as her latest novel, *N'Zid* (Paris: Seuil, 2001).

32. Thiher, *Revels in Madness*, 144.

33. Thiher, *Revels in Madness*, 133.

34. Frantz Fanon, *Les Damnés de la terre* (Paris: François Maspéro, 1961); *The Wretched of the Earth*, translated by Constance Farrington (New York: Grove Press, 1963). Tunisian Albert Memmi also discussed the effects of colonial oppression in psychological terms in his work *Portrait du colonisé* (1957).

35. Frantz Fanon, *Les Damnés de la terre*, 300; *The Wretched of the Earth*, 250.

36. Tracy Sharpley-Whiting, *Frantz Fanon: Conflicts and Feminism* (Lanham, Md.: Rowman & Littlefield Publishers, 1998), 16. Sharpley-Whiting notes, however, that in 1956 Fanon did collaborate on a paper presented at the fifty-fourth session of the *Congrès des médecines alienistes et neurologues de France et des pays de langue française* with Charles Geromini on women's mental ailments. The paper was titled: *"Le T.A.T. chez la femme musulmane: Sociologie de la perception et de l'imagination"* (16).

37. Frantz Fanon, *A Dying Colonialism* (New York: Grove Press, 1965); translated from *L'An Cinq, de la révolution algérienne* (Paris: François Maspero, 1959), 66.

38. Fanon, *A Dying Colonialism*, 66.

39. Fanon, *A Dying Colonialism*, 50.

40. Teresa Ebert, *Ludic Feminism and After: Postmodernism, Desire, and Labor in Late Capitalism* (Ann Arbor: University of Michigan Press, 1996), 8.

41. Algerian women throughout French occupation were repeatedly portrayed in French literature and art through a *lens of seduction*. The orientalized, harem diva, veiled, cloistered, hidden away from the foreigner male's eyes is a figure par excellence in the European exotic-erotic literary and pictorial fantasy. Authors and artists

such as Fromentin, Loti, Délacroix, and Ingrès, among others, systematically forged a lasting image of the Arab woman that persists today. From the first colonial missions of 1830, French authorities believed that total submission of Algeria would be achieved if Algerian women could be Europeanized. They were, however, sorely mistaken, as the revolution proved.

42. Lazreg, *The Eloquence of Silence*, 132.

43. Lazreg, *The Eloquence of Silence*, 176.

44. Assia Djebar, *Les Enfants du nouveau monde* (Paris: Julliard, 1962), 312.

45. Assia Djebar, *Oran, langue morte* (Paris: Actes Sud, 1997), 371–2. My translation.

46. Awa Thiam, *La parole aux négresses* (Paris: Denoël. 1978), iii.

47. Carole Boyce Davies and Anne Adams Graves, *Ngambika: Studies of Women in African Literature* (Trenton, N.J.: Africa World Press: 1986), 26.

48. Maryse Condé, *La Parole des Femmes* (Paris: L'Harmattan, 1993), 3–4. My translation.

49. Condé, *La Parole*, 40. My translation.

50. Karen Smyley Wallace, "Women and Alienation: Analysis of the Works of Two Francophone African Novelists," in Davies and Graves, *Ngambika*, 65.

51. Condé, *La Parole*, 45.

52. Wallace, "Women and Alienation," 72.

53. Sandra M. Gilbert and Susan Gubar, *The Madwoman in the Attic* (New Haven, Conn.: Yale University Press, 1979), 55.

54. Gilbert and Gubar, *The Madwoman*, 55.

55. Gilbert and Gubar, *The Madwoman*, 20.

56. Shoshana Felman, "Women and Madness," in *Feminisms*, ed. R. Warhol et al. (New Brunswick, N.J.: Rutgers University Press, 1991), 7.

57. Hélèn Cixous, "The Laugh of the Medusa," in Warhol, *Feminisms*, 338.

58. Cited by Anne Adams in her article "To Write in a New Language: Werewere Liking's Adaptation of Ritual to the Novel," *Callaloo* 16, no. 1 (1993): 153–168, 153.

59. Elisabeth Mudimbé-Boyi, "Narrative 'Je(ux)' in Kamouraska and Juletane," in *Postcolonial Subjects: Francophone Women Writers*, ed. M. J. Green et al. (Minneapolis: University of Minnesota Press, 1996), 137.

60. Mudimbé-Boyi, "Narrative," 137.

61. Gilbert and Gubar, *The Madwoman*, 19.

62. Paul de Man, "Autobiography as De-facement," in *MLN* 94 (1979): 925.

63. Interview with Assia Djebar in *Le monde* 12 (1993), n.p.

64. Astbury, *Crazy for You*, 83.

65. Astbury, *Crazy for You*, 69–70.

66. Astbury, *Crazy for You*, 71–72.

67. Sigmund Freud, "The Ego and the Id," in *The Standard Edition of the Complete Psychological Works of Sigmund Freud*, vol. 19 (London: Hogarth, 1961).

68. Grosz, *Volatile Bodies*, 34–35.

69. Grosz, *Volatile Bodies*, 34–35.

70. Freud, "The Ego and the Id," 25.

71. Freud, "The Ego and the Id," 27.

72. M. Merleau-Ponty, *Phenomenology of Perception* (New York: Routledge, 1996), 154.

73. Grosz, *Volatile Bodies*, 145.

74. Grosz, *Volatile Bodies*, 148.

75. Thiher, *Revels in Madness*, 302.

76. Thiher, *Revels in Madness*, 302.

77. Mudimbé-Boyi, "Narrative," 138.

78. Jürgen Habermas, *Moral Consciousness and Communicative Action* (Cambridge, Mass.: MIT Press, 1993), 122.

79. Gayatri Spivak, *In Other Worlds: Essays in Culture and Politics* (New York: Routledge, 1988), 103.

80. Gilbert and Gubar, *The Madwoman*.

81. Habermas, *Moral Consciousness*, 135.

82. See Gilles Deleuze and Félix Guattari's *A Thousand Plateaus* for an explanation of the *becoming* principle. There is a becoming-animal, a becoming-woman, and a becoming-imperceptible. All these becomings are possible as an entity travels on the plane of consistency, territorializing and deterritorializing on plateaus between becomings-stages of identity transformation.

83. Juliet Flower Maccannell, *The Hysteric's Guide to the Future Female Subject* (Minneapolis: University of Minnesota Press, 2000), 29.

84. Maccannell, *Hysteric's Guide*, 206.

85. Calixthe Beyala, *Your Name Shall Be Tanga* (Portsmouth, N.H.: Heinneman, 1996); originally published as *Tu t'appelleras Tanga* (Paris: Editions Stock, 1986), 127.

86. Beyala, *Tanga*, 129.

87. Gilles Deleuze and Félix Guattari, *Anti-Oedipus: Capitalism and Schizophrenia* (Minneapolis: University of Minnesota Press, 1983), 2.

88. Makward, 118.

89. Homi K. Bhabha must be credited for conceptualizing the idea of the "Third Space." See his work, *The Location of Culture* (New York: Routledge, 1994).

90. Sandra Gilbert and Susan Gubar, *Madwoman in the Attic* (New Haven, Conn.: Yale University Press, 1979), 50.

91. Gilbert and Gubar, *The Madwoman*, 51.

92. Julia Kristeva, *Strangers to Ourselves*, 23.

93. Michel Foucault, *Histoire de la folie à l'âge classique* (Paris: Gallimard, 1972), 50.

94. This is true for West African and North African authors. However, Martinique in the 1920s and 1930s produced several prominent women authors who participated (albeit on a limited basis) in the Négritude movement. These authors included Suzanne Césaire; Suzanne Lacascade; and Paulette, Jane, and Andrée Nardal. For a profound study of these women, see T. Denean Sharpley-Whiting's book *Negritude Women* (Minneapolis: University of Minnesota Press, 2002).

STATE I

MEDIATING IDENTITY IN FOREIGN SPACES

What is theoretically innovative, and politically crucial, is the need to think beyond narratives of originary and initial subjectivities and to focus on those moments or processes that are produced in the articulation of cultural differences.

—Homi K. Bhabha, *The Location of Culture* (1994)

Chez moi c'est là où je mange mon pain.

[Home is where I eat my bread.]

—Leila Houari, *Zeida de nulle part* (1985)

Introduction to State I

Being in two, divided by two languages, two cultures, and/or two continents characterize the environments of the heroines of this study. This duality, this space of disjunction—*étrangeté*—is so often experienced by women authors writing from the francophone diaspora. As the authors, the heroines are exiled from their countries of origin and isolated because of their difference and their incessant search for liberty. Suzanne Lacascade and Leïla Houari define worlds where their heroines must mediate their identity in foreign spaces. These women are caught in the in-between, a third space that is both liberating and frightening. Claire-Solange and Zeida, operating in the in-between, transgress traditional cultural boundaries in order to confront their emotions, longings, and self-doubts. The third space is where the lives of Claire-Solange, in Martinican Suzanne Lacascade's *Claire-Solange, âme africaine*, and Zeida, of Moroccan Leïla Houari's *Zeida de nulle part*, are defined. These authors, although from different regions and origins, write about women who share a common denominator: they must live in a nomadic in-between space that represents both liberty and self-sacrifice. The irony of the nomad, the multiple-selved woman, is that she becomes implicated in a larger sphere of discovery, while, at the same time, she is alone, cut off from family and tribe, faced with the prejudice of others. As Julia Kristeva writes "belonging to nothing, the foreigner can feel affiliated with everything." The foreign nomad, because she is marked by her difference (whether it be skin color, nationality, views, or beliefs), lives in continuous exile and feels "constantly the hate of others."[1]

Alienation drawn along racial, ethnic, and/or gendered lines is a common theme found in the works studied in this section. Each heroine is caught up in a foreign world that she tries to understand and of which she wants to be a part. Yet, as the protagonists realize in the two novels considered here, discovering their own identities in a foreign environment means also negotiating endless adversities. Each woman desires to belong to a group and to be accepted because she knows that groups and association with a larger social order play important roles in the makeup of an individual's identity. As members of a group, women (as well as men) are expected to contribute to the foundation of a *cultural code* by which all individuals in the group must live.[2] Discovering the foreign cultural code of her adopted foreign society is the key to becoming part of it. As Leïla Houari's protagonist Zeida, of *Zeida de nulle part*, discovers, she is entangled in between two cultural codes, neither one of which is truly her own. On the one hand, she must insert herself into the urban, multicultural identity of Brussels and, on the other, the traditional village life of her parents' Morocco. Claire-Solange, of Suzanne Lacascade's 1924 novel *Claire-Solange, âme africaine*, is labeled "The Créole," locked in a no-man's land between white and black cultural spheres, both with which, at varying times, she identifies and despises. Being unable to break the cultural codes of these foreign spheres obliges the heroines of these novels to struggle against the ominous presence of mental distress that comes from nomadic wanderings and lack of integration into the indigenous societies with which they want to identify. Difference marginalizes these women on the borders of the norm, the accepted, and the nominative of cultural definition.

The novels studied here span sixty years and are testaments to the fact that, regardless of the era, women from different backgrounds are still confronted with the arduous task of carving out a place for themselves. "A room of their own," as Virginia Woolf would contend, is often unattainable but is necessary for women in order to construct their own unique, individual identity devoid of phallocentric oppression, traditional conventions, and social and cultural constraints.

An additional commonality these heroines share is an incessant need to cope with transcontinental separations and arduous relationships with men who do not understand them and who, more often than not, manipulate them in order to fulfill their own self-interests. Families also shape and mold the identity and lives of the protagonists discussed here. Claire-Solange's biracial identity is melded by two opposing family groups that are at constant odds with each other, forcing her to form allegiances along color lines. As evidenced in the forthcoming chapters, discovering their place and space not only ultimately determines Claire Solange's and Zeida's subjectivity, but also how they cope with the trauma of fighting the cultural codes that have been forced upon them. They learn that, even when forced to live within the foreign, fashioning another image for themselves, reflective of their own volition, will be inevitably difficult, but possible.

NOTES

1. Julia Kristeva, *Strangers to Ourselves*, 50. My translation and my emphasis.
2. Teresa Cristina Carreteiro, *Exclusion sociale et construction de l'identité* (Paris: L'Harmattan, 1993), 35. My translation.

1

The Politics of Race and Patriarchy in Suzanne Lacascade's *Claire-Solange, âme africaine*

> La Créole est d'une beauté plaisante, d'une grâce distinguée parmi ses politesses crues et banales, et d'une douceur excessive. Les blancs sont les biens-reçues des familles créoles et, après quelques jours de résidence, comptés comme les amis de la maison.
>
> [The Creole possesses a pleasant beauty, a distinguished grace among her raw and banal politenesses, and an excessive softness. Whites are well received by Creole families and, after some days in residence, counted among the friends of the house.]
>
> —Pétrus Durel, *La Femme dans les colonies françaises: Etudes sur les moeurs au point de vue mythologique et social* (1898)

> Mme. Pol Hucquart, sous un sourire figé, luttait contre une défaillance. Résisterai-je jusqu'à la fin? Trop de chocolat pour mon goût.
>
> [Madame Pol Hucquart, with a fixed smile, fought against feeling faint. Will I resist up to the end? Too much chocolate for my taste.]
>
> –Suzanne Lacascade, *Claire-Solange, âme africaine* (1924)

Racial discrimination, the bestiality of colonialism, marginalization, and imperial politics are the components of Martinican author Suzanne Lacascade's 1924 novel *Claire-Solange, âme africaine*. This little-known work, of which only thirty copies were printed by the Eugène Figuière Parisian publishing house, is shrouded in mystery. Less information is available about the author or under what circumstances she conceptualized and completed her novel. Based on the paltry sum of documents referring to her work, it may be surmised that this was the only novel Lacascade ever wrote. The author probably contributed to various reviews and journals of the first days of the Négritude movement, working with other women from Martinique, such as the Nardal sisters, Jane and Paulette, and Suzanne Césaire. Although the novel viewed through a postmodern lens seems rather melodramatic, Guadeloupian novelist Maryse Condé, the first scholar to study the work in depth, does remind us that it "is the first literary attempt by a woman of color from the Antilles that seeks out original qualities." Condé continues stating that "this novel was published in 1924, before the cries of Négritude and [therefore] it must be considered as the fruit of [the author's] personal development [as a novelist]."[1] The original qualities evident in Lacascade's novel to which Condé alludes are particularly bound up in the discourse of race, racial mixing and hierarchy, colonialism as construed by blacks and whites, and the power of men over women. Racialized parameters are synthesized, most significantly, through the protagonist Claire-Solange's view of, and opinion on, two environments: the first is France, whose language she speaks fluently but in which she feels foreign; and the second is Africa, a mythical place to which she is drawn due to her African ancestry filtered through her island home of Martinique. Although Claire-Solange reiterates time and again her "passion" and dedication to the defense and glorification "de la Race Noire" [of the Black Race], she eventually realizes that she will always be detached from being truly African and will never travel to African shores.[2] The detachment felt by her heroine alludes to Suzanne Lacascade's own feelings of *étrangeté*; a disjunction between woman-author-writing-in-French and her native country. Julia Kristeva defines this disjunction as a result of "not belonging to any place, any time, any love. A lost origin, the impossibility [of taking] root, a rummaging memory [haunted by] the present in abeyance. The space of the foreigner is a moving train, a plane, in flight, the very transition that precludes stopping."[3] This haunting foreignness and rootlessness manifest in the deep recesses of Claire-Solange's identity as she seeks to justify her mulatto skin as well as reject everything associated with the white race. She is the *anomalous* subject of Deleuze and Guattari's *Mille Plateaux* who is "an exceptional individual" and who no longer associates herself with "the pack. . . . [She] represents a power of another order, potentially acting as a threat as well as [an] outsider."[4] The anomalous woman author threatens social stability defined by masculine prerogatives. She insists on going against tribe, tradition, and established norms. She is the nomad who destabilizes as she establishes her own place that is new and uncharted. She is a femme fatale who makes men lose their self-control. At the end of Lacascade's novel, the anomalous Claire-Solange succeeds in cutting herself off from all racial ties—black or white—to exist in a no-(wo)man's land of racial ambiguity.

The protagonist's racial allegiances are problematic from the beginning. We are told in the first pages of the book that her mother, Aurore, a young *mulâtresse* "de nos vieilles colonies" [of our old colonies][5] embarks with her family for Paris for the 1889 Exposition. She falls in love and marries Etienne, a young Frenchman who "reniant son passé, brisant son avenir, rompant les liens du sang, [et] . . . s'expatriait, pour l'amour d'une fragile créole!" [gives up his past, breaks with his future, cutting blood ties, (and) . . . becomes an expatriate for the love of a fragile creole].[6] Returning in 1893 to Europe from Martinique (where Etienne is a high-ranking diplomat in the colonial mission of the French West Indies), he brings with him their infant daughter, Claire-Solange; their baby boy; and Aurore. Even though they take flight to the southern, more mild Midi region of France to escape the "frissons" of cold that affect the warm-blooded islanders during their stay in northern France, disaster strikes. First the baby and then Aurore fall ill and die. Claire-Solange returns to Martinique with her father.

As a woman author ahead of her time who produced a phenomenal novel for the 1920s, Lacascade pays close attention to the minute details that draw barriers between racial groups, nationalities, and gender of early twentieth-century Parisian life. Instead of portraying her character as a "typical" mulatto woman of her time (i.e., playing into the popular stereotypes of the day), Claire-Solange Duflôt Hucquart wields her African heritage to confront the white (masculine) world, drawing strength from her difference with re-sounding determination. The protagonist flaunts her skin color to construct a visible presence and an active voice in the *foreign* environment into which she is introduced. She divides her world in terms of color and then acts accordingly, even if it means going against prescribed norms of practice in the white, bourgeois Parisian world of 1914.

Lacascade probably relied on personal experience to create her work. She definitely attempts to draw out the racial prejudices of the day as well as the misconceptions the *colons* had about the *colonisés*. Her commentary on these misconceptions leads us to conclude that she did not see any possibility of mutual racial harmony or hope of equality in a non-color-blind world. Through her work, Lacascade makes it clear that the early twentieth century, for people of color living in France, was highly problematic. The author clearly describes how the French people viewed the black race (inclusive of its various shades) as inferior, colonized, and in need of being saved culturally, intellectually, and linguistically. It is for these reasons that her novel is a valuable resource, shedding light on the intricacies of the politics of race in early-twentieth-century Paris as well as in the colonies.

Lacascade's *Claire-Solange* breaks with the typical writing style of the *assimilé*. These authors from the colonized Francophone diaspora, raised and formed in the French education system, strove to write like Frenchmen, modeling their prose on popular European styles of the time. Conversely, Lacascade exposes readers to the dialogue, the unaltered voice, of *real* people of color from the Islands. She constructs her novel in the local French créole of the heroine's milieu, exposing the uninitiated reader to a speech that is a mélange of African dialects and French West Indian idioms. The French, white reader of the time is forced to contemplate otherness as he/she is exposed to Claire-Solange's world. As the impending doom of World War I draws nearer, this whole new world is transported on the same boat with the heroine as she and "tous les Duflôt et leurs alliés" [all the Duflôts and their allies], créole aunts and uncles, and her grandmother (on her mother's side) arrive with her white father, Etienne Hucquart, at the Paris mansion of the widow Madame Pol Hucquart (Etienne's dead brother's wife).[7]

As one of the first feminists of color, Lacascade constructs a politically charged text (calling for a dialogue on race) while offering a staunch message on women's subjugated roles in society. The author comments openly and critically on the restriction of (both white and black) women's intellect by the societal structures forged by men in France and the Antilles. Despite its melodramatic flair, *Claire-Solange* is certainly an advanced treatise for its era, both for white and black women living in France. Lacascade's novel is filled with creole sentences and sayings translated by Claire-Solange who attempts to enlighten her white family about the charms and actualities of the Martinican heritage from which she comes. Dispelling stereotypes, the heroine defines her speech with phrases such as "comme nous disons" [as we say], marking territory along ethnic lines between the Creoles of the house and her aunt's stuffy, bourgeois, white society.

Claire-Solange's powerful voice interjects not only into white, bourgeois circles, but also into the tight male cliques of masculine salon society normally off-limits to women. When the protagonist breaks into these forbidden spaces, Lacascade peppers Claire-Solange's speeches with creole maxims, songs, and poems as well as very vivid visual descriptions of the Islands, all the while offering sociocultural and political commentary on the human condition of those of color who live (and historically were enslaved) in the colonies. Lacascade's novel opens up the world of the Creole as never before. Adding to the revelations of creole culture that her heroine imparts, Lacascade includes three "bel-airs des Antilles" (*Mardi-Gras, Le Clair soleil,* and *Dis-moi Doudou*), complete with piano scores, to further instruct her audience at the end of her novel. The inclusion of these short musical scores makes Lacascade's novel effective in three different registers: the linguistic, the visual, and the auditory. We not only read of the life of the Creole, we *experience* it.

Claire-Solange is, above all, a novel about seeking a place in the margins of society and about the disconnected isolation felt by one woman caught in the in-between space of race and identity. The young heroine is neither black nor white nor French nor African. She is defined by her difference in both racialized worlds. For whites whom she encounters, she is exotic, for black Africans, she is viewed as French, white, and an *assimilée* of the Martinican elite, imbued with the Parisian, bourgeois haute-culture of the time. Even Claire-Solange's name evokes conflict and racial ambiguity. "Claire," meaning "light" in French, further complicates the protagonist's identity. She is unsure whether to seek out and embrace her whiteness—her lightness—or reject it.[8] From the moment she sets foot on French soil, she fights to secure herself in a definitive category, defining for her white cousin, the dandy Jacques Danzel, the nuances of racial type in the colonial world and the dissent between "*bequés* and *mulâtres, capres* and *quarterons*":[9]

> Claire-Solange prend la parole:—Créole: né aux colonies, exemple: boeuf créole, cheval créole, liriez-vous dans un dictionnaire. Mulâtre vient de mulet, veut dire: incapable de créer une famille. Les blancs aiment à nous donner ce nom et nous l'acceptons en riant,—moi du moins,—comme une preuve de leur suffisance.
>
> [Claire-Solange interjects:—Creole, born in the colonies, example: creole beef, creole horse, you'd read in the dictionary. Mulatto comes from mule, which means: incapable of creating a family. Whites like to give us this name and we accept it laughing,—I do, at least,—as proof of their self-importance].[10]

Not only does her articulation of the categorization of race and its colonial lexicon force the reader to remark on the bestiality of the colonial enterprise, she also demonstrates her outspoken nature as a woman with a mind, intellect, and political savvy ready to comment on the sociocultural inadequacies of her time. The young heroine leaves her audience, her cousin, Jacques Danzel, his godmother, Mme. Pol Hucquart, and her father, Etienne Hucquart, speechless. They are more incredulous when she follows her laundry list of definitions with a direct statement claiming her affinity to the black race ("moi je suis nègre") as well as to Jews, whom she also views as "une . . . race opprimée" [a . . . race that is oppressed].[11] Mme. Pol Hucquart is surprised at Claire-Solange's affection for both races from which she views the young heroine as being disassociated not only by color but also by nature and class. Her aunt asks her point-blank, "Pourquoi te dis-tu nègre?" [Why do you call yourself black?], to which Claire-Solange responds:

> Pourquoi? Voyez mes cheveux crépus, je ne saurais les lisser en cadenettes contre mes joues, comme les Juifs d'Aden, je ne pourrais les relever en chignon 1830. . . . Mes cheveux de nègre, il faut les séparer en bandeaux, les tordre tant bien que mal sur la nuque. . . . Régardez-moi bien. . . . Pour renier l'origine africaine, il me faudrait vivre sous un voile, ne laissant passer ni mes yeux, ni mon nez. Allons, tante, un sourire. Acceptez telle quelle une femme de couleur qui donnera de la variété à la famille.
>
> [Why? Look at my frizzy hair, I wouldn't know how to smooth it out in long curls laid against my cheeks like the Jews of Aden, I could never pull it back in a bun (in the style of) 1830. . . . Take a good look at me. . . . In order to deny (my) African origin, I would have to live under a veil, not letting my eyes nor my nose show. Come on Aunt, smile. Accept that a woman of color adds a little spice to the family.][12]

Again, Lacascade makes reference to the exotic nature of the French colonial enterprise as it is construed through the seduction of race. Playing on the idea of the veil (which particularly calls attention to the French fascination with veiled North African Arab women, ideas of the harem, and sexual licentiousness) and Africa as a continent veiled in darkness and in need of enlightenment by French culture and intellect, Claire-Solange challenges the popular imperial politics of the early twentieth century. Curiously, where she allies herself with Jews as one of the oppressed, in the succeeding paragraph she defines the sociocultural incongruence between Jews and blacks by drawing on their hair texture as a deciding factor for what is considered "white" and "black." Lacascade's confused views on racial categories can hardly be condemned here, since she is relying most probably on the popular ethnographic/demographic strategies of the French colonial missions in Africa, which were popular in the late nineteenth and early twentieth centuries. The plethora of information sent back from the colonies in the form of ethnographic and natural histories shaped the minds of the French population. This information provided evidence, as it was believed at the time, of the inferiority of those of color and led to the labeling of these same peoples as exotic, much to the delight of the mystified French public. Frédéric Cuvier and Geoffroy St. Hillaire's *Histoire naturelle des mammifères* and Cuvier's *Discours sur les révolutions du globe,* published in 1824 and 1864, respectively, paved the way for a century of racial categorization that was based, according to these scientific studies, on fact.[13] Even after Claire-Solange's speech on racial categories, the heroine's aunt, still unable to understand her niece's division of the races (Lacascade poignantly makes us aware that the French *just don't get it*), responds, "Laisse donc reposer tes instincts de lutte; en France la question de couleur compte si peu" [Leave aside your fighting instincts; in France the question of color counts for so little].[14] Clearly, difference for her aunt is based on *malcompréhension* rather than any prejudice. Lacascade embodies in Aunt Hucquart the typical French reaction to the problem of race: categorize and then assimilate all difference, because once a *colonisé* is incorporated into the French Empire, he/she is considered French. Mme. Pol's reaction to her niece's views reflect the author's awareness of the bitter lessons of assimilationist politics endured by people of color in the colonies; policies originally mandated by the republican tenants of the French revolution.[15] The colonized were assimilated into the French realm and expected to embrace their adopted Frenchness, or *Francisation,* as the process was known, with open arms. Those foreigners living in France were also expected to kowtow to French republican ideology, which promoted the solid centralization of the French state. National decrees such as the 1888 Decree sought to "grant immigrants the same type of civil status as French nationals" with the understanding that these immigrants would adopt "new Christian name[s]" in order to adhere to the "logic of republican law [that struggled] to eliminate all traces of origins."[16] Today, as it was during Lacascade's time, at the heart of France's nation-state model is the need to promote unity, gather all citizens under one republican umbrella, and assimilate and eradicate all markers of difference within the population. This model is based on the belief that, through the *machine à francisation,* as minister Adophe Landry expressed in 1914, France would be protected from "the formation of non-indigenous cores that might alter our race."[17]

Within the quagmire of the white/black racial divide and assimilationist politics, Lacascade throws her volatile young heroine into the fray of a paternal/colonial, slave/master dialectic. Claire-Solange rejects the white race she sees as the enslavers of those of color, yet she sets her father (who is white) apart from the oppressors. For the young girl, the stoic patriarch of the colonial regime in Martinique, Monsieur Hucquart, sacrificed a brilliant career in France to be with his beloved Aurore and work as a notable functionary in the French Colonial Bureau. He is not implicated historically as a *colon* and is above the malicious behavior of whites in the colonies. For his daughter, Hucquart *is and isn't* white. The heroine even reveres him for having fought "depuis un siècle pour la cause de couleur" [for a century, for the cause of color].[18] Metaphorically, patriarchy operates on two levels. On the one hand, Claire-Solange rejects France, the fatherland of the assimilated creole and promoter of the *mission civilisatrice,* an imperial policy said to be necessary to educate and assimilate the indigène. Yet, on the other, she embraces this same fatherland because it is her father's homeland. According to Claire-Solange, her father is patient, indulgent, and, even though he works for the system, cannot be considered as someone who has profited from it.

With the outbreak of World War I, Claire-Solange realizes that she loves Jacques (who is drafted to the Front). Her father's self-sacrifice for a special mission to an undisclosed military outpost and her decision to volunteer as a nurse in a Parisian hospital contribute to her change of heart with respect to France. This foreign country becomes a metaphor for a beloved, complaisant, father-symbol worthy of her love. In the end, France embodies an archetypical accepted father as the young woman changes her hostile views toward the father['s]land in favor of love for her adopted *patrie.* This fatherland image melds in symbiosis with the *personnage* of her own biological father: "Pourquoi faut-il, Papa, que j'aie attendu le malheur pour comprendre!" [Why father did I have to wait until catastrophe in order to understand!] she declares in a letter to Etienne Hucquart while working in a hospital where she tends wounded from the Front.[19] Later in the letter she admits that it wasn't until she had heard "le tocsin d'alarme parmi les paysans, en priant Sainte-Geneviève avec les civils, en circulant à travers Paris . . . qu'elle a connu la vraie France" [the alarm bell among the peasants, praying with the people in Sainte-Geneviève, navigating around Paris . . . that she came to know the true France].[20] War generates her compassion for a country that, before, was synonymous with abjection and oppression.

Her sermons of love sent to Jacques at the Front go unanswered; yet this lack of acknowledgment causes her to embrace even more an "ardeur de sacrifice" as she resigns herself to never leave France, but to stay and claim her beloved hero when he returns.[21]

The protagonist's about-face and ideological changes are shocking and take the reader by surprise. How could this militant woman of color, who espouses the tenants of a new black consciousness and feminism, succumb to the tutelage of white patriarchy? Frantz Fanon would suggest almost thirty years later in *Black Skin, White Masks* that giving up one's blackness is a result of the imperfections of love, as well as its perversions.[22] Fanon's critique of Martinican Mayotte Capécia's 1948 novel *Je suis martiniquaise* in his work *Black Skin, White Masks* may apply to Lacascade's novel. Fanon criticized Capécia for devaluing black men in her aspirations for whiteness. Upon a first reading, it does seem that Lacascade falls into the same trap as Capécia of succumbing to what Fanon defines as black women's need to become white (thus, according to his hypothesis, obtaining financial gain as well as increased social standing) through liaisons with white men. He states that Capécia's penchant for white men is based on the fact that, for her, it is "customary in Martinique to dream of a form of salvation, that consists of magically turning white."[23] Fanon condemned Capécia for "valorizing whiteness in her aspirations to privilege."[24]

By contrast, Lacascade's novel dissolves any similar criticism, offering a heroine who is sure of herself and able to make her own way in the world without the aid of men, white or black. Claire-Solange, unlike Capécia, never views herself as inferior with respect to the white part of her family or French society, nor does she believe she was underprivileged. On the contrary, as Emilienne, the protagonist's Martinican aunt, remarks to her: "c'est ta double hérédité qui te rend si vaillante" [it's your double heredity that makes you so valiant].[25] Claire-Solange's love for Jacques is based not on attraction because of his white skin (which in fact she views as beige and ugly), but rather pure love. At no point does she experience feelings of inadequacy because of her race, nor does Claire-Solange hypothesize that her life would have been less difficult if she had been white, as Mayotte Capécia states in her 1948 novel: "Si [ma grande-mère] avait épousée un blanc, peut-être aurais-je été tout à fait blanche . . . ? Et la vie aurait été moins difficile pour moi" [if my grandmother had married white, perhaps I would have been totally white and life would have been less difficult for me?].[26] Nor does Claire-Solange feel that marrying a white man will give her status or "make her more white," as Mayotte contends when she admits: "J'aurai voulu me marier, mais avec un blanc" [I wanted to marry, but with a white man].[27] We can only speculate on the impact Lacascade's novel would have had on Fanon's hypothesis concerning sexuality, women, and race. If anything, the reason Claire-Solange's love for Jacques Danzel is heightened at the end of the war and the novel is because of his infirm, broken body. She feels it is her duty *as a woman* and as a nurse to love him. As feminists and scholars of race, we cringe at the heroine's need to give into the persona fashioned for her by the patriarchal/colonial system as nurturer and caregiver to her white man. We might surmise that Lacascade's heroine falls into "a symbolic order," as francophone literary scholar and critic Françoise Lionnet would suggest. This symbolic order, Lionnet contends, often influences the outcome of heroines' destinies in francophone novels written by women of the Antilles.[28] Yet unlike the protagonists of later novels, such as Myriam Warner-Vieyra's *Juletane* and Michèle Lacrosil's *Cajou* (both analyzed in the following chapters), two women who die as a result of investing too much in men (black and white, respectively) and false promises, Claire-Solange survives intact mentally and physically at the end of Lacascade's novel. Out of her own volition, the heroine makes a series of choices to which she adheres.

Within the postmodern framing of francophone literature, where race is often a principal issue, we may conclude that Suzanne Lacascade's work fails to be the manifesto championing freedom and equality for the colonized that it started out to be. In the end, Claire-Solange abandons her staunch views about the necessity of breaking the chains of racial oppression in order to embrace the love she feels for a white man. However, I argue that we must consider the novel as reflecting the views of its era. If understood solely as a commentary on the way things were and how they stood with regard to gender divisions and racial stereotypes, Lacascade's work is a valid reflection on the patriarchy and dominant male codes that ruled both black and white women's lives in early-twentieth-century France. In the end, it is obvious that, like her heroine, Lacascade considered change along gender and racial lines to be elusive, something for future generations to undertake. She set out to provide a commentary on the social prerogatives of race and gender in France during the World War I era, giving credence to the fact that, as Lionnet suggests, "women writers are often especially aware of their task as producers of images that both participate in the dominant representations of their culture and simultaneously undermine and subvert those images by offering a re-vision of familiar scripts."[29]

Claire-Solange opens a window to how things were in pre– and post–World War I France, not how they should be. The heroine comments on events as an elite Creole woman perhaps might have at the time, admitting that she had become transformed by "the French sun."[30] This colonizing, imperial country molded her like a father molds a daughter. Claire-Solange *becomes* French, adopting the French assimilé view of her colonial past. Lacascade reveals the painful truth about the colonial situation: the colonized could not escape the influence of francisation and the power of the imperial machine. Claire-Solange's francisation, the change in the way she views France and her home island, are construed through the metaphorical interplay of theme and language. Metaphors abound when describing the dialectic colony/France and are defined in terms of nature. The young woman gives into the identity that is fashioned for her by Parisian bourgeois society, realizing that sacrifice is everything and that "son bonheur, lorsque la Patrie est dans le besoin, ne convient pas à un héro" [her happiness, when the Fatherland is in need, is not admirable for a hero].[31] Instead of effacing lines between colonized and colonizer, clear distinctions between the two spaces become more distinct. Martinique becomes something where "rien n'est réglementé" [nothing is ordered], where everything "se reproduit spontanément" [is reproduced spontaneously], while the opposite is true of "ordered" and "civilized" France, where "un jardinier . . . n'accorde pas à la nature la liberté de rester spontanée, fougueuse, luxuriante" [a gardener . . . does not let nature have its freedom to remain spontaneous, spirited, luxurious].[32] Claire-Solange eventually even views the war in a positive light because it has forged a "union sacrée" [sacred union] between "blancs et mulâtres dans les oeuvres et les comités" [blacks and mulattos in tasks and in committees].[33] Just as a promoter of assimilationist politics would hope, Claire-Solange, in her desperate situation of waiting without word from Jacques, treating other men whom she declares resemble her lover as they lay dying in their hospital beds, begins to "contemple ce symbole de la vie d'Europe" [contemplate this symbol of European life] which, from her privileged milieu, she sees now as not much different than what she had known in the Antilles. It is the universal and "vrai foyer de famille" [true family home] that creates "l'intimité" [intimacy], she concludes.[34] Within this intimacy, race and ethnic strife are forgotten. Claire-Solange sets everything aside (as she totally assimilates into her bourgeois life) for Jacques and the ideal of the nuclear family: "elle aime, exclusivement, farouchement, tragiquement, comme une Africaine, et elle acceptera l'existence emprisonnée d'Europe, cette vie de bourgeois dont elle connaît le tissu beige, à l'envers sanglant" [she loves exclusively, ferociously, tragically, like an African woman, and she will accept the imprisoned existence of Europe, this bourgeois life whose beige cloth she knows has a bloody lining].[35]

Love of family and *patrie* become the centering forces that dictate the heroine's actions for the rest of the novel. Claire-Solange's militant *métissage* takes a backseat to her assimilation into the French elite bourgeoisie class of Paris. Lacascade regards the world of the métis through an exterior diegesis wherein, as Françoise Vergès explains in *Monsters and Revolutionaries: Colonial Family Romance and Métissage*, "the emergence of a new identity" takes place. This new identity insists on "the productive quality of discourse" and does not seek to radically change the racist status quo.[36] At the end of the novel, Lacascade's heroine chooses not to discount her white heritage, albeit born of pain, suffering, and slavery. Through the voice of Claire-Solange, the author deconstructs colonialism and its markers upon her subjectivity through a "process of anamnesis," which assumes that "the past has the value of representing what is lacking" by proposing a new discourse wherein a "heterological position of the subject [is favored]."[37] This heterologically positioned subject situates him/herself within "a social and cultural matrix of race, gender, class, and sexual difference."[38] Within the matrix, the Creole woman scrutinizes "suspicion toward the ideals brought by Europe and the Enlightenment [and, at the same time, recognizes an affiliation with] these ideals."[39] If we place Claire-Solange within this matrix—this new identity that she views as constructed, not out of a denial of the past, but rather an embrace of the facts of the present, which do not discount the privilege of her class—her change in attitude at the end of the novel becomes more comprehensible. The heroine, as did Lacascade, sets herself within this convergence of racial ambiguity, a place the author seems to acknowledge that only the métis can understand. Claire-Solange speaks with the knowledge that she must, as Vergès states in her study, "work within her own history, away from the ideological discourse of European feminism about patriarchy and power relations . . . [she must] resist the *altericide* (destruction of otherness) led by the French state" in order to carve out her own specific identity in the world.[40]

Lacascade embraces her métis identity, which she views as unique and special in the world. Maryse Condé remarks that Claire-Solange fashions her identity out of what she is and the love she is able to give because of who she is: "According to [Lacascade] . . . Claire-Solange captures for her benefit the warmth, the generosity and the abundance of her [island]. She also carries within herself an Earthly Paradise that only asks to blossom."[41] Although the heroine regrets that she must remain and live with her husband in France, she admits that she draws strength from the knowledge that she possesses a certain "vrai soleil . . . en moi-même" [a true sun . . . within myself].[42] Lacascade truly believes, as she foregrounds the thoughts of her heroine, in the "greatness of Africa and the African man," yet she also accepts "the white world [and co-opts] possession of the very elements that are inherent in racist mythology."[43] Lacascade definitely wishes to efface the stereotypes attached to women of the Antilles, whom Condé suggests are viewed by whites in popular lore as "servants, charged with taking care of the white man's child, [as] enslaved fieldhands turning the soil under the sun, [and as] forever humiliated concubines." In place of these archetypes, the author seeks to build a new identity that will promote another type of "woman of the Tropics."[44] This strong and independent woman of the Tropics is not like Mayotte Capécia, who considers being white the summit of a perfect ideal she wants to obtain. In contrast, Claire-Solange's view of whiteness throughout Lacascade's novel is synonymous with death and foreboding; a death "more deathly than a mortar-shell."[45] Whiteness for the heroine is the equivalent of a void—an abyss—into which she does not want to fall. By the end of the novel, readers are well aware of the heroine's metaphorical suffocation and, on a certain level, do identify with her plight. Claire-Solange is able to "pull back the curtain of snow" in order to let her African "smile of hope" come through, but she pays a price.[46] The author grounds a new heterological subject within the identity of Claire-Solange and overturns privileged whiteness, offering another version of a woman of color's story in a white man's world. Yet, as the author duly notes in the tone of the closing pages, in the end, her protagonist is unable to avoid the reality of the sociocultural and racial constructs of the time.

Lacascade's novel does not offer a prescription for racial liberation. Claire-Solange does not conquer the purviews of masculine domination or succeed in vocalizing a strong argument against colonial assimilationist theory. The work remains purely a commentary on the *way things were* for one Creole woman of the elite class of Martinique during the early part of the twentieth century; an era stratified by war, colonialism, racism, and French bourgeois idealism about race. At the end of the novel, Claire-Solange, for her love for Jacques (who is wounded for life and embittered by the war and human carnage he witnessed on the battlefield), remains to take care of him in this beige in-between world set at the crux of white and black, where *étrangeté* will forever define the young heroine's identity as, indeed, it must have the author's.

NOTES

1. Condé, *La Parole*, 29. My translation. To my knowledge, and after careful research and correspondence with Maryse Condé, she is the only literary scholar to have read and studied Lacascade's work in depth. In 1999, scholar Tracy D. Sharpley-Whiting refers to Lacascade's novel in her study *Black Venus: Sexualized Savages, Primal Fears, and Primitive Narratives in French* (Durham, N.C.: Duke University Press, 1999). The novel is practically impossible to find because there were only thirty copies printed. Two libraries contain the edition in their collections—Yale Library and the Bibliothèque Nationale in Paris.

2. Suzanne Lacascade, *Claire-Solange, âme africaine* (Paris: E. Figuière, 1924), 75.

3. Julia Kristeva, *Strangers to Ourselves* (New York: Columbia University Press, 1991), 7–8.

4. Gilles Deleuze and Félix Guattari, *A Thousand Plateaus* (Minneapolis: University of Minnesota Press, 1987), 245–46.

5. "Old Colonies" refers to the first French colonial settlements in the West Indies dating back to the late seventeenth century. These included Martinique, Guadeloupe, and Haiti.

6. Lacascade, *Claire-Solange*, 13–14. All translations of Lacascade's work are my own.

7. Lacascade, *Claire-Solange*, 19.

8. My words in French.

9. The four racial groups that make up Martinican society. Lacascade, *Claire-Solange*, 35.

10. Lacascade, *Claire-Solange*, 35–36.

11. Lacascade, *Claire-Solange,* 36.

12. Lacascade, *Claire-Solange,* 36–37.

13. T.D. Sharpley-Whiting, *Black Venus: Sexualized Savages, Primal Fears, and Primitive Narratives* (Durham, N.C.: Duke University Press, 1999), 22.

14. Lacascade, *Claire-Solange,* 37.

15. France has anchored its identity, its being in the world, in the modern age—that of the *Lumières* of the late eighteenth century. Great philosophers such as Jean-Jacques Rousseau promoted the philosophical idea of "ontological security" based on racial and ethnic origins and hierarchies. A century later, France led the way in constructing its imperial identity by drawing on anthropological-sociological structures as proposed by great French ethnologists of the nineteenth century, such as renowned zoologist and author of *Discours sur les révolutions du globe,* Georges Cuvier (Sara Bartmaan's dissector). French statesmen's penchant interest in mixing science and politics throughout the late eighteenth, nineteenth, and most of the twentieth century solidified policies on race through study of the colonized world. The French civilizing mission in Africa, the Americas, and Asia—from the *vieilles* colonies in Guadeloupe and Martinique to Algeria and the Maghreb (colonized in the nineteenth century)—provided a testing ground for anthropological hypotheses of the day held in high esteem in Europe. Upholding doctrines such as the "First Order of Nature," Donna Haraway suggests, became "a colonial affair," where African men, women, and children found themselves under a "system of unequal exchange" held at bay by an "extractive colonialism" that categorized every aspect of the colonial world (Donna Haraway, *Primate Visions* [New York: Routledge, 1989], 119). North African colonization propelled the French scientific world toward leaps and bounds of discovery, following on the heels of military conquests that inevitably sparked the public's interest in further study of the exotic flora and fauna of the newly founded colonies. The enthusiasm of Napoleon III for the scientific ventures of the colonial missions accumulated eventually into the founding of the Société Zoologique d'Acclimation in the spring of 1855. Frantz Fanon later wrote in his work *Les Damnés de la terre* (*The Wretched of the Earth*) that "Le language du colon, quand il s'agit du colonisé, est un language zoologique" [The language of the colonizer is a zoological language]. The link between science and colonialism took on its most heinous attributes toward the end of the nineteenth century, when "human zoos" became the rage in Paris. After the successful "dog exhibition" in 1874, human exhibitions boasting African specimens became widely popular. Humans behind bars, put on display, became a common occurrence across Europe. In Berlin in 1879, six Zulu warriors were displayed, and from 1877 to 1893, several "tribes" were exhibited in the Jardin d'Acclimatation in Paris. Such fascination, however, does not end with the nineteenth century. As recent as 1994, a zoo near Nantes, France, wanted to create a "village ivorien" [Ivory Coast Village] but were discouraged by a wave of antiracist organizations ("Zoo humains," *Le Monde,* 17 January 2000).

Anthropological classifications based on race dissimilated any potential chaos within the French psyche over racial-ethnical questions and created a sense of security for the white colonials of late-nineteenth-century France. Even later into the twentieth century, François Mittérand himself declared that "Algeria would always be part of France," it had been conveniently assimilated, and its cultures—Arab and Berber—had been classified within the strata of ethnic boundaries according to French science; Algerians would forever be French.

16. Gérard Noiriel, *The French Melting Pot: Immigration, Citizenship, and National Identity* (Minneapolis: University of Minnesota Press, 1996), 74.

17. Noiriel, *French Melting Pot*, 84–85.

18. Lacascade, *Claire-Solange*, 37.

19. Lacascade, *Claire-Solange*, 180.

20. Lacascade, *Claire-Solange*, 181.

21. Lacascade, *Claire-Solange*, 181.

22. Frantz Fanon, *Black Skin, White Masks* (New York: Grove Press, 1967), 42.

23. Fanon, *Black Skin*, 44.

24. T. Denean Sharpley-Whiting, *Frantz Fanon: Conflicts and Feminisms* (Lanham, Md.: Rowman & Littlefield, 1998), 37.

25. Lacascade, *Claire-Solange*, 189.

26. Mayotte Capécia, *Je suis martiniquaise* (Paris: Corréa, 1948), 59.

27. Capécia, *Je suis martiniquaise*, 202.

28. Françoise Lionnet, *"Geographies of Pain: Captive Bodies and Violent Acts in the Fictions of Myriam Warner-Vieyra, Gayl Jones, and Bessie Head," Calaloo* 16, no. 1 (1993): 132–152, 132.

29. Lionnet, *Geographies*, 132.

30. Lacascade, *Claire-Solange*, 202.

31. Lacascade, *Claire-Solange*, 202.

32. Lacascade, *Claire-Solange*, 202.

33. Lacascade, *Claire-Solange*, 179.

34. Lacascade, *Claire-Solange*, 179.

35. Lacascade, *Claire-Solange*, 205.

36. Françoise Vergès, *Monsters and Revolutionaries: Colonial Family Romance and Métissage* (Durham, N.C.: Duke University Press, 1999), 12.

37. Vergès, *Monsters*, 16–17.

38. Vergès, *Monsters*, 17.

39. Vergès, *Monsters*, 17.

40. Vergès, *Monsters*, 20. Author's emphasis.

41. Maryse Condé, *La Parole des femmes: Essai sur des romancières des Antilles et de langue française* (Paris: L'Harmattan, 1979), 30.

42. Lacascade, *Claire-Solange*, 5.

43. Condé, *La Parole*, 31.

44. Condé, *La Parole*, 30.

45. Lacascade, *Claire-Solange*, 220.

46. Lacascade, *Claire-Solange*, 193.

2

Home Is Where I Eat My Bread

Multiculturality and Becoming Multiple in Leïla Houari's *Zeida de nulle part*

L'Ecriture décentrée rendrait compte de développements à l'intérieur de l'Hexagone d'une littérature marquée par des différences linguistiques et culturelles ancrées en partie dans l'origine étrangère des écrivains.

[Decentered writing takes into consideration the developments inside the Hexagone (France) of a literature marked by linguistic and cultural differences anchored, in part, in the foreign origins of the authors.]

—Michel Laronde, *L'Écriture décentrée: la langue de l'Autre dans le roman contemporain* (1996)

"Beur" est un mot bizarre, à la construction peu rationnelle, produit d'une manipulation complexe de "verlan": à partir d'arabe, on arrive à "Beur," ce qui permet les jeux de mots sur "petits beurres," et même le féminin "beurette." Mais le sens est clair: il s'agit d'un jeune né en [Europe], dont les parents sont immigrés. Le langage officiel ne propose que la lourde et longue périphrase: "jeune issue de l'immigration."

["Beur" is a strange word, based on a very irrational construction, produced by a complex (linguistic) manipulation known as "verlan" (backwards talk): taken from the Arabic "Arabe" in French we get "Beur," this allows word play such as "petits beurres" (which are cookies) and even the feminine form "Beurette." But the sense of the word is clear: it means an adolescent born in France (or Francophone Europe) whose parents are immigrants. The official language only offers a heavy and long circumlocution: "an adolescent born out of immigration."]

—*Parler au Quotidien. Les Archives Inofficielles* (2001)

Charles Taylor explains in his work *Multiculturalism* that contemporary discourses in multicultural politics are grounded in recognition and in the idea "that my own identity crucially depends on my dialogical relations with others."[1] However, as Taylor further contends, these dialogical relations do not provide the subject's automatic recognition a priori, "[he/she] has to win it through exchange, and the attempt can fail."[2] Beur novels, written by the sons and daughters of North African immigrants who now reside in France, Belgium, and parts of Switzerland, best exemplify these contemporary dialogical relations as grounded in these authors' demands for recognition and the right to be different.[3] The Beur author seeks to blend several reference points while searching to define his/her identity. This identity is construed on the liminal edges of hegemonic discourse (French space in Europe), while also drawing on the past life experiences of the parents' homeland, which, for the Beurs', is Algeria, Tunisia, or Morocco. Through the act of writing in French from this a-centered space, the Beur author defines a new sense of being and a new discourse. Michel Laronde contests that this new discourse is "de-centered," favoring

> writing that, with regards to a centered Language and a Culture, produces a Text that maintains linguistic and ideological gaps . . . this writing is produced at the interior of a Culture by authors who are partially removed from it, this removal (both of the writing and of the author) exerts a twist on the form and the value of the message.[4]

Such de-centered writing changes the dynamic not only of the French language, but also the relationship of cultures to history and what has been written about the Other by dominating Eurocentric and, I might add, colonial discourse. Furthering this hypothesis, Keith Walker remarks in his book *Countermodernism and Francophone Literary Culture* "that the challenge of the francophone writer is to translate, in the archaic sense of *translatio studii*—that is, to carry over into the French language or the culture of the Other—the particularity of self and culture, as well as the sense of home."[5]

"Home" in terms of multiculturality for the Beur author is a problematic emblem, something that is not quite defined at the outset of the author's introspection, but must be discovered. Finding stability within the multicultural is achieved through a nomadic process of self-discovery. There are often what seem like endless roads to follow before one finds, at last, one's place. Home must be sought out through the understanding of how multiculturality influences the field of reference of the author. The Beur author asks, How do I reconcile my parents' traditional life with my European world? Like Lacascade's Claire-Solange, Zeida, of Leïla Houari's 1985 novel *Zeida de nulle part*, must navigate between two spaces, finding few clues to her true identity in either one. As did Claire-Solange, Zeida must negotiate European ideals and values placed upon her by whites. Although Houari wrote her novel sixty-one years after Lacascade's work was published, many of Zeida's feelings of isolation also stem from marginalization because of skin color or cultural determinates that codify her as "different." Postmodern ideals promoted in the late 1980s and 1990s fostering the appeal and positivity of multiculturalism perhaps make Zeida's choices somewhat more easy to make than those of Claire-Solange. However, her underlying feelings of étrangeté—being foreign and out of place in a cold, beige world—still prevail in Houari's novel, haunting the heroine who knows that she will always exist in the "nulle part," the no-(wo)man's land between two cultures.

Locating a sense of home by negotiating multicultural space is something author Leïla Houari grew to accept from personal experience. The oldest of seven children born in Casablanca, Morocco, in 1958, Houari experienced the painful process of immigration when her family moved to Belgium in 1965.[6] Zeida, the author's young heroine, finds herself searching for her identity somewhere in between her family's immigrant apartment in Brussels and her homeland, Morocco. Houari emphasizes the heroine's feelings of *déracinement*—uprootedness—which are so great that Zeida feels as if she has no real substance, no identity. She exists "nowhere," as the title suggests, caught between European and Moroccan worlds. Zeida is constantly threatened with the possibility of losing all sense of her Self and falling into the abyss of "nulle part." She is unable to root herself totally in her adopted country, Brussels. Yet, when she does finally go to Morocco (which she left at age five), she finds that she is considered a foreigner, unable to fit into the village life of her parents because she has been Europeanized. Zeida literally exists on the margins of two identities, one Moroccan and one European. However, somewhere in the middle—within the "nowhere"—she discovers that there is a compromise. As the young girl's mother tells her: "chez moi c'est là où je mange mon pain" [my home is where I eat my bread].[7] In the end, the protagonist finds that her identity is located in a multicultural space where fragments of experience on both sides of the Mediterranean make up a whole. She exclaims: "j'ai voulu rejeter mon histoire et voilà qu'elle me poursuit, me harcèle, me rit au visage et me laisse perdue" [I wanted to reject my history and voila, here it is pursuing me, antagonizing me and laughing in my face, leaving me lost].[8] The girl discovers that she cannot escape her history, she must accept it, refashion it, and find a place in the nowhere to make it a somewhere of importance. That somewhere is not located in the home world of her parents or in the French speaking world of her European peers, it is situated in the middle; in the overlap of two cultures. Zeida's "overlapped" identity is constructed in terms of what Homi K. Bhabha calls a "cultural globality," defined as a reality found "in the in-between space of double-frames" of reference.[9] In Zeida's case, these reference points are Morocco and Belgium.

In order to emphasize her heroine's feelings of being lost and what it is like to be from *nowhere*, Houari plays linguistically with her character's development. In the beginning of the novel, Zeida's name is not disclosed; she is simply "elle" [her] or "la jeune fille" [the young girl]. The story often switches narration between first and third person. The third person's voice provides the reader with commentary on personal family issues and clashes with her father. He is a man who has made Zeida understand that, as a teenager, she "had become a woman" and, therefore, must keep herself from "becoming a bad girl."[10] The tumultuous relationship between the heroine and her father symbolizes the dualistic lives of Europe's young Beurs. Alec Hargreaves remarks that the multiple narrators' voices of the novel are due to Houari wanting to make the reader experience the feelings of her own family's immigrant turmoil as well as that of the protagonist. Through this tension, the author forces the reader to understand what it is like to live in the in-between of two cultures:

> When I discussed these twin narrators with the author, it became clear that Houari had initially adopted a homodiegetic approach because she wanted to recreate as vividly as possible the emotional turmoil which she herself had experienced as an adolescent. The switch to a less emotive heterodiegetic narrator was a token of the increased psychological control enjoyed by the more mature Houari and, eventually, by the protagonist herself.[11]

"Elle" [she], as the author demonstrates for her readers, is a pronoun synonymous for all the young Maghrebine women caught in the middle of immigrant families trying to hold onto their traditions in a Western, white world that repeatedly threatens the very cultural fibers dear to them: honor, women's chastity, and the predominance of patriarchal prerogatives. As the story progresses, the reader learns about the nameless heroine's history through flashbacks at her school in Brussels and narrated conflicts between the young girl and her father. Zeida's name is finally disclosed on page 25 when, as a little girl, she accompanies her family on her first trip "back home" to Morocco. The homeland of her parents represents a pure place, a true reality for Zeida. It is a place about which she has learned only from the snippets of stories and mythical histories her parents have passed down to her. Yet, it is here also where the reader glimpses the girl's tormented feelings about her dual life, which is an existence in flux, the dissonant sphere of two cultures caught in the in-between of two worlds. The young woman believes that Morocco represents the potential for her self-discovery, a place that she feels will allow her to seek out and, hopefully, come to know her identity. Unfortunately, the traditionalism of the inhabitants of her father's village puts up constant hurdles, impeding her identity quest. Zeida's presence there, like in Brussels, is viewed as *dérangeant*—upsetting. Her disconnectedness from her country of origin is underscored by her inability to understand her parents' culture. Upon her arrival in Morocco she remarks, "Qu'est-ce qu'ils sont mal organisés, ici, au moins pour ça, là-bas, ça va plus vite" [Boy are they unorganized here, at least for that, over there things go more quickly].[12] The schism between "là-bas"—Europe—and "ici"—Morocco—slowly becomes a vast chasm as she realizes that there is no way to breach the gap between the two cultures. Throughout this first encounter with her father's family in the small village of Ba Sidi, her point of reference remains "là-bas," a standard by which to judge and be judged.

Déracinement characterizes not only Zeida but her entire family. For the villagers, the heroine's family has cut all ties with their homeland and will never again be totally a part of the Moroccan village community. Leaving and settling in Europe labels the family as nomads; they are the *kharidj* (which in Arabic literally means "the outside"). The kharidj changes an emigrant forever. As Abdellatif Chaouite and Azouz Begag explain, those who become the kharidj are "those who leave and never come back as before, even if they leave for a short time." He who leaves "comes back with a new way of looking, and another experience of time . . . the displacement of the body modifies the angle of seeing."[13] The kharidj, outside space, is also a familiar foreign space for the Maghrebian traveler. It connotes "a fantastic space . . . a space of the imaginary where one may find success in the foreign space [francophone Europe]."[14] Yet often, as Begag and Chaouite explain, success for the immigrant family is elusive, and happiness is nonexistent. Back in Brussels, the pain of exile and what the young heroine's mother sees as the cause of her daughter's estrangement from the family (because of the conflicts with her father, Zeida has moved out of the family's apartment) take their toll on them all. The girl's mother laments that if she had been told that, one day, exile would force her to lose one of her children, she would have stayed in Morocco and "mendiait plutôt que de venir dans ce pays de malheur, qui nous fait payer cher notre pain" [begged rather than come to this country of unhappiness which makes us pay dearly for our bread].[15]

As Houari concludes her novel, the feelings of helplessness Zeida experiences as a result of not having a "home" place to root herself prompt the girl to reconcile with her parents as well as come to terms with her identity as one that is neither Moroccan nor Belgian, but somewhere in the middle. Morocco is just as foreign as Brussels, yet in the middle, there is compromise. Homi K. Bhabha remarks that this in-between is a space of "negotiation rather than negation, it is to convey a temporality that makes it possible to conceive of the articulation of antagonistic or contradictory elements [making up the subject's life]."[16] Compromise for the protagonist is a positive enterprise and allows her to at last define who she is: "Il ne fallait pas s'en faire, elle avait ramené un peu de menthe fraîche et des fleurs d'oranger pour les donner à sa mère . . . elle souriait mais ne rêvait plus" [She shouldn't worry about it anymore, she was bringing back a little fresh mint and orange flowers to give to her mother . . . she smiled, but didn't dream anymore].[17]

Coming to terms with the compromises that she has to make in order to live between these two conflicting, culturally defined spaces is a gradual process for Zeida. She must first pass through a series of stages, or plateaus, of self-discovery. The first stage involves the rejection of her parent's history and traditionalism. The second stage is one of reconciliation in which Zeida seeks to understand her parents by embracing their world. Finally in stage three, where resolution is imminent, Zeida finds that neither total rejection nor complete reconciliation will help her form her identity. Happiness exists between the world of her parents and that of the "here and now," which is Brussels, Belgium, and not Ba Sidi, Morocco. At the end of the novel, the heroine admits that it is possible to incorporate her *Moroccanness* into her *Europeanness*, or to "make and eat her bread" in one multicultural space.

In stage one, Houari's character rejects her parents' world. The author's prose is disconcerting, constantly switching narrative voices in an effort to interpret the protagonist's feelings of being lost in a teenager's world of chaos. It is a world in which Zeida feels no attachment whatsoever to her family, their space, or even that of her adopted city, Brussels. Jumping from "elle," "il," "moi," "tu," and "je," Zeida puts her story together for the reader as one of exile in every voice. Noting the switching of lexicons in one paragraph, the reader realizes to what extent Zeida feels detached from the world of her parents and their history. However, at the same time, the heroine tries to understand what her family left behind in Morocco:

> Elle avait peur de son père et n'osait rien dire, pourtant elle l'aimait beaucoup, mais il ne le voyait pas: le froid de l'exil a reculé ton passé, mon père, a meurtri ta fierté. . . . Tes mots qui sont durs, ont la dureté de ton expérience. Si tu m'avais battue, cela m'aurait fait moins mal. Sur son cheval un cavalier doit rester errant, une famille, des enfants, l'Europe, le béton, l'exil ne remplaceront jamais le vent parfumé d'encens, l'odeur de lavande sur les femmes voilées que tu aimais.
>
> [*She* was afraid of her father and didn't dare say anything, however she did love him a lot, but he didn't see it: the cold of exile removed *you* from your past, my father, killed your pride. . . . *Your* words which are hard, are as hard as your experience. If you had beaten me, it would have hurt me less. On *his* horse the cavalier must stay errant, a family, kids, Europe, concrete, exile will never replace the incense perfumed wind, the smell of lavender on veiled women whom you loved.][18]

Her memories of home-place/space clash with exile. Living in Europe, her father watches over his daughter with vigilance, accusing her of being "une petite révoltée qui déshonore sa race" [a little rebel girl who dishonors her race].[19] Yet, Zeida wonders, what is her race? Can she even hope to share the ethnic identity of her father, when she doesn't really know it? She tries to mediate her reality between the closed Moroccan world of her parents' tiny apartment and the larger looming Brussels of neon lights and graffiti-littered walls that remind her that she is not in *her* country.[20] She chooses to leave her family. After some reflection, memories of her extended family in Morocco seem to speak to her from the past, causing her to question her actions. Houari tells us that while Zeida was estranged from her father and mother she "n'avait jamais essayé de dialoguer avec ses parents" [never tried to talk to her parents], but that also "elle ne supportait plus cette solitude loin de ses frères, loin de sa mère" [she couldn't stand the solitude anymore, far away from her brothers and mother].[21] Zeida decides to reconcile with her history and her family by seeking out a compromise. She proposes a trip "home" to Morocco in an attempt to bridge the gap that alienates her from them.

Houari pushes her character to find the limits of her identity in the second stage of the novel, the reconciliation stage. Zeida travels farther (metaphorically and physically) in this section of the novel, seeking an identity-space for herself. She realizes that her trip to Morocco "n'était qu'une fuite, elle le savait, mais vivre autre choses et ailleurs, cela pouvait peut-être l'aider à échapper à toutes les contradictions dont elle souffrait" [was only running away, she knew, but to live other things and in another place, that might help her to escape all the contradictions from which she suffered].[22] Instead of denying her father's cultural heritage, she embraces it. Returning to the Morocco of her parents, she hopes, will enable her to erase the isolation she feels in Brussels. Among her relatives, aunts, uncles, and cousins she desires to find a new purity of being, generated from belonging to a group and "the knowledge that [she is part of a] cultural reality" and this reality will serve her well as a "reference point."[23] Zeida's identity will become whole and individualized, as she gains perspective on her heritage and the customs of her people: "je veux vivre dans mon pays, c'est tout ce que je demande" [I want to live in my country, it's all I ask], she states.[24] The young girl will form her identity by associating with her larger clan or her "collective peripheral identity."[25] Painfully, Zeida realizes that the Moroccan (collective) community will under no circumstances accept her. From the moment she sets foot in her father's native village, she is treated as "une fille d'Europe" [a European girl]. Adding to this stereotype, her cousin Mustapha points out: "ceux qui partent n'appartiennent plus à leur pays" [those who leave (for Europe) don't belong to their country anymore].[26] She is treated differently because of her European ideas and, as her aunt claims, her loose ways with men, in particular with Wantabi, a local boy for whom she feels a certain affection. Her aunt acidly points out: "Ici quand un garçon parle à une fille cela veut dire qu'il veut se marier ou alors il est avec une fille pas très sérieuse" [here, when a boy talks to a girl that means he wants to marry her or that he is with a loose girl].[27] The more she tries to understand the demarcation of space between men and women of the village, the more difficult it is for Zeida to continue her search for identity in her parents' homeland. She finds that she is unable to adapt to Moroccan village ways, she is *too* foreign. She also recognizes that "beaucoup de choses lui étaient permises parce qu'elle n'était pas du pays" [she was permitted a lot of things because she was not of the country].[28] When Wantabi tells her "tu n'es ni européenne ni arabe" [you are neither European nor Arab], she realizes that her place is not, nor ever could be, among her father's people.[29] She learns that even the villagers thought that one day or another she would return *home* to Europe.[30] Her idealization of her parents' homeland slowly erodes as she accepts the impossibility of ever living as a "native" in her father's village. Zeida would forever be considered "l'Etrangère." She decides to return to Europe, accepting the fact that "l'exil était et serait toujours son ami, il lui avait appris à chercher ses racines" [exile was and would forever be her friend, it had taught her to look for her roots].[31]

In the last stage of Houari's novel, the resolution stage, the heroine acknowledges that her identity lies in her own backyard in Brussels, where two cultures met and have resided together all along. Zeida learns that her identity is individual, but also that she is who she is because of two cultures. The young heroine recognizes, however, that this individuality is rooted in knowing her cultural heritage.[32] In the end, Zeida is convinced that this cultural heritage has taken on new forms because of her exile. In the final stages of the novel, the heroine comes to terms with her multicultural space by constructing a dialogue with her parents in their emigrant world of the present. Her cultural binarism allows her to embrace a new hybrid space of blended Moroccan and European fields of reference. The realization that she can be an individual in the collective of her heritage is enriching, erasing her original feelings of exile and isolation: "Rien n'était à justifier, ni ici, ni là-bas, c'était comme cela, un point c'est tout! Chercher et encore chercher et trouver la richesse dans ses contradictions, la réponse devait être dans le doute et pas ailleurs" [Nothing needed to be justified, neither here nor there, that's how it is, period! Repeatedly to look for and find richness in contradictions, the response must be found in doubt and not elsewhere].[33] Landing at the airport in Brussels, her mother's words come back to her: "Chez moi, c'est là où je mange mon pain" [Home is where I eat my bread].[34]

Leïla Houari, like so many Beur and francophone authors currently writing *in* the multicultural space they now call home, seeks to negotiate a new multiple identity. This multiculturality, Keith Walker remarks, reminds us that "ultimately, [this] literature is a representation of a liminal state [where] there is a yearning for reconciliation of the warring strivings and paradoxical impulses as one lives on the hyphen of cultural identity."[35] Beur literature as an established genre has existed for less than twenty years, therefore it remains to be seen where this yearning and reconciliation will take authors such as Leïla Houari who writes from a space that connotes both exile and home.

Despite their diverse backgrounds and historical time periods, Suzanne Lacascade and Leïla Houari share commonalities in the way in which they explore exile and marginalization and how these factors impact the lives of their heroines. These protagonists, although living on the liminal edge of the accepted, expected, and the routine of the foreign societies in which they are supposed to function, never lose total sight of their own inner true selves; their passions, secrets, and harbored desires. Claire-Solange and Zeida incorporate part of the foreign into their own Selves in order to explore étrangeté and displacement. They come to terms with understanding what it is to be foreign within the cultures in which they must live. How much do displacement and the feeling of being split in two impact the mental well-being of the heroines? Claire-Solange gives up her radical ideologies for love and succumbs to patriarchal structures that leave her with few options in a white world, whereas Zeida must renounce her ethnic origins and accept the fact that, although her skin color is dark, she has been totally Europeanized. Despite the enormous demands placed on them, which are the results of having to negotiate between two cultures, these women never lose the desire to take charge of their own destinies. They make the choices that take them down various paths of enlightenment, discovering in the end who they really are. Unlike the women in the following chapters, who are victims of madness because they are restricted bodily and/or mentally from making their own choices, or cannot find a means to liberate themselves from the environments in which they live, the heroines discussed here have overcome the duality and alienation in their lives and, subsequently, found their place.

NOTES

1. Charles Taylor, *Multiculturalism* (Princeton, N.J.: Princeton University Press, 1994), 34.

2. Taylor, *Multiculturalism*, 35.

3. The word "Beur" means "Arabe" in a code language (a type of slang) known as "verlan." Verlan is popular among the youth of immigrant groups marginalized on the peripheries (often ghettos) of large urban centers in France. Two syllable words in French lend themselves best to be "verlanized." Following the pattern, a word such as "femme" (woman) becomes "meuf," "pourrie" (rotten) becomes "ripoux." Beur culture has adopted this code language as a means of resistance to French authority as well as to champion their cause against racism, marginalization, and inequality.

4. Michel Laronde, *L'Ecriture décentrée: La langue de l'Autre dans le roman contemporain* (Paris: L'Harmattan, 1996), 8.

5. Keith Walker, *Countermodernism and Francophone Literary Culture: The Game of Slipknot* (Durham, N.C.: Duke University Press, 1999), 42.

6. Alec Hargreaves, *Immigration and Identity in Beur Fiction* (Oxford: Berg Press, 1997), 14.

7. Leïla Houari, *Zeida de nulle part* (Paris: L'Harmattan, 1985), 84. All translations are mine.

8. Houari, *Zeida*, 39.

9. Homi K. Bhabha, *The Location of Culture*, (New York: Routledge, 1994), 216.
10. Houari, *Zeida*, 17.
11. Hargreaves, *Immigration*, 97.
12. Houari, *Zeida*, 26.
13. Azouz Begag and Abdellatif Chaouite, *Ecarts d'identité* (Paris: Seuil, 1990), 41.
14. Begag and Chaouite, *Ecarts*, 43.
15. Houari, *Zeida*, 31.
16. Bhabha, *Location of Culture*, 25.
17. Houari, *Zeida*, 84.
18. Houari, *Zeida*, 17. My emphasis.
19. Houari, *Zeida*, 17.
20. Houari, *Zeida*, 19.
21. Houari, *Zeida*, 29–30.
22. Houari, *Zeida*, 41.
23. Laronde, *Autour le roman beur* (Paris: L'Harmattan, 1993), 42.
24. Houari, *Zeida*, 48.
25. Laronde, *Autour le roman beur*, 43.
26. Houari, *Zeida*, 68.
27. Houari, *Zeida*, 57.
28. Houari, *Zeida*, 69.
29. Houari, *Zeida*, 61.
30. Houari, *Zeida*, 69.
31. Houari, *Zeida*, 83.
32. Laronde, *Autour le roman beur*, 17.
33. Houari, *Zeida*, 83.
34. Hoauri, *Zeida*, 84.
35. Walker, *Countermodernism*, 37.

STATE II

WRITING IN MADNESS

Ai-je de la fièvre? Tant mieux! J'appelle le délire. Il m'aidera à vivre ma mort par anticipation. J'ai l'habitude de m'enterrer moi-même. C'est consolant, ces plongées dans le néant. Elles m'épargneront, je l'espère, les affres de la réalité.

[Do I have a fever? All the better! I call out to delusion. It will help me live my death by anticipation. I have the habit of burying myself. It's consoling, these dives into nothingness. They will save me from, I hope, the torments of reality.]

—Marie Chauvet, *Amour, colère, et folie* (1968)

Francophone women novelists have frequently represented female illness and the topos of madness. . . . Madness functions rather [in their works] as a metaphor of the female social condition and alienation.

—Elisabeth Mudimbé-Boyi, "Narrative 'Je(ux)' in Kamouraska and Juletane" (1996)

Insanity comes in two basic varieties: slow and fast.

—Susanna Kaysen, *Girl, Interrupted* (1993)

Introduction to State II

"Every voyage is potentially a voyage into exile, a voyage to the 'end of the night.'"[1] Women novelists agree that written expression is inspired by wanderings of both the mind and the body. Algerian novelist Malika Mokeddem attests that subjecthood is formed through writing down experiences gained through nomadic passages that take the author/heroine out of her sociocultural established realms of womanhood, or "womanbeing."[2] Scholar Thérèse Michel-Mansour notes that these nomadic passages encourage "mobility of memory," allowing women to transgress the "prescribed codes" of their own cultures. Malika Mokeddem observes that embarking on a nomadic journey (literarily or physically) means both "a quest to and a flight from" feminine identity structures, both positive and negative, construed in terms of society, culture, history, and politics.[3] Indeed, as Georges Van Den Abbeele remarks, "just as travel poses the danger of loss so also does it propose the possibility of gain (whether this gain be in the form of greater riches, power, experience [or] wisdom)."[4] As the heroine of the francophone novel flees prescribed codes of conduct honed for her by the society in which she lives, the floodgates of speech are opened for her. She is presented with new arenas in which to refashion her identity. For Yasmine, heroine of Mokeddem's *Le siècle des sauterelles*, daughter of an Algerian nomadic tribesman and a black African woman, constant motion brings new experiences, while also providing answers to the young girl's questions about her mother's sub-Saharan African roots, a mother brutally murdered when Yasmine was but a small child:

[E]lle a traversé le désert vers la noire source de sa mère. Ils disent que là, dans l'antique Afrique, elle a nourri son chant des rythmes noirs. On dit qu'elle va d'amant en amant parce qu'aucun amour n'a su la retenir ni l'apaiser. . . . Et les

odyssées de l'imagination qui, tous mythes allumés, labourent la lumière, par-
courent furieusement le désert, ne sont que fallacieuses marches quand le corps
est contraint à sa plus grande terreur, l'immobilité.

[She crossed the desert towards the black source of her mother. They say that
there, in the Africa of her antiquity, she nourished her song with black rhythms.
It is said that she goes from lover to lover because no love knows how to hold
and appease her. . . . And the odysseys of imagination that all illuminated myths,
slashing the light, furiously traversing the desert, are only journeys of fallacy
when the body is constrained by its grandest terror, immobility.][5]

Mokeddem's novels *Les Hommes qui marchent* (1990), *Le siècle des
sauterelles* (1992), *L'Interdite* (1993), *Des rêves et des assassins* (1995), *Une
nuit de la lézarde* (1998), and *N'Zid* (2001) promote her view that it is necessary for the female novelist to "rester nomade" [remain nomadic] in order
to enjoy a "*desertification* of the mind" which offers a tabula rasa on which
to build a new identity, constantly changing her socioculturally coded
slate.[6] Mobility is essential for the francophone African woman who writes,
as attests Yasmine of *Le siècle des sauterelles*: "Il nous faut fuir le piège de
la vengeance dans lequel, sans jamais le nommer, nous avons piétiné
depuis si longtemps. Nous irons en pays étranger où je pourrai marcher et
écrire" [We must flee the trap of vengeance in which, without ever naming
it, we have slid for such a long time. We will go to a foreign country where
I can walk and write].[7] Yasmine knows that the key to her independence
and her identity depends on constant movement, *déplacement*, allowing
her to inscribe her experiences on paper whether they are positive or abject, revealing sanity or madness.

In past history (Western European included), women confined in their
rooms and houses wrote of the world outside their windows, freeing
their minds to go places that were forbidden to them:

Literally confined to the house, figuratively confined to a single "place," enclosed in parlors and encased in texts, imprisoned in kitchens and enshrined in
stanzas, women artists naturally found themselves describing dark interiors and
confusing their sense that they were house-bound with their rebellion against
being duty bound. . . . Inevitably, too, they expressed their claustrophobic rage
by enacting rebellious escapes.[8]

From the Brontë sisters and Emily Dickinson to Virginia Woolf, Zelda Fitzgerald, and Sylvia Plath, anglophone women poets and novelists of the nineteenth and twentieth centuries, confined to the physical architecture of their
homes as well as the purviews of the societies in which they lived, plotted
strategies to explore a world outside the shackles of domesticity. For some,
no exploration could counter the results of their confinement: depression,
hysteria, madness. Some of the women novelists cited above suffered psy-

chological stress (Woolf, Fitzgerald, and Plath) because of their lack of empowerment and curbed physical liberty outside the home. The contemporary francophone authors considered in the following chapters are also not clinically mad (although Chauvet suffered from depression). Yet, their heroines do succumb to madness and, more often than not, death. African and Caribbean female novelists use the madness of their protagonists as a thematic state through which to articulate the sociocultural, historical, and postindependence constraints that women have had to endure from the latter part of the twentieth century to our present time. No such investigation of the use of madness by female authors of the francophone diaspora to represent the complexities that postcolonial societies pose for women has been done. Thus, this study is timely. The francophone postcolonial authors considered here use the madness of their heroines as a symbolic reference point to study and analyze the sociocultural conditions of their contemporary milieus. Supporting this hypothesis, Jill Astbury claims in her book *Crazy for You: The Making of Women's Madness* that "the concept of woman is socially constructed [expressing] the values and expectations cultures assign to being female."[9] Not only are these women novelists writing within a "francophone literary culture . . . concerned with transitional social realities and the ever-shifting construction of the francophone identity as it responds to the pressures of the political, the economic, the social, and the legal,"[10] they are also determined to reveal to their readership that their fiction concerns the "universal condition of women, whether Black, white, yellow, red, brown, European, American, or third world."[11] This universal condition is one that is experienced, albeit in differing stages of severity, by all women. The pressures of politics, traditional sociocultural norms, historical events (colonial wars, occupation, independence revolutions, famine, and poverty), religious fundamentalism, as well as contemporary Western European and African feminist views all impact the way African and Caribbean francophone women live their lives within contemporary societies.

Not only do these authors discuss the problematic positions of women in contemporary francophone cultures—positions that often lead to anxiety about their own place and roles—they are also taking to task men and women's traditional views on identity within family and social structures. The protagonists figuring in these novels suffer from an "ontological insecurity" wherein they lack "the sense of unquestioning, self-validating, integral selfhood and personal identity that 'normal' people take for granted."[12] The ontologically secure person, explains psychoanalyst R. D. Laing, takes on life "from a centrally firm sense of his own and other people's reality and identity." When these two elements are diminished, or lacking in one's own field of reference, questions arise and insecurity ensues. Protagonists such as Myriam Warner-Vieyra's Juletane, Michèle Lacrosil's Cajou, and Nina Bouraoui's Fikria suffer from a lack of ontological security. They feel cut off from any sense of social rootedness within their respective environments. They are alienated from their past and feel disconnected from others and thus have no "validating certainties" in their lives.[13] Madness is a refuge to escape the daunting realities in their daily environments. Dementia offers release, a false self, a shell in which one can feel "normal," albeit temporarily. The false self, explains Laing, is a "way of not being oneself."[14] For the female protagonists studied in this work, adopting a false self is also a way of coping and assuring their self-preservation, while confronting what is typically expected from their milieus. For the novelist telling her story, madness serves as a metaphor for "anxiety about social and sexual roles" within her society; roles that women are required to play but that are often detrimental to their own individuality or even identity.[15]

Reiterating my introductory thesis and, once again, referring to Elisabeth Mudimbé-Boyi's hypothesis that "Madness . . . functions rather as a metaphor of the female social condition and alienation,"[16] I stress the importance of francophone women novelists' use of madness as a catalyst to explore, not only the psyche of their heroines, but also the sociocultural, political, and historical parameters that influence the protagonists as well as the environment from which the author is speaking. Madness offers a mirror image of unreality for the female heroine seeking relief from the sociocultural arenas and political repressions in which she finds herself entrapped. The mirror image, this false self, affords the heroine a means of observation; a privileged area from which to gaze inward and outward. Indeed, the use of mirrors and windows by the heroines in these novels is interesting. Claire, of Chauvet's *Amour*, peers out between her bedroom curtains to observe the streets below in order to comment on the sociopolitical unrest that characterizes Haiti during the Duvalier years. Juletane, heroine of Warner-Vieyra's novel *Juletane*, locks herself in her room, preferring to withdraw from her husband's culture in order to watch her in-laws passing underneath the sill of the single window of her tiny chamber. Fikria, of Nina Bouraoui's *La Voyeuse interdite*, is forced to stay in a locked bedroom, her only salvation being a closed window through which she contemplates the streets of Algiers below. Watching and waiting, she comments on the decrepit state of Algerian society in the post-independent years immediately following the war of liberation. These windows are "the glass coffins of patriarchy" through which the heroine must look in order to imagine an ontological security that escapes her.[17]

In the following literary analyses, I consider to what extent confinement, and subsequent madness, influence the heroines' demise. Lack of any possibility of *becoming* a nomad, and, therefore, unable to free themselves from the abject power structures that relegate women to the margins of sociopolitical power, truncates these heroines' agency, forcing them to live in constant despair, rage, hysteria, and dementia. Conversely, as Mokeddem and other francophone women novelists profess, nomadism allows a woman to be a polyglot and to exist between languages while she resists "settling into one, sovereign vision of identity." Not only does she wander, exploring the freedom she finds in outside space, "the nomad's identity is a map of where [she] has already been."[18]

Feminist philosopher Rosi Braidotti remarks that women must be migrant nomads to "plot" their identities (both historically determined by men as well as those yet to be formed), drawing on their own feminine prerogatives. "The migrant," she notes, is not exiled because "she has a clear destination: she goes from one point in space to another for a very clear purpose."[19] In contrast, death comes from sedentary lives and curtailed activity. Power is movement, like the path of Gilles Deleuze and Félix Guattari's *rhizome*, a root that grows haphazardly with no beginning or end. This root simply travels, not stopping. It is a force that shakes and uproots "the verb 'to be.'" Movement and nomadic quests help answer the questions: Where are you going? Where are you coming from? To what are you heading? It aids the heroine to do away "with foundations [and to] nullify endings and beginnings"[20] as she establishes her ontological security, a state that allows her to explore all factors (negative and positive) that make up her being.

Sedentary and socially cut off from the outside world, the heroines studied here find themselves living in the obeisant areas of their respective societies. Containment in prisons of socially determined mores and designated codes that define women's existence are the reasons for which women fall into the abyss of madness. This is particularly evident in Caribbean women's depiction of mad female protagonists. Novelists from this region are particularly sensitive to "poverty . . . [and the] resultant negative self-image[s] of failure . . . [that women endure] largely [as] the results of the class-structure which shapes identities and which exercises considerable power over [people]" in the Caribbean.[21] For Haitian novelist Marie Chauvet's heroines Claire and Rose, in her triptych *Amour, Colère, et Folie*, a combination of social obligations, antiquated views on women's place in Haitian society, postcolonial violence, lost love, and personal sacrifice force the protagonists into worlds of mental anguish and absolute dementia. Juletane, heroine of Guadeloupian Myriam Warner-Vieyra's novel *Juletane*, finds herself bound up in a polygamous Senegalese marriage devoid of any power due to sociocultural, as well as language, barriers. Juletane, too, becomes engulfed in madness. Senegalese author Mariama Bâ's Mireille, of *Un Chant écarlate*, lives in a world where she is marked as an outcast due to the color of her skin, her language (French), culture, and faith. Mireille, a white woman married to a Senegalese black man, lives with him in Dakar in post-independent Senegal of the 1970s. Bâ exposes a heroine eventually suffocated by her difference and marginalized from her in-laws due to the impossibility of assimilating into Senegalese society. The author's novel has a bloody outcome, the result of Mireille's violent hysteria. Algerian Nina Bouraoui, in *La Voyeuse interdite*, narrates the life of a young woman living within the confines of a four-walled room where her only view of the outside world is through a small window. Although Bouraoui tells us that the city is Algiers and that the time frame takes place sometime after Algerian independence in 1962, the book is meant to offer a universal commentary on women's curtailed sociocultural and political status with regard to *shari'a* law in ultra-conservative, fundamentalist Islamic societies. Bouraoui's novel draws attention to countries such as Algeria where stringent conservative laws adopted both in the past and in contemporary times have restricted the physical movement and development of women living across the Arab world.

When considering madness in works written by francophone feminine novelists who are sane, the task at hand is to determine if, through the examples of her heroines, these authors succeed in exposing the sociocultural ills that hinder women's well-being in their own societies. By exposing the insanity inherent in certain areas of postcolonial cultures in Africa and the Caribbean (as mentioned previously, this is problematic for Guadeloupe and Martinique, which still cannot be defined as part of the postcolonial world since they are considered part of France), are women able to find constructive ways in which to plot new strategies to counter phallocentric structures detrimental to their socioeconomic development? Do women, as Mudimbé-Boyi suggests, achieve a new form of speech that allows them to "say the unsayable," dislodging themselves from their disenfranchised positions? Does writing really mean power both politically and culturally for women in oppressive environments? It is true that at present more women are writing than have at any other period of our history, and francophone women are no exception? Yet can we measure the impact of this writing on their respective societies? Has the madness used by authors to explore the feminine condition in the francophone world aided or hindered women's emancipation from their socioculturally determined roles? Why does the francophone author have to resort to a mad heroine in order to make her point? The questions seem endless, rendering the task at hand daunting for a scholar to explore. In order to answer these questions, I would humbly offer the following response. To effect drastic change within sociocultural and economic sectors of society, particularly in developing countries, necessitates that a woman act publicly. As Juliana Makuchi Nfah-Abbenyi remarks, even though a woman speaks from the margins, she

can create new spaces and social locations for [herself] within the dominant culture, marginality (be it represented as racial, sexual, historical, or cultural difference) will therefore be the point of intersection for identity politics, the location where identity politics finds full expression. By creating these new spaces and locations, women take the margins to the center and visa versa.[22]

Women therefore must engage in the "unsayable" in order to find solutions to what seem like unsurmountable problems. The voice of the hysteric is often the only voice that can express the many un-uttered words that will unlock larger areas of discourse touching upon subjects such as female genital mutilation, polygamous marriage, obligatory veiling, infanticide, domestic abuse, child abuse, rape, torture, and the mental psychoses all of which are bound up in the works considered here.

The novels analyzed in this section are grouped thematically around the subject of confinement and how it influences the heroines. I chose not to organize the works regionally or chronologically, but rather in terms of varying degrees of truncated liberty in order to determine how this lack of freedom impacts women's agency in sociocultural spheres and causes mental instability and/or outright madness. As these works attest, madness is the result of varying constructions of restraint. I have ascertained, based on the following novels, that three different modes of confinement can cause a woman's madness. Insanity is the result of self-imposed, socioculturally determined, and/or institutionalized confinement (constructed in terms of legislative phallocentric laws manipulated to victimize women). The heroines in these novels will never enjoy the freedom of nomadic quests and emancipation that comes through self-discovery as a result of physical and mental freedom.

In the following works, these three different forms of confinement are at the heart of the heroines' insanity. In order to be "balanced" mentally, a person must live in harmony with the inside and the outside of his/her field of reference or sociocultural milieu. Factors which curtail choice over one's own actions inside and outside one's field of reference lead to insanity, as these heroines demonstrate. Hindering a person's freedom influences his/her psychological state. Thomas Szasz, famous psychologist and author of numerous studies on insanity, notes that:

> A person's ability to make uncoerced choices is contingent on his internal and external conditions. His internal conditions, that is, his character, personality, or "mind"—comprising his aspirations and desires as well as his aversions and self-discipline—propel him toward, and restrain him from, various actions. His external conditions, that is, his biological makeup and his physical and social environment—comprising the capabilities of his body, and the climate, culture, laws, and technology of his society—stimulate him to act in some ways, and inhibit him from acting in others. . . . In general, the more control man gains over his internal and external conditions, the more free he becomes; whereas, if he fails to gain such control he remains enslaved, or, if, having gained it, he loses it, he becomes enslaved.[23]

It is imperative for women to maintain an equilibrium between the external and internal factors that mold their lives. According to Szasz's observations we are not whole unless we are masters of these two realms: "[I]ndividual liberty has always been, and is likely to remain, a hard-won prize, requiring a delicate balance between self-assertion sufficient to safeguard personal autonomy, and self-control sufficient to protect the autonomy of others."[24]

The novels studied here expose worlds where feminine autonomy, individuality, and liberty are effaced. Whether freedom to be an individual is hindered due to physical confinement or by sociocultural mores that restrict a woman's movement and/or role within her respective society, the heroines discussed in State II of this work are unable to enjoy an equilibrium between self-assertion and self-control or strike a peaceful balance between the interior and exterior environments that make up the worlds around them.

In the first instance, mental instability is the result of self-imposed sequestration, which hinders the actions of the heroine, disavowing any possibility of mobility in the outside realms of society. Two novels whose characters most acutely reflect the results of self-imposed confinement are Michèle Lacrosil's *Cajou* and Myriam Warner-Vieyra's *Juletane*. In both novels, the protagonists slip slowly into madness as a result of their self-loathing, lack of confidence, vulnerability, loneliness, and self-imposed exile, cutting themselves totally off from the outside world and any possibility of happiness. Both novelists are from Guadeloupe and draw on the multifaceted problematic of being a French woman of color. Their psychological stress is rooted in trying to exist in what these women feel is a hostile, foreign society. Assimilation is impossible for Cajou, living in Paris in the 1960s, and for Juletane who moves to her husband's native Senegal from Paris.

In novels where confinement of the heroine is purely ideological (i.e. culturally and socially determined), madness is the result of being unable to cope with mores and/or events of the time that restrict a woman's personal development as an individual who can profit from liberty and freedom of choice. The novels *Amour, Colère, et Folie*, by Haitian author Marie Chauvet, and *Un Chant écarlate*, by Senegalese Mariama Bâ, best enunciate the psychological trauma of socioculturally determined sequestration. Both heroines are not physically hindered from enjoying the *outside* spaces of their homes and families by the societies in which they live, but they do suffer mental instability due to sociocultural mores and traditions that force them ultimately to commit bloody crimes. In Chauvet's novel, the bourgeois structures in which Claire must live during the Duvalier epoch in Haiti stifle her independence and any possibility of love and happiness. Racial difference, which succeeds in totally marginalizing Mariama Bâ's heroine, Mireille, terminates any hope of living peacefully with her mulatto son in Senegal. Neither heroine is left with an outlet, and both suffer mental strains that, in the end, have dire consequences.

Institutionalized confinement is perhaps the most insidious of the three modes of truncated liberty that are discussed in this section. "Institutional" I define as the physical areas of sequestration (prisons, locked rooms, asylums) where a woman is cut off from her family, loved ones, and all possible active arenas of her life. More often than not, these tangible areas of confinement are phallocratically fashioned. They take the form of prisons managed by overbearing, violent men, as in the case of Cameroonian Calixthe Beyala's *Tu t'appelleras Tanga*. Or women are confined in rooms with locked doors, the keys to which are held solely by men, such as in Algerian Nina Bouraoui's *La Voyeuse interdite*. The effects of crippled liberty, violence, and horrible physical abuse end in death for the former heroine and dementia for the latter.

Although I have grouped these novels in terms of the varying constructions of their heroines' confinement, I do not disregard the fact that parallels can be made and comparisons drawn between the novels on many different levels. The affinities shared by Bâ's protagonist, Mireille, and Warner-Vieyra's Juletane are striking. Fikria, of Bouraoui's novel, and Lacrosil's Cajou also suffer from the same self-loathing that is generated from the adverse societal influences that surround them. Close readings of these novels lead us to determine certain commonalities between the heroines' psychic states. Often we are led to wonder if we can classify these marginalized women as suffering from pure insanity, or if they are even insane in the clinical sense. In the case of Juletane, although dementia causes her to slip away from reality, she still remains lucid enough to write daily in her diary, chronicling the progression of her madness. Scholar Jonathan Ngate ponders whether or not Juletane fabricated her insanity for personal gain and as a means of survival in a foreign country.[25] If authors such as Warner-Vieyra use insanity to demonstrate that "mad" women can be faulted for their cold and calculating actions, then can we always view insane women as victims? Once again, I will argue that use of madness by African and Caribbean women authors is but a means through which to filter other issues that are inherently important in our postcolonial era. Madness unlocks the words to express the sociocultural conditions of women who daily struggle to remain sane in the face of life-threatening experiences.

NOTES

1. Georges Van Den Abbeele, *Travel as Metaphor: From Montaigne to Rousseau* (Minneapolis: University of Minnesota Press: 1992), xvii.

2. See Renée Laurrier's *Francophone Women Writers of Africa and the Caribbean* (Gainesville: University Press of Florida, 2000), 5.

3. Quotes are cited from a talk given by Thérèse Michèle-Mansour at the Conseil International d'Etudes Francophones annual conference in Portland, Maine, May 26–June 3, 2001. Translation of Mansour's work is mine.

4. Van Den Abbeele, *Travel as Metaphor*, xvii.

5. Malika Mokeddem, *Le Siècle des sauterelles* (Paris: Ramsay, 1992), 279. All translations of Mokeddem's work are my own.

6. Michèle-Mansour, my translation.

7. Mokeddem, *Le Siècle*, 259.

8. Gilbert and Gubar, *Madwoman in the Attic* (New Haven, Conn.: Yale University Press, 1984), 84–85.

9. Jill Astbury, *Crazy for You*, 13.

10. Keith Walker, *Countermodernism and Francophone Literary Culture: The Game of Slipknot* (Durham, N.C.: Duke University Press, 1999), 127.

11. Walker, *Countermodernism*, 137–138.

12. Evelyn O'Callaghan, "Interior Schisms Dramatized: The Treatment of the 'Mad' Woman in the Work of Some Female Caribbean Novelists," in *Out of Kumbla: Caribbean Women and Literature*, ed. Carole Boyce Davies and Elaine Savory Fido (Trenton, N.J.: African World Press, 1990), 92.

13. R.D. Laing, *The Divided Self* (New York: Pantheon, 1960), 40.

14. Laing, *The Divided Self*, 102.

15. O'Callaghan, "Interior Schisms," 101.

16. Mudimbé-Boyi, "Narrative "je(ux)" in Kamouraska and Juletane," in *Postcolonial Subjects: Francophone Women Writers*, ed. M. Green et al (Minneapolis: University of Minnesota Press, 1996), 137.

17. Gilbert and Gubar, *Madwoman in the Attic*, 44.

18. Rosi Braidotti, *Nomadic Subjects* (New York: Columbia University Press, 1994), 14.

19. Braidotti, *Nomadic Subjects*, 22.

20. Gilles Deleuze and Félix Guattari, *A Thousand Plateaus* (Minneapolis: University of Minnesota Press, 1987), 24. See this work for further information on the philosophical concept of the rhizome.

21. Evelyn O'Callaghan, "The Bottomless Abyss: 'Mad' Women in Some Caribbean Novels," *Bulletin of Eastern Caribbean Affairs* 11, no. 1, (March/April 1985): 45–58, 56.

22. Juliana Makuchi Nfah-Abbenyi, *Gender in African Women's Writing: Identity, Sexuality, and Difference* (Bloomington: Indiana University Press, 1997), 32.

23. Thomas Szasz, *Ideology and Insanity: Essays on the Psychiatric Dehumanization of Man* (New York: Doubleday, 1970), 1.

24. Szasz, *Ideology and Insanity*, 2.

25. See Jonathan Ngate's, "Reading Warner-Vieyra's Juletane," *Callaloo* 9, no. 4 (1986): 553–563.

3

Self-Loathing, Self-Sacrifice

Michèle Lacrosil's *Cajou* and
Myriam Warner-Vieyra's *Juletane*

> I believe that human happiness, or well-being, is possible—not just for a
> select few, but on a scale hitherto unimaginable. But this can be achieved
> only if many men, not just a few, are willing and able to confront frankly,
> and tackle courageously, their ethical, personal, and social conflicts.
>
> —T. Szasz, *Ideology and Insanity* (1970)

Although a twenty-one-year span separates Guadeloupian authors
Michèle Lacrosil's *Cajou* (1961) and Myriam Warner-Vieyra's *Juletane*
(1982), similarities between their heroines abound. Self-loathing leads Cajou and Juletane to self-imposed exile where they eventually succumb to
madness. Insanity is the outcome of these heroines' stories, caused in part
by their inability to assimilate into the foreign environments in which they
have to live. Each heroine experiences a dementia that, in the end, causes
total psychological unraveling and, eventually, death. These heroines are
destabilized by what François Lionnet defines as "deculturation" and a
"lack of [a feeling of] authenticity"[1] which inhibits the development of
their identities. Cajou and Juletane long to disappear, ridding themselves
of what they perceive as acute shortcomings and a debilitating difference
housed in bodies they view as prisons. The body for these women is a
hindrance, acting "as animal, as appetite, as deceiver, as prison of the soul
and confounder of its projects."[2] In short, these women desire "a shrinking from all bodily contact"[3] with the outside world. As if to counter this
shrinking and melting away of feminine identity, the authors use their
heroines' names as titles for their books, thus challenging each woman's
total disappearance. Lacrosil and Warner-Vieyra strive to keep their alienated heroine's materiality intact, only to renounce this goal at the end of

their respective novels. Questions which arise in these works about feminine materiality take on lager proportions, becoming synonymous with
not just a single heroine but an entire feminine ontology. By analyzing
these heroines' mental instability, we are instructed on many different levels about the conflicts of race, class, and gender faced daily by women in
the postcolonial world. Through the individual heroines' stories, many,
more general, feminine issues emerge which are pertinent to not only
women of color, but to Western, white, Anglo-European women as well.
Although their heroines fail, Cajou and Juletane demonstrate that marginalization creates a new space in which the authors maneuver to draw attention to issues surrounding feminine identity in the postcolonial world.
Noting this fact, African scholar Juliana Makuchi Nfah-Abbenyi suggests
that "marginality (be it represented as racial, sexual, historical, or cultural
difference) [is a] point of intersection for identity politics, the location
where identity politics finds full expression."[4]

Lacrosil and Warner-Vieyra, like many women authors of the Caribbean,
are committed to discussing larger questions of identity through the psychological turmoil of their heroines. Their work reveals a frequent theme
found in Caribbean literature written by women exposing, most particularly, the heroine who "is often left without choice" and whose life contains
few options other than those that lead to her own destruction. This thematic
trajectory is a common motif in Caribbean literature, particularly written by
women.[5] In these novels, lack of choice leads to dependence on men, self-
loathing, and the profound feeling that, because of her difference, each
heroine is barred from being a part of a community (Juletane is unable to
integrate into Senegalese culture and Cajou cannot assimilate into Parisian
life of the 1960s). These factors lead to mental destabilization and, eventually, madness. Juletane's and Cajou's identities are caught up in their *victimhood*, fostered by the masculine sociocultural forces which bind them.
The varying degrees of the heroines' victimization are scrutinized by both
authors. Certainly, alienation and lack of self-confidence, traits evident in
both protagonists, lead to their demise. More importantly, and on a larger
global note, Lacrosil and Warner-Vieyra call our attention to the ontological
insecurity that many women experience in their daily lives. Diminished feelings of self-worth eventually lead to madness.[6] These heroines are forced to
live lives behind false selves in order to mold themselves to the expectations people have of them. "Behind the facade of the false self/selves, the
isolated 'true self' becomes more and more empty," giving way to cycles of
dementia where unreal fantasies are the only means to experience om-
nipotence and self-worth.[7]

These mad heroines' victimization is explored on several levels by the authors. In Lacrosil and Warner-Vieyra's novels, we hear the voices of colonized women of color who have had very little say in how their history has

been written down. Their voices express an existence that has been manipulated by men and stripped of agency within the environments in which they are forced to live. These factors lead each heroine over an abyss into inescapable insanity. Their subjecthood "bears the double burden, material and ideological, of colonial and patriarchal society, [they have] difficulty in conceiving of [themselves] as a subject who controls knowledge, and hence as a subject endowed with either agency or power."[8]

In both *Cajou* and *Juletane*, we return to the theme of madness as a determinant that leads author and reader (at the expense of the heroine) to gain a new understanding of the sociocultural constraints placed on women living in postcolonial Africa, the Caribbean, and France. The theme of victimization, as a result of alienation, is used not only to paint a picture of these heroines' demise, but also to expose everyday limits placed on them in postcolonial societies or in France, where they live in exile. Through the voices of their protagonists, Lacrosil and Warner-Vieyra instruct readers on the general feminine malaise often found within phallocratic-traditional postcolonial societies. These women are "affected by" what Jill Astbury defines as "the stress of living as someone in constant opposition to the status quo."[9] The theme of women as victims touches off a plethora of other issues which these authors compel us to consider in more global terms. Madness is brought to the forefront through the demise of the heroine. Her reflections on her declining mental state urge readers to consider the complexities of life faced by people, particularly women, in the postcolonial world. Jonathan Ngate argues that madness in *Juletane* is "domesticated" and serves the heroine as a "vehicle for self revelation, enabling her to write about and ponder her own experiences."[10] In both instances, Lacrosil's and Warner-Vieyra's works open up larger issues prevalent in the postcolonial world. From race and gender to politics and postcolonial socioeconomic dilemmas, these novels demonstrate a complete "metonymic chain of otherness" which characterizes the feminine condition in francophone Africa and the Caribbean. This otherness is something very different from what white, Anglo-Saxon, and/or Western European women describe in their novels. Unlike their Anglo-European sisters, Cajou and Juletane are *othered* on several levels as: "the Other of man, the Other of the West, the Other of other (Western/non-Western) women."[11]

Both women fight preconceived images that have been construed for them either by their own societies or by foreign environments to which they seek to adapt. They are not mothers (Juletane loses her unborn child when she is hit in the street by a car, and Cajou kills herself, even though she is pregnant), nor do they play by the sociocultural rules of their respective environments. Cajou rejects assimilation despite her love for her white fiancé and accomplishments made in her professional life as a bio-technician in a laboratory in Paris. Juletane refuses to accept her husband's traditional Senegalese culture and its mores which uphold his right to a polygamous marriage. Although she is finally granted the option to return to Paris, in the end she prefers to stay locked in her room. Despite her yearning to understand Africa, a continent she perceives as her distant place of origin, Juletane cannot renounce her Euro-Westernized independence and French upbringing.

Most importantly, through the theme of madness, Lacrosil and Warner-Vieyra call our attention to the many failures in communication which emanate when Hegemonic meets Other. These breakdowns in communication are the result of several imposing factors: gender, geography, psychology, as well as skin color. In both novels, the authors, through the travesties of their heroines, ask *What, then are other options for modern women of color living in the postcolonial world?*[12] Can women who choose alternative paths to those of motherhood and matrimony survive in traditional societies with their sanity intact? If we view madness and general self-destructive behavior as metaphors for lack of social power, then use of insanity as a prevalent motif in the works of women novelists of the francophone diaspora takes on new contours.[13]

Guadeloupe boasts a long list of women novelists who have scrutinized women's lack of social power as being at the root of a *feminine malaise* in the Antilles. This malaise often cumulates into the portrayal of a feminine victimization that is unequaled elsewhere. Although not overly feminist, Guadeloupian women's writing has been militant in pointing out that Antillian women's positions are often tenuous in society, both in France and in Guadeloupe. Women, more often than men, are alienated from mainstream power structures. As authors such as Lacrosil and Warner-Vieyra contend, although Guadeloupian women are educated and make significant contributions to society, they are still not viewed in socioeconomical and political terms as having power. Indeed, the protagonists of these works are "haunted by a deep sense of failure, of dislocation and alienation. . . . [T]hey are like 'baleines échouées,' lost whales washed up on the beach."[14]

On a historical level, Lacrosil and Warner-Vieyra write against the voice of Négritude which they consider has done little for women authors and less for promoting women's voices in the Caribbean.[15] Michèle Lacrosil, one of the first Guadeloupian women authors to write counter to the Négritude movement beginning in the 1950s, recognized that assimilation into French society would be impossible. In her works *Sapotille et le serin d'argile* (1960), *Cajou* (1961), and *Demain, Jab-Herma* (1967), the sociopolitical commentary about race in her works (particularly that racism in metropolitan France is inevitable and that cultures and races different from mainstream France will always be incompatible) cannot be overlooked.[16]

Cajou's and Juletane's self-loathing and lack of confidence, which lead them to self-sequestration and eventual madness, are the focal points through which I will analyze to what extent mental instability influences their demise. Self-hatred and an inability to take charge of their own lives are the consequences of not only having to live and assimilate into a foreign society, but also to individual crises faced at an early age. These women's crises, in turn, influence and subsequently foster each heroine's dementia. Cajou, from childhood, is mentally unstable. She blames her anxiety on her mixed-race heritage. Although her widowed white mother loves and supports her daughter in every way, Cajou succumbs to feelings of inadequacy stating "je ne me suis jamais aimée" [I never loved myself].[17] She both despises the white otherness of her mother and aspires to possess it, admitting that she gives into "ce sentiment singulier, composé d'une furieuse envie d'être l'Autre" [this unique feeling, composed of a furious need to be the Other].[18] Although her mother seeks psychiatric help for her daughter, what Cajou perceives as her inadequacy due to the dark color of her skin (attributed to her deceased black father) detrimentally rules her life. No psychological treatment cures the young girl who further distances herself from those around her as she creeps slowly into a no-man's land of depression where she is haunted by the idea of suicide.[19]

Similarly, Juletane is orphaned at an early age in her island home. As a young girl she is sent to live with her godmother, "une vieille fille" [a strict, old maid], and, in turn, is raised isolated and naive as "une ingénue . . . ignorante et sotte" [an ingénue, an ignorant and foolish girl].[20] Set in the early 1960s, in the heyday of decolonization, the young woman admits that she has been sheltered all her life and is ignorant with respect to the political events going on around her. When she meets Mamadou, a young student from Senegal who is studying law at the university, Africa is opened up for her. Caught up in the African student movements of the day and invited to discussions centered around the topic of Senegalese independence, Juletane concedes that, before meeting Mamadou, Africa was but a myth, a place about which she knew nothing. She maintains that as far as colonialism was concerned: "j'avais vécu bien loin de tout écho du monde colonial. Aussi, l'indépendance ou autonomie étaient des mots tout à fait nouveaux pour moi" [I had lived very far indeed from any echo of the colonial world. Hence, independence or self-government were words which were quite new to me].[21] This revelation accentuates Juletane's confusion over her place within French society (to which she always claimed affinity) and, for the first time, problematizes race. Although she is from the West Indies, she considers herself French (from metropolitan France) and admits that her identity is bound up in the education she received while in Paris—"une éducation bourgeoise." It is not until she meets Mamadou that she discovers her *difference*. Recognizing this difference for the first time brings her to the realization that she is alone and isolated from mainstream France, a place to which she had always felt some attachment, despite the fact that her godmother discouraged any ties with people her own age and subjected the young girl to a strict, isolated upbringing.

Lacrosil and Warner-Vieyra make a point of examining the French idea of *assimilation,* a political ideology that always served imperial France well and continues to be a platform for right-winged legislation made by French government officials (including current president Jacques Chirac) today. Some would argue that assimilationist politics were implemented to dismiss the gravity of colonialization. The entire French Civilizing Mission was based on the nineteenth-century belief that assimilation of the colonized into the great empire of France would confer on them a culture and a language of which to be proud. Such reasoning made subjugation of foreign peoples much more palatable to the French public at the time. Throughout the colonial years (roughly spanning from the end of the seventeenth century to 1962), the policy mandated that colonialism was actually good for the *colonisé* since, through France's tutelage, all people of color would be brought up to be an *évolué* [elite/educated in French] through exposure to the magnificence of French culture and civilization. According to this ideology, the colonizing mission would efface the colonized's identity, prompting him/her to renounce his/her own culture. In both novels, assimilation, or lack thereof, is posited as a theme on numerous levels. Conflicts arising because of skin color are the most prevalent. Cajou is black, but according to Lacrosil, the heroine has been accepted—assimilated—as an equal in her professional milieu and praised for her intelligence. Color for her French, white coworkers does not seem to hinder their respect for the heroine, nor does it *seem* to limit their appreciation for her as a person. However, for Cajou there is an underlying racism constantly present that places her in either of two camps. She believes that French whites perceive her as either exotic, thus an object of sexualized fantasy adhering to the typical stereotypes placed on women from the Antilles, or she feels that she is perceived by whites as an enigma because of her singularity in achieving a diploma at the Sorbonne and because she is the only woman of color in her scientific field. Lacrosil effectively reveals how both whites and people of color considered each other at a time when writing about race was virtually unknown in France. The author thus is a pioneer and must be credited for aiding the launch of race-consciousness writing within the francophone literary diaspora of the 1960s.

Juletane, although the same color as her husband, does not share any other common traits with him, his family, or tribe. She becomes progressively isolated from all the people who make up her Senegalese household. Color is not so much the cause of her isolation, but rather it is caused by her background, her French upbringing, her lack of being able to communicate in Wolof, and her inability to adapt to the foreign environment. These hindrances contribute to her feelings of inadequacy and eventually cause her to slowly waste away in a mental institution.

CAJOU

The difficulties that arise in Cajou's life, because of trying to assimilate into various environments, force the heroine to analyze her difference on several levels. Questions surrounding her own race and origin finally lead the protagonist to doubt her own self-worth. Flashbacks of early memories of Guadeloupe and the many negative experiences she has due to the color of her skin (which she feels is too dark, making her feel "laide" [ugly]) result in her constant apprehensions. Divisions between black and white for Cajou become reasons, both real and imaginary, for second-guessing her own identity as an adult woman of color living in Paris in the 1960s. Color defines Cajou on two levels: first, it marginalizes her on the outside of white society; second, she feels her dark skin draws attention, making her the object of constant scrutiny. Her brilliant scholarly and professional accomplishments are cheapened by her self-devaluation, as evidenced here when she explains to her fiancé, Germain, who is white, that she has only succeeded in Paris because she is an oddity, an exception: "Ma thèse de doctorat et mes travaux ont fait du bruit parce que je suis une fille de couleur, et non en proportion de leur valeur intrinsèque. Tout ce qui vient de moi semble insolite et prend l'ampleur du scandale."[22] [My doctoral dissertation and my work were recognized because I am a woman of color, and not because of their intrinsic value. Everything that comes from me seems unusual and is amplified into scandal]. Cajou's continued self-pity and self-loathing become so acute that by the end of the novel she has cut herself off from friends, colleagues, and her lover. She even withdraws from the infant in her womb, choosing to commit suicide in the final pages of the novel.

Cajou's self-imposed isolation is the result of several prevalent themes, which Lacrosil seeks to exploit in her work. Although written in 1961, during decolonization in Africa and the civil rights movement in the United States, Lacrosil's message is one filled with universalisms that continue to be important today in feminine francophone writing. As previously noted, the author is staunchly anti-assimilationist, favoring instead the humanist theme of the Diaspora, a theory that encompasses the right to be different. The word "Diaspora" is continuously heard, ringing in Cajou's ears as she slips in and out of demented states in the closing pages of the novel. "Une phrase musicale, venue je ne sais d'où, m'imposait son rythme; les syllabes du mot DIA-SPO-RA éclataient en fanfare, faiblissaient, et reprenaient leur crescendo" [A musical phrase, coming from who knows where, imposed its rhythm on me; the syllables of the word DIA-SPO-RA burst in fanfare, growing faint before taking up their crescendo].[23] This pluralistic view of racial harmony, which champions the tolerance of ethnic diversity and the right to be different, is echoed in later writing across the francophone world.[24] Although Cajou is a victim of her self-loathing, within the diasporic context, she glimpses the possibility of individuality and enjoyment of cultural specificity. We suppose that if Cajou had not committed suicide, she would have definitely continued to take a stand against the assimilationist practices of the French milieu in which she lived. The protagonist is not so blinded by her vulnerability that she lacks a voice with which to critique the inadequacies around her. This voice becomes stronger over the course of the novel as she continually contests the hypocrisy prevalent in the Parisian milieus of her workplace and social sphere. From the racist rhetoric of a colleague, to her boyfriend Germain's malicious, generalized "exotification" of her (reminiscent of French colonialists' attitudes toward the colonized), the reader constantly learns lessons on what it is like to be a woman of color trying to survive in the Western, white, European world.

Cajou's madness, as previously acknowledged, is the impetus that enables Lacrosil to introduce a plethora of issues pertinent to Caribbean and African women at the time of decolonization. In a sense, through her madness, we *see* what the heroine does. Her self-loathing becomes a meeting point—a platform—for larger, global themes such as the exotification of the Other by the West, the adverse socioeconomic divisions between white and black worlds, racism in the French population, as well as the abuse and manipulation of women by men (those of color as well as white).

Ironically, as Cajou slips further into madness, she also becomes exceedingly more clear in defining her views on and about assimilation, racism, difference, and marginalization during her time in Paris. Madness affords Cajou a medium through which to articulate what it means for her to exist in a world divided in terms of white and black. The more her dementia takes hold, the more clearly she sees that the idea of the diaspora is the only means by which to break the chain of oppositions between the white and black spheres that have characterized her life. Within the realm of the diaspora—a third space situated between White and Other—there is no hierarchy of difference and all humanity is on equal footing. Unfortunately, the beauty of the possibility of the diaspora is only revealed to her in the closing pages of the novel, as her madness engulfs her rational thinking. The drive to end her life is too great. Cajou's self-loathing is too intense and her lack of confidence too unbearable to be countered with the positive ideals of the multicultural.

Lacrosil's novel is divided into four "soirs," although throughout the story we are privileged to flashbacks detailing the events of the heroine's life as a child in Guadeloupe. The medium of the dark, insensitive night generates a milieu of reflection for Cajou. Painful memories from her difficult childhood are juxtaposed with events that take place in Paris which define her present tumultuous affair with Germain, a man she both loves and despises. Overlying these events and memories is Cajou's increasing angst over whether or not she should marry Germain and have his baby. Her insistence that she is "laide," and her assumption that her ugliness "scandalizes people," further propels her toward the climax of the novel.[25] It is not until "le dernier soir"—the last night—that Cajou makes the decision to end her life and, thus, that of her baby's, stating that the only important thing for her is "n'être pas vue. Me supprimer" [to not be seen. To do away with myself] and with it, her color.[26] In the closing pages, Lacrosil's thoughts on the impossibility of assimilation and her increasingly intense fixation on her color become more acute, driving her to the ultimate decision of suicide:

> Après tout, la forme, ici, importe peu. Que je sois maigrelette, ou au contraire obèse et défformée, cela ne signifie pas grand-chose et n'influerait pas sur ma place dans la société. Ce qui compte, c'est la couleur. Le rang social en dépend; elle crée les catégories humaines et l'espèce dont relève l'individu; c'est elle qui oppose de façon définitive un Scandinave, un Latin, un Israélite, un Eurasien, un Jaune, un Noir. . . . L'Habitude me prend la main. Elle exige que j'exécute les gestes quotidiens. Elle ignore que voici le temps de la diaspora. Il faudrait, avant tout, tuer l'Habitude.

> [After all form, here, is unimportant. If I'm skinny, or on the contrary obese and deformed, it is of no consequence and does not influence my place in society. What counts, is color. Social position depends on it; it creates categories of humans and animals out of which the individual emerges; in a definitive fashion, it opposes a Scandinavian, a Latin and Israelite, a Eurasian, a Yellow and a Black. . . . Habit takes my hand. It requires that I execute daily gestures. It ignores that it is the time of the diaspora. One must, before all else, kill Habit.[27]

The heroine's need to "kill" the habitual, standardized, coded concepts of white and black, which include the misconception, misunderstanding, and stereotypes associated with the Other, so prevalent in the Western, white European psyche, defines Lacrosil's commentary here. The author reveals the truth for her readers, exposing them to not only the complications of race for those who are not white (and French), but also to the influences of class and gender on the relationships the heroine has with others around her. Her protagonist strives to protect her true self, to overcome her insecurity, and to break the bonds of the stereotypical that have been construed in terms of colonial history and postcolonial events, yet to no avail. Cajou cannot exist in the white man's Parisian world.

Maryse Condé interprets Cajou's reactions to her environment as those of someone seeking to dispel the white man's colonial myth of the beautiful *mulâtresse* who is happy with herself and her color. Such a personnage was a favorite in works by nineteenth-century authors such as Pierre Loti, Eugène Sue, and Honoré de Balzac. In Lacrosil's novel, we see another side of race defined by someone who believes that her whole identity is bound up in what she perceives as ugliness uniquely due to her color. Cajou views herself as suffering from marginalization because she is too dark. Her color ultimately causes the degradation of her sanity, while also dispelling the enchanted myth whites fabricated for women like her in "the songs and the ditties [that promoted] a whole exotic mythology, [wherein] mulâtresses have been generally sacred, the most beautiful women of the world, more captivating than white women and more seductive than black." Cajou, on the other hand, "seems, ignorant of this myth and lives enclosed inside herself."[28] In the end, the heroine's ideas surrounding her own physical appearance become metaphors for the inadequacies of assimilationist theories which disfavor the majority of people of color living in the white world. Although Cajou understands this at the end of the novel and realizes that the diaspora is the *Au-delà*, a beyond that would wipe away difference, her self-loathing is too great. The pressure to conform to the codified white world, and, thus, her false selfhood, is too strong. Her life, she claims, has been tainted by one fall after another as she strives to flee the ambiguity of being of mixed race.[29] In the end, she realizes that neither world offers total refuge because both are part of her heritage and have contributed to who she is.

The heroine's confusion over the alliances she must make with white and black worlds begins at an early age and later influences her negative views about her own body. In focusing on the racial politics that are ever present in Guadeloupian society, Lacrosil comments on how skin color is a constant reminder of where one must situate oneself with respect to others. Reflecting on this issue, Maryse Condé contends, "slave roots are regarded as a curse [in Guadeloupe and Martinique]. . . . Up to the present time, no other society has been more obsessed by its past than the societies [of these two islands].[30] Added to racial divisions in her own society, Cajou suffers from a deformed view of her own body which, in turn, affects how she interacts within both her family and social environments.[31] Feminist philosophers such as Elizabeth Grosz contend that, in general, if a woman is able to "transcend corporeality," and, thus, the physical negative attributes she perceives as detrimental to her selfhood (body and mind), then she frees her identity from the purviews of the social codes in which she lives and, eventually, fashions her *being in the world* on her own terms.[32] However, the discordance between Cajou's own body image and how she is perceived (her "lived body") is too acute. Despite the fact that her "lived body" (an amalgam of perceptions that others have about her) is basically positive (she is continuously hailed in her work as a leading researcher in her field), her lack of confidence and her self-loathing dictate the outcome of her life.

Transcending her physical and psychological turmoil is impossible for Cajou. Her demise reflects psychologist Thomas Szasz's hypothesis that psychological stability is only achieved when internal and external conditions are in balance. Only then can a subject freely make her way in the world. Cajou's desire to commit suicide, which she has harbored from puberty, is due to an inner need to annihilate her split identity, thus overcoming the tortured, divided self she feels is so overbearing. Her world is caught between others' perceptions about who she is (accomplished researcher and/or exotic "Other") and her imagined failures.

As the novel progresses, the conflicts between white and black within Cajou's life are revealed. From the first instances of her childhood, the heroine is obsessed with the beauty of her white Parisian mother who, widowed at a young age, raises her daughter herself. No matter the love and support of her mother, Cajou constantly compares herself to her. The heroine decides that her inadequacies are uniquely due to not being white enough like her mother. Her embarrassment about the dark color of her skin is blamed on her deceased father who, as Maryse Condé points out, is "doubly killed by the child, because he personifies the part of herself which she hates."[33] Metaphorically, the father represents more than simple color, but also her "ancêtres esclaves" [enslaved ancestors], about whom Cajou feels only embarrassment.[34]

Cajou's story is enlarged into a universal treatise on race and racial prejudice, making us believe that perhaps she will come to reason since, in the latter part of the novel, she is able to finally see the beauty of her diasporic identity. In the second and third "soirs" of the story, the heroine embraces her blackness and begins to counter the misnomers about racial tolerance that the French around her constantly are promoting. Her militancy leads her to alienate herself further from all that is white, including Germain, whom she classifies as "un échantillon d'Aryen'" [an Aryan sample] par excellence.[35] Despite his protests that he is not privileged because of his color, that she should regard him as an individual, that he loves her, and that Parisian society does not have any preferences for skin color, she recoils from him: "Open your eyes" Germain tells her, "Paris is around you," yet she cannot avoid the grip of despair.[36] In a proclamation reclaiming her individuality, Cajou states that the Parisian world is like a paternal father. This world, after all, is the father of her white mother who was Parisian. Although the heroine professes that she loves her mother's country, she holds no particular personal ties with it. Paris is not the world of her extended family, as she proclaims to Germain, because the rest of her relatives are disseminated across the continents, following the model of the diaspora. Unlike Germain, who traces his *français de souche* (French roots) family back generations, Cajou's relations are "dispersed" and their origins are unknown to her. Recognizing that she is not French, nor white, nor even really Parisian, further alienates her from Germain and the identity that he wants her to adopt. He counters her claims, stating "tes réactions se comprendraient si tu vivais en 1900, ma pauvre Cajou. Mais aujourd'hui!" [Your reactions would be comprehensible if you lived in 1900, my poor Cajou. But today!][37] As much as Lacrosil forces her heroine to negotiate her identity within the realms of racial ambiguity, Cajou stands alone and isolated, unable to refashion herself. She is disassociated from the white man's world, while also cut off from her own ancestors. It is impossible for her to reestablish links to her past and her people who were destroyed because of white imperialism and slavery.

Lacrosil's commentary on France's postcolonial relationship with the for-merly colonized cannot be overlooked. Even more problematic is the au-thor's hidden condemnation of Guadeloupe's dependent status on France which surfaces through the voice of her heroine. Like Guadeloupe, Cajou is caught in the middle of the colonial past and the present Frenchified iden-tity she has inherited—an identity that, no matter how much she tries, she cannot refute. Germain is the Paris-France-White-Pro-Assimilation archetype against which Lacrosil writes in her effort to educate her readers on the com-plications of the postcolonial world. He plays both sides of the fence in his white liberal skin. On the one hand, he professes to love Cajou despite her color, yet on the other, he is drawn to her by the captivating exoticism he believes she represents, thus replaying French stereotypes associated with colonized women: "Je t'apprendrai, Cajou. . . . Tu est terriblement excitant" [I'll teach you, Cajou. . . . You are terribly exciting].[38] His tenderness toward the end of the novel, where he claims that "the gap" between them can be bridged, however, does not diminish the violence by which he "captured" Cajou in the first place. In the beginning of their affair, Germain's behavior is synonymous with that of the white plantation owners of the *vieilles colonies* of France's eighteenth-century empire. In the venue of the mas-ter/slave dialectic, he forces himself upon her; "Ma petite, il faudra bien que tu y passes tôt ou tard. Alors, pourquoi pas moi? Tu avais compris ce que je te voulais depuis le temps, non?" [My little one, you have to eventually suc-cumb now or later. So, why not me? You have known what I've wanted for a long time, right?].[39] Germain's overzealous sexual advances turn into rape. His violation of Cajou's body, both physically and mentally, is channeled through his wanting to make her into something other than what she is, to whitewash her, as he masters her body and soul: "Ce n'est pas le moment d'entamer une discussion. Quand je t'aurai contentée, tu ne te feras plus d'idées noires" [It's not the moment to begin a conversation. When I have satisfied you, you won't have any more *dark ideas*],[40] he tells her as he forces himself upon her.[41] Lacrosil's play on words here is significant in ex-posing Germain for who he really is. Problematic innuendos emanate from these two words as the author obliges her readers to subconsciously add "des" to Germain's phrase. "Idées [des] noires" in French signifies "ideas of Black women" and "idées noires" literally means "dark, foreboding ideas." This double meaning expressively defines how Germain, on the one hand, seeks to "whitewash" her, erasing her color and her foreign identity, and on the other, how he desires to conquer any independent ideas she might har-bor that would be contrary to those of his hedonistic, white, Parisian milieu. Germain's world is Christian and devoid of the haunting dark spirits which whites often associate with island peoples. Despite her protests, Germain wins: "Il emploie les mots les plus crus. La honte me brûle les oreilles." [He uses the most crude words. Shame burns my ears]. He overpowers her and

Cajou admits that she inevitably submits to his caprices.[42] Germain views her as his whore and his slave, disregarding the pain of her deflowerment:

C'est la première fois? Tu en redemanderas, ma petite, je m'en charge. . . . Une fille qui se donne aussi facilement que ça, on est sûr de la ravoir. Je reviendrai demain soir. Dis donc, ton lavabo. . . . Le bruit de l'eau qui coule me semble une humiliation de plus.

[It's your first time? You'll ask for it again, my little one, I'll see to it. . . . A girl who gives herself so easily as that is sure to be taken again. I'll come back to-morrow night. Hey, where's your sink. . . . The sound of the water running seemed like one more humiliation to me.][43]

Cajou, reduced to a *femme-objet*, is colonized by Germain. As his object, she is "mastered" by him: "Ma chérie, je ne songeais qu'à te maîtriser. . . . Une autre fille aurait jugé ma violence flatteuse, ou bien elle m'aurait haï si elle estimait que je n'étais pas assez bien pour elle. Toi, tu ne parlais pas de 'réparation'; tu acceptais d'être une amusette" [My dear, I only dream of mastering you. . . . Another girl would have judged my violence flattering, or she would have hated me if she hadn't thought I was good enough for her. You, you didn't mention reparation; you accepted to be a plaything].[44] These violent scenes are disturbing, melding present time with past plantation/slave history as Lacrosil draws our attention to the brutality suffered by women at the hands of white men in the West Indies. In linking the past with the present, Lacrosil alludes to the precarious lives of women even in the postcolonial era. Women of the Antilles continue to be physically enslaved in the French psyche, manipulated by the Germains of the white world. The author's scene does not let us forget that history repeats itself, lessons are never learned, and white and black worlds will always be disharmonious. Germain's behavior forces Cajou to embrace her ultimate demise: total effacement. When she asks him point-blank: "Germain? J'ai peur que tu ne me voies plus" [Germain, I am afraid that you do not see me anymore],[45] Lacrosil's voice dovetails that of her heroine's as her subtext demands, "Does the white man see the black woman ever?" and "Can racial difference be erased given that brutality based on race and gender persists in our modern era?"

In the concluding "dernier soir," Cajou takes the only way out she feels is possible to escape the false self she has lived: suicide. She leaves behind the idea of the diaspora which is double-edged with negative and positive themes. On the one hand, the concept favors the beauty of difference, yet on the other, it is synonymous with "dispersion, dissolution, déstruction."[46] The possibility of the positive intermingling of all colors, the dissolution of racial tensions, and the destruction of hierarchy based on class, gender, and color, although fleetingly mulled over by the heroine, mean nothing to her in the end because she cannot overcome her psychological distress. If her mental faculties had been stronger and had she not succumbed to the voices in her head and what she defines as a "peur de [soi]-même" [fear of the self][47] which ultimately transforms into insanity, then she would have perhaps fought for the right to be different in a multicultural world, succeeding in her individuality as a talented woman from Guadeloupe.

JULETANE

In her 1982 novel *Juletane,* Guadeloupian author Myriam Warner-Vieyra, like Michèle Lacrosil, uses the theme of madness to allude to larger sociocultural issues influencing the lives of women not only in the postcolonial world but also in France.[48] In a 1993 interview with Mildred Mortimer, Warner-Vieyra indicated that her novel was more than simply the story of a young Caribbean woman driven insane from the love (or lack of it) of a man. Juletane is a person doubly hindered because she has never formed her own individuality, her own identity, and "has no relatives, no attachments in France [or her country of origin]. Her whole raison d'être is her husband."[49] Women's sociocultural isolation is brought to the forefront as the author explores a very real and widespread problem for women who find themselves manipulated because of their economic as well as political dependency on men. Madness and economic-political power are inextricably linked in Warner-Vieyra's novel. The author brings to light the very real, timeless problem of women exploited economically, politically, and socioculturally by their lack of power in phallocratic societies—this is true for African, Caribbean, and Western European and American women. Phyllis Chesler contends that women in general will tend to

> "stick" by their men sooner than they will "become" their own men, i.e., sooner than they will incorporate "male" [characteristics associated with assertiveness]. The real sexual revolution is harder and more threatening to people of both sexes, and of all classes and races, than are even other extremely difficult revolutions.[50]

Isolation, exile, the domination of her husband, and financial impoverishment drive Juletane insane. The novel is a testament of how "women become prisoners of other people's distorted perceptions," traditions, and oppressive cultural mores, and of how one woman seeks to write herself into a place of subjecthood while confronting daunting odds.[51] These barriers, as well as her overwhelming naiveté, eventually lead the heroine to self-destruct.

Unlike Cajou, Juletane does not suffer from self-loathing but rather male manipulation and a personal lack of interest in her life. Her world is the world of her young Senegalese husband, whom she marries without thinking about the consequences. Subsequently, she finds herself caught in a polygamous marriage and living in a village where no one speaks her language (French). The customs of her husband's village also prove to be difficult to adopt. Like Cajou, Juletane gives up, locking herself away in her bedroom where she can spy on her in-laws through one tiny window while she writes in her diary. Her writing becomes her only friend: "Ecrire écourtera mes longues heures de découragement, me cramponnera à une activité et me procurera un ami, un confident, en tout cas je l'espère" [Writing will shorten my long hours of discouragement, will be something for me to cling to and will give me a friend, a confident, at least I hope it will].[52] Juletane's withdrawal physically into her room and psychologically into madness lead inevitably to her death. Curiously, in a very clear manner, the protagonist meticulously writes down her slippage into insanity and all its turmoil day by day in her diary. We are privileged to moments of lucidity as well as periods of utter dementia. Her diary becomes a meeting point between these two psychological extremes. Juletane's self-imposed isolation is disregarded by her husband's family which automatically labels her "la folle" [the crazy one]:

> Ici, on m'appelle "la folle", cela n'a rien d'original. Que savent-ils de la folie? Et si les fous n'étaient pas fous! Si un certain comportement que les gens simples et vulgaires nomment folie, n'était que sagesse, reflet de l'hypersensibilité lucide d'une âme pure, droite, précipitée dans un vide affectif réel ou imaginaire?
>
> [Here, they call me "the mad woman", not very original. What do they know about madness? What if mad people weren't mad? What if certain types of behavior which simple, ordinary people call madness, were just wisdom, a reflection of the clear-sighted hypersensitivity of a pure, upright soul plunged into a real or imaginary affective world?][53]

Particularly, Ndèye, Mamadou's second wife, succeeds in alienating Juletane by constantly calling her mad. Mamadou's family thus subsequently inserts her into a particular place (which becomes familiar and establishes a certain order) within the family; she is "folle," but tolerated as such. Juletane is left to her own devices primarily because she is viewed as foreign and therefore unable to adapt to African culture. Warner-Vieyra draws our attention to a universalism essential to the basis of human community which, as Thomas Szasz notes, stipulates that "calling a person mentally sick . . . implies that [her] behavior is unacceptable and that [she] should conduct [herself] in other, more acceptable ways."[54] These "acceptable ways" are bound up in cultural and gendered roles that Warner-Vieyra's heroine realizes she is expected to perform but cannot. Cultural misunderstandings abound between Juletane, her husband, Mamadou, and his family, implying that stable mental health of a subject is a sign of adaptation and adherence to certain social rules: "In some societies, adaptation to society has tended to be highly valued . . . as a sign of mental health; and failure to adapt has been even more strongly regarded as a sign of mental ill-health."[55] In lieu of finding a means of somehow fitting in, or leaving, Juletane stagnates, accepting her mad label without protest. We are left to ponder if Juletane is really mad or simply fulfilling the family's designated expectations of her as a foreign, demented newcomer, caught in a web they weave for her.

Not only does the label mark Juletane as different, but her "Western ways" determine her status as an outcast—*une toubabesse* (a white woman)—in the eyes of the traditional society of Senegal. Unlike Cajou, Juletane professes that in France "je n'avais jamais été peinée quand on faisait allusion à ma couleur; je me rappelle avoir toujours accepté ma différence fièrement" [I had never been offended when people referred to my color. I remember I always accepted proudly the fact that I was different].[56] Warner-Vieyra is thus complicating ideas about race, since the concept of difference encompasses not only skin color, but also culture. Although Juletane is black like her husband, because she does not speak his language and is generally ignorant of Africa and its history, she feels that she will never fit in. Again, Françoise Lionnet's definition of *déculturation* is pertinent.[57] In the eyes of the society around her, Juletane, like Cajou, lacks authenticity with regard to origin, clan, and possessing a general idea of where she comes from. This *dépaysement*—uprooting from their origins, their identities—cuts both heroines off from any hope of ever feeling like they belong to a group, clan, country, or continent. The only identity Juletane possesses is the one she has formed within the confines of her Parisian godmother's upbringing. She knows little of her parents, both deceased in the "islands," or of her extended family there, the members of which she has never met. Her identity is entangled between two foreign worlds—her unknown homeland and the impossible-to-embrace world of her husband.

Juletane's vulnerable and weak identity is countered by an antithesis-heroine, Hélène, a young Antillean woman who works as a social worker in a hospital in Senegal. Hélène is everything Juletane is not. She was educated at home in the Antilles, pursues a multicultural life and lives in Paris, the Caribbean, and Dakar. In contrast to the heroine, Hélène had a happy childhood, knew her parents and her homeland, and was never lonely as a little girl. Hélène Parpin finds Juletane's diary among forgotten objects she has packed up to move to a new apartment. The diary came to her by way of her job as a social worker in a hospital. Juletane's story becomes an object "possessed" by Hélène. Juletane's words are not directly uttered to the reader but are imparted via the pages on which she has written her story that, in turn, are read by Hélène. Throughout the novel, Warner-Vieyra continuously plays the individualist Hélène opposite the vulnerable and victimized Juletane. Hélène is liberated by her nomadic life crossing between the islands, France, and Africa. Physically and psychologically, Hélène has incorporated a certain "maleness" (she speaks her mind, makes decisions, and likes to "décide, dirige" [takes the lead]) in her attitude toward life. Her family roots are strong, yet she does not feel the need to rely on anyone to help her make her way in life. Unlike Juletane, Hélène has picked the time, place, and conditions in which she wants to devote herself to a man having "décidée depuis peu de se marier, dans l'unique but d'avoir un enfant tout à elle. Elle [. . .] aimait bien [son amant]. Il était plus jeune qu'elle de dix ans . . . Elle le dominait financièrement et intellectuellement. Trop indépendante, elle n'aurait pas pu supporter un mari qui commande" [decided to get married, for the simple reason that she wanted a child of her own. She was fond of her husband-to-be. He was ten years her junior . . . she was his superior financially and intellectually. Too independent by nature, she could not have tolerated a husband who would dominate her].[58] The reader is constantly aware that Hélène is in control of her own story as well as that of Juletane's, since we "read" the victim's diary only when the young social worker does. Hélène's opinions and reflections on Juletane's journal are rendered distinctly clear by her self-assured voice which comments on the journal. Yet, as the stories play themselves out, each counter-punctual to the other, we are left wondering in the end who is really a victim. Victimhood for Warner-Vieyra serves in a larger capacity to expose the ills suffered by women when they are unable to adapt to foreign sociocultural parameters. Both Juletane's and Hélène's bodies "become texts . . . on which pain can be read as a necessary physical step on the road to a higher moral state, a destiny, or a way of being."[59] Although Hélène's suffering, she admits, is not as great as that portrayed in the diary of her defunct compatriot, she does recognize that, as far as men and love are concerned, she has had her share of woe. She was abandoned by her first fiancé, Hector, for a white Frenchwoman. The lost love made her cold and distant as well as led her to avow that she would never again suffer because of men.[60] From that time on, love became something detached from emotion; a vengeful experience where "elle s'était appliquée à se venger d'Hector sur tous les hommes qu'elle avait connus. Elle se servait d'eux pendant quelques temps, puis dès qu'ils semblaient s'attacher, elle les abandonnait sans aucune explication" [she had set out to pay Hector back through every man she met. She would use them for a while, then as soon as they seemed to be becoming involved, she would stop seeing them without any explanation].[61] As Hélène continues to read Juletane's story, she becomes more convinced that "tous les hommes, quels que soient leur niveau culturel ou leur origine sociale, étaient de parfaits égoïstes qui ne valaient pas une seule larme de femme" [all men, no matter their class or their social origin, (were) perfect egoists who (didn't) merit (a) single tear of a woman].[62] She decides her life will be devoted to avenging all that was lost with Juletane's death.[63]

Although Hélène views Juletane as a victim, caught up in a life over which she has little control, Warner-Vieyra does not describe her heroine's victimization as we would expect. Juletane's lack of will, rather than total, overwhelming sociocultural forces, causes her demise. She is perfectly aware that she is slipping into dementia. Scholar Jonathan Ngate argues that Juletane is always conscious of her mental state. By writing in her diary as a "victim" she "is not only acknowledging the presence of the victimizer, she is also recognizing his authority, looking outward to him in a way that helps one see clearly why this story that is supposed to be a diary is very much an autobiography which, Juletane hopes, will help her husband understand her better."[64]

Despite her suffering from cycles of dementia, Juletane is somewhat in control of her actions and often makes sociocultural remarks that are lucid and forthright. Based on her judgments about African society, she decides early on not to accept the hand she has been dealt. Through her Western (and French-influenced) observations, she does become aware of an insufferable inequality between men and women in her husband's society, something which she refuses to accept:

> Quand nous sortions, il me présentait, puis m'oubliait dans un coin, comme une vieille chose, au milieu d'un tas de femmes, souriantes et gentilles, mais qui ne parlaient pas le français. Je le voyais plus loin, volubile avec les hommes. Je ne comprennais pas non plus cette forme de ségrégation où les femmes semblaient n'avoir aucune importance dans la vie de l'homme, sauf au moment de ses plaisirs, ou encore, comme mères des enfants. Elles n'étaient pas les compagnes complices et confidentes. Une ombre de mystère entourait les affaires du mari qui [était le] seul maître.

> [Whenever we went out he would introduce me, then forget me in a corner, like some discarded object, surrounded by a group of women who were smiling and kind, but who spoke no French. I saw him at a distance, chatting with the men. Neither could I understand this sort of segregation where women seemed to have no importance in a man's life, except for his pleasure or as the mother of his children. They were not companions and confidants. An aura of mystery surrounded the husband who (was the) sole master]. [65]

Over the course of time, this once shy, young ingénue becomes slowly aware of herself and her situation. Polygamy is Mamadou's downfall and is viewed by the heroine as "a kind of relationship [that] secretes the poison that helps destroy his whole household."[66] Juletane, entangled in this abject domestic web, overcomes her passivity. The fact that she loses her child, which would have granted her more sympathy from her husband's traditional family, turns her into a "vicious" schemer who is convinced that she must plot the demise of her co-wives.[67] Even though Mamadou, after the loss of the child and Juletane's first slip into dementia, offers to send her back to

France, she decides to stay, admitting that she doesn't see the point of returning since she has no taste for anything anymore and no family. She has
become used to her "vegetative" life.[68] This life is tangible only through
meanness, hate, and cowardness, transforming into what she defines as her
normal cycle of existence.[69] The demented otherness that characterizes the
irrational side of Juletane, fashioned from her alienation in this foreign environment, creates another persona that allows her to act in ways she never
would have if she had stayed in France.

Even though Juletane professes a certain tolerance for Mamadou's first
wife, Awa, and loves and enjoys Awa's children, Diary, Oulimata, and
Alioune, avenging her situation at their expense becomes the heroine's singular aim. Her rage and hate accumulate in her detestation of Ndèye, the
second wife. It is hate that eventually transforms into full-blown madness
and, subsequently, causes Juletane's violent outbursts. Curiously, her dementia also reveals the idea of writing in a diary. She confesses that writing leads to her rebirth and is "une bonne thérapeutique pour mes an-
goisses; je me sens déjà plus sûre de moi. . . . Aujourd'hui, ma seule
certitude est de renaître à la vie. J'écoute battre mon coeur d'excitation,
frémir le sang qui court dans mes veines" [good therapy for my anxieties.
Already I feel more secure. . . . Today my only certainty is having come to
life again. I listen to my heart beating excitedly, and my blood rushing
through my veins].[70] The journal becomes her focal point, a place where
reality and unreality are negotiated as she seeks to dissimilate the differences between her dreams and real life events.

It is not until Awa's three children are found dead that we understand to
what extent Juletane lives in an unreal world. The heroine is not a suspect
because she is insane, yet, as she notes in her diary, she is unsure whether
or not she is guilty. Mamadou's family's tolerance for Juletane's insanity (she
is never blamed for the death of the children, nor is she a suspect) is exem-
plary of African tribal beliefs about madness. Senegalese psychiatrist
Bougoul Badji explains that "in Black Africa, generally, mental sickness, bad
luck which seems inexplicable, [is viewed as] an act of an exterior agent to
the victim-subject."[71] Badji notes further that "at no time is contact between
the mad person and the group disrupted, despite the disorder caused by the
mad person."[72] Although Juletane is condemned as a foreigner and never totally accepted by Mamadou's entourage, she is, nevertheless, because of her
madness, not blamed when adversity strikes.

Juletane's journal again is the only insight Hélène (or the reader) gains
into the heroine's demented actions. In her writing she recounts horrific
and seemingly fictitious scenes where she kills Ndèye with a knife. Although apparently fabricated, as she reads her own entries, she becomes
doubtful of her innocence: "Et la mort des enfants. Qui est responsable
de leur mort? . . . Ne m'avait-on pas prescrit des gouttes?" [And about the

children's death. Who is responsible for their death? . . . Didn't they pre-
scribe drops for me?].[73] Every incident, lucid or imaginary, is noted. We are
privy to the denouement of the heroine's demise as Hélène reads, imparting to us the last few months of Juletane's existence. We do learn that Juletane did not stab Ndèye, but as for the death of the children, we are never
sure. It is not until Tuesday, September 5, 1961, that the heroine admits
that she is in a psychiatric hospital once again. Her crime? Having thrown
"une casserole d'huile bien chaude" [a saucepan full of very hot oil] in
Ndèye's face.[74] Her revenge is complete. Following the disfigurement of
Ndèye, Awa throws herself into a well, killing herself. Juletane confesses
that, although she did not remember having done it, she probably left the
barbiturates within reach of the children. Despite her confession and her
sadness over the loss of the children, she still selfishly remarks that
"Cependant leur disparition ouvrait une brèche dans la cuirasse d'indif-
férence de Mamadou" [However, their death had pierced Mamadou's ar-
mour of indifference].[75] She obtains what she had wanted all along; her
husband's attention.

From her hospital bed, the protagonist tells us that she has never felt more
in possession of her faculties, her vengeance has appeased her. When she
learns that Mamadou lost control of his car and was killed, the sweet taste of
this revenge dissipates, there is now no one to love and no one to hate. Her
world has stopped: "Ma vie valait-elle la peine d'être vécue?" [Had my life
been worth living?] she asks, declaring that her singular wish is to "se
réveiller dans un autre monde où les fous ne sont pas fous, mais des sages
aux regards de justice" [To wake up in another world where mad people are
not mad, but wise and just].[76]

For Juletane, love and independence prove impossible to obtain. Yet,
her journal—the story of her life and her madness—remains a legacy to the
power of words in the process of inscribing feminine subjectivity. By writing down her story—her speech—Juletane has formed connections with
the women who later read her diary. Myriam Warner-Vieyra's novel reminds us of the importance of the link between women's power and their
speech. Those who have access to the pen rule the writing of their history.
It is, thus, important for women to understand this power and to find a way
to divert its masculine eminence in order to mold it to their own specifica-
tions. "Power and knowledge are mutually conditioning"[77] and lead to development of the ego, the very heart of logos: subjectivity. For women,
development of the ego (and thus identity) is extremely important when
considering madness, loss of subjectivity, and women's subjugation due to
oppressive patriarchal systems. Development of the ego for men and
women relies on the *inscription* of events and experiences from outside
life on the surface of the Being. In contrast, isolation, as Juletane exempli-
fies, means death for women.

Juletane and Cajou individually fail in dealing with the adversities and injustices in their lives. They serve as archetypes as well as metaphors for the larger sociocultural ills that plague women. These ills are revealed through madness, turning women into monsters and medusas.[78] Through their heroines, Lacrosil and Warner-Vieyra expose the sociocultural conditions that adversely influence the lives of women and determine how, ultimately, they cope with their own existence. As Phyllis Chesler remarks, women need to "effect . . . crucial changes in their economic and reproductive lives" in order to take charge of their mental as well as physical health. Lacrosil and Warner-Vieyra do not make excuses for their heroines; rather they use madness as a tool, a window, through which to assess what is often wrong with the socioeconomic and cultural parameters in which women find themselves bound throughout the world. Literature melds with sociocultural realities, exposing the hard, cold fact that "women who engage in self-destructive behavior in order to compensate for their lack of social power" are prevalent in all societies.[79]

NOTES

1. François Lionnet, "Inscriptions of Exile: The Body's Knowledge and the Myth of Authenticity," *Callaloo* 15, no. 1 (1992): 30–40, 31.

2. Susan Bordo, *Unbearable Weight: Feminism, Western Culture, and the Body* (Berkeley: University of California Press, 1993), 2.

3. Bordo, *Unbearable Weight*, 148.

4. Juliana Makuchi Nfah-Abbenyi, *Gender in African Women's Writing: Indentity, Sexuality, and Difference* (Bloomington: Indiana University Press, 1997), 32.

5. Nfah-Abbenyi, 37.

6. Evelyn O'Callaghan, "Interior Schisms Dramatized: The Treatment of the 'Mad' Woman in the Work of Some Female Caribbean Novelists" in *Out of Kumbla: Caribbean Women and Literature*, ed. Carole Boyce Davis et al. (African World Press, 1990), 89–109.

7. O'Callaghan, "Interior Schisms," 92–93.

8. Evelyn O'Callaghan, "The Bottomless Abyss: 'Mad' Women in Some Caribbean Novels," Bulletin of Eastern Caribbean Affairs 11, no. 1 (March–April 1985): 45–58.

9. Astbury, *Crazy for You*, 36.

10. Ngate, "Reading Warner-Vieyra's *Juletane*," Callaloo 9, no. 4 (1996): 556.

11. Nfah-Abbenyi, 31.

12. Nfah-Abbenyi, 56. See her chapter "Gender, Feminist Theory, and Postcolonial (Women's) Writing" (pp. 16–34) in her new book, *Gender in African Women's Writing*.

13. Lionnet, "Inscriptions," 33.

14. Betty Wilson, introduction to the English translation of *Juletane* (London: Heinemann Press, 1987), vii

15. In general, Guadeloupian women authors are more numerous than their Martinican compatriots. It is speculated that this is due to Guadeloupe's more militant nationalistic arena which, in turn, has fostered women's movements and dialogue

around feminine issues. In contrast, Martinican society has historically been more white, sharing close ties with France. The island therefore has not produced a strong, independent feminine literary voice (see Betty Wilson's introduction to the English translation of *Juletane* [London: Heinemann Press, 1987]), vii.

16. Jack Corzani et al., "Antilles-Guyane," in *Littératures francophones: Les Amériques: Haïti, Antilles-Guyane, Québec* (Paris: Belin-Sup, 1998), 120.

17. Michèle Lacrosil, *Cajou* (Paris: Gallimard, 1961), 21. My translation.

18. Lacrosil, *Cajou*, 30.

19. Lacrosil, *Cajou*, 32.

20. Myriam Warner-Vieyra, *Juletane* (Dakar: Présence Africaine, 1982), 21; translated by Betty Wilson under the title *Juletane* (London: Heinemann, 1987), 7.

21. Warner-Vieyra, *Juletane*, 30, 12.

22. Lacrosil, *Cajou*, 18.

23. Lacrosil, *Cajou*, 199.

24. Promotion of the idea of racial harmony and the diaspora are particularly evident in Aminata Sow Fall's *Douceurs du bercail*, studied in part three of this book.

25. Lacrosil, *Cajou*, 210.

26. Lacrosil, *Cajou*, 229.

27. Lacrosil, *Cajou*, 225.

28. Maryse Condé, *La parole des femmes: Essai sur des romancières des Antilles et de langue française* (Paris: L'Harmattan, 1979), 21. Condé, drawing on Jack Corzani's thoughts in *La littérature des Antilles-Guyane Françaises*, notes that originally Lacrosil wanted to center her novel around the universal theme of ugliness above and beyond race, however it was her editors at Gallimard who required, for purely commercial reasons, that she modify her character to be a mulatto woman (21–22).

29. Lacrosil, *Cajou*, 229.

30. Condé, *La parole*, 11.

31. Elisabeth Grosz, *Volatile Bodies: Toward a Corporeal Feminism* (Bloomington: Indiana University Press, 1994), 75. The philosopher notes that: "[T]he body image is in continuous process of production and transformation. It changes orientation or inflection as the child develops into adolescence and adulthood. Adolescence is also of significance in understanding the development of the body image, for this is a period in which the biological body undergoes major upheavals and changes as an effect of puberty. It is in this period that the subject feels the greatest discord between the body image and the lived body, between its psychical idealized self-image and its bodily changes" (75).

32. Grosz, *Volatile Bodies*, 75.

33. Grosz, *Volatile Bodies*, 22.

34. Lacrosil, *Cajou*, 2.

35. Lacrosil, *Cajou*, 3.

36. Lacrosil, *Cajou*, 213.

37. Lacrosil, *Cajou*, 202.

38. Lacrosil, *Cajou*, 166.

39. Lacrosil, *Cajou*, 182.

40. My emphasis.

41. Lacrosil, *Cajou*, 181.

42. Lacrosil, *Cajou*, 182.

43. Lacrosil, *Cajou*, 183.

44. Lacrosil, *Cajou*, 218.

45. Lacrosil, *Cajou*, 213.

46. Lacrosil, *Cajou*, 209.

47. Lacrosil, *Cajou*, 209.

48. Warner-Vieyra's previous novel, *Le Quimboiseur l'avait dit* (1980), also uses madness as a theme to explore the results of exile, self-loathing, and alienation as reasons for her heroine's mental demise.

49. Mildred Mortimer, *"Interview with Myriam Warner-Vieyra," Callaloo* 16, no. 1 (1993): 108–15, 111.

50. Phyllis Chesler, *Women and Madness*, (New York: Four Walls, 1997), 238.

51. Chesler, 112.

52. Warner-Vieyra, *Juletane*, 18; Wilson, *Juletane*, 5.

53. Warner-Vieyra, *Juletane*, 13, 2.

54. Szasz, *Ideology and Insanity*, 50.

55. Szasz, *Ideology and Insanity*, 37.

56. Warner-Vieyra, *Juletane*, 80, 43.

57. Lionnet, "Inscriptions," 31.

58. Warner-Vieyra, *Juletane*, 11–12, 1.

59. Lionnet, "Inscriptions," 30.

60. Warner-Vieyra, *Juletane*, 56, 28.

61. Warner-Vieyra, *Juletane*, 56, 28.

62. Warner-Vieyra, *Juletane*, 82, 44.

63. Warner-Vieyra, *Juletane*, 85, 46.

64. Ngate, "Reading *Juletane*," 560–61.

65. Warner-Vieyra, *Juletane*, 49, 24.

66. Ngate, "Reading *Juletane*," 561.

67. Ngate, "Reading *Juletane*," 561–62.

68. Warner-Vieyra, *Juletane*, 77, 41.

69. Warner-Vieyra, *Juletane*, 77, 41.

70. Warner-Vieyra, *Juletane*, 94, 51.

71. Bougoul Badji, *La Folie en Afrique: Une rivalité pathologique* (Paris: L'Harmattan, 1993), 21.

72. Badji, *La Folie*, 36.

73. Warner-Vieyra, *Juletane*, 125, 69.

74. Warner-Vieyra, *Juletane*, 131, 73.

75. Warner-Vieyra, *Juletane*, 133, 74.

76. Warner-Vieyra, *Juletane*, 141, 78.

77. Grosz, *Volatile Bodies*, 148.

78. Cixous, "The Laugh of the Medusa," 337–338.

79. Susan Bordo, "Anorexia Nervosa: Psychopathology as the Crystallization of Culture," in *Feminism and Foucault: Reflections on Resistance* (Boston: Northeaster University Press, 1988), 87–118; as cited by Françoise Lionnet (36).

4

Out(in)side the Confinement of Cultures

Marie Chauvet's *Amour, Colère, et Folie* and Mariama Bâ's *Un Chant écarlate*

Exile is that fragile moment when the outside world separates the self from the other and drives them apart.

—Derayeh Derakhshesh, "Un Chant écarlate: The Song of Exile" (1996)

Claire, a dark-skinned bourgeois in a world of light-skinned, nearly white mulattoes, seems unable to affirm her power as a plantation mistress because of the things she is not: male and white.

—Lizabeth Paravisini-Gebert, "The Alienation of Power: The Woman Writer and the Planter-Heroine in Caribbean Literature" (1998)

Where Juletane suffers from lack of control over her life and Cajou from alienation and self-loathing, Marie Vieux Chauvet's heroines (particularly Claire) and Mariama Bâ's Mireille are repressed through a type of "disciplinary power" constructed from social rules and regulations that are essentially "invisible" yet present enough in society to harm them. This disciplinary power fabricated by men and wielded against women eventually either entraps them in worlds where few options remain, or totally engulfs them, ending their lives. Chauvet's Claire of her first novella, *Amour* (in a collection of three), possesses wealth she would lose if married due to the mores of the bourgeois society in which she lives. Rose, principal protagonist of the second novella, *Colère*, prostitutes herself in order to keep her family's property. The power that men hold over women in these novels varies from being subtle to violent, but is always definitively rooted in socioculturally defined gendered roles pertaining to women's place in the social order. The heroines in this chapter are condemned because of what their gender means for their respective societies. Their insignificant power assures that men (lovers, rapists, police, fathers) will forever rule them.

Within the male dominator's space "disciplinary power manifests its potency, essentially, by arranging objects," and, we might add, "subjects" to fit its prerogatives.[1] The heroines in the novels discussed here are constantly watched and scrutinized because they choose to refute the roles they have been given. They are criticized by their respective societies for locating themselves on "the periphery: invisible, lucid, dangerous, unmarried, [and in Chauvet's heroine Claire's case] childless."[2] These women are also effaced in the sense that they have very little voice and their actions do not change the unfavorable status they endure in the societies in which they live. Chauvet's and Bâ's primary aim is to use the obsequious spaces occupied by their heroines to expose the violence (Chauvet) and the xenophobia (Bâ) that is possible in the environments in which their novels take place. Chauvet denounces the evils of the Duvalier regime in her native Haiti, and Bâ comments on the phallocentric and patriarchal ideologies that rule traditionalist Africa, truncating women's liberation in Senegal. In both novels, the heroines are constantly monitored by the sociocultural and domestic spaces in which they live. They exist in a state of continued surveillance because they are also marked as different (even among their peers). Claire, in *Amour,* is considered too black for her mulatto bourgeois family, and Mireille, in *Un Chant écarlate,* is white and foreign, barred from assimilating to her Senegalese husband's traditional family. Difference renders these women not only more visible than the other "accepted" characters in these novels, but also more vulnerable because they are the targets of apprehension and spite which lead to misunderstanding, alienation, madness, and death.

Although the marginalization that these heroines experience propels them toward abjection, these women leave behind a cogent commentary on the societies which engulf them. Each heroine "lays herself bare" by "physically materializ[ing] what she's thinking; she signifies it with her body . . . she draws her story into history."[3] Both Marie Vieux Chauvet's triptych *Amour, Colère, et Folie* and Mariama Bâ's *Un Chant écarlate* are formidable novels that emphasize how women's bodies, minds, souls as well as history are melded with the narrative text. These "corporeal" texts are conceptualized and written in the margins of society. Both authors' novels are neither totally autobiographical nor entirely fictitious, but rather they are a melange of both that offers larger sociocultural commentaries on issues that have determined how women lead their lives. These narratives are the media through which their authors articulate the loathsome histories of feminine madness that force their protagonists to commit violent acts. The dementia from which these women suffer in these novels is more subtle than that of Cajou's and Juletane's. Chauvet's and Bâ's novels are studies of women who have been confined ideologically by the societies and sociocultural groups in which they are forced to live. Questions of skin color (both Claire and Mireille are faulted for their color which renders them "visible" objects marked by their difference from others around them), class, and gender have evident roles in the novels considered here. Yet, these factors are but a part of a larger commentary each writer offers on the contemporary human condition and the universal truths that are exposed when classifications of people are drawn along lines of race and gender. Claire and Mireille are unlike Juletane and Cajou, who withdraw and surrender to the environments in which they live because they are unable to adapt. Marie Chauvet's Claire, Rose, and Cécile and Mariama Bâ's Mireille do not suffer from self-loathing, nor succumb to vulnerability. In contrast to Juletane and Cajou, these heroines act within their environments, confronting adverse societal forces that have pushed them to their psycho-physical limits. Claire's and Mireille's stories force our reflection on sociocultural brutality and political turmoil as well as the inconsistencies in race and class consciousness that are prevalent in the postcolonial world.

Both authors considered here write from not simply a Caribbean or African perspective, but from a human one. The issues which they debate in their works affect not only their heroines, but the humanity around them. These novels insist on "social reality as background, on the repeated surfacing of collective conscience, on individual destinies being supplanted by national destinies."[4] With respect to women, these authors ask the principal question, Where do women fit into the phallocratic structures of the postcolonial world? Women cannot be forgotten and their voices need to be heard if socioeconomic as well as political changes are to take place.

Destabilizing the masculine world yet also finding a way in which to live with men are prevalent themes in these women authors' works. As Haitian scholar and novelist Yanick Lahens contends, women's writing from the francophone world is global in its context, particularly in Haiti, because women are constantly considering "L'autre dans nous-mêmes" [the Other in ourselves].[5] Lahens echoes Cixous who states that "there is hidden and always ready in woman the source; the locus for the other."[6] Discovering the other within the self is particularly important for Haiti, whose culture has been crisscrossed by a multitude of races and origins. For Chauvet, as for many other exiled Haitian authors writing in French, drawing out the multiethnic in order to understand the bloody history that has characterized the island (and its impact on women) has been a focal point of the modern Haitian francophone novel in recent years.

In contrast to Warner-Vieyra's and Lacrosil's novels, in which the heroines look from the *inside* out of their environments, allowing themselves to be overwhelmed by their own sequestered worlds and consumed by their own failures, Chauvet and Bâ position their protagonists' on the *outside* to look in. Chauvet's commentary is focused (from exile in the United States where she wrote *Amour, Colère, et Folie*) on the political demise of Haiti, its violent history, and debilitating class/race structures. Bâ's *Un chant écarlate* makes us aware, through the voice of her white French heroine Mireille (who moves from France to Senegal to live with her Senegalese husband), that African independence did not succeed in reforming colonial structures which continue to stratify people along race and gender, particularly to the detriment of women. Nor did the Négritude movement, promoted among the intellectual black elite of Africa (which was supposed to allow for one to rediscover one's roots, *enracinement*, while also fostering the opening up of a positive métissage of language and culture) accomplish anything positive, as Bâ suggests, for the African woman. Bâ takes to task the paucity of women's rights that came out of African intellectualism within postcolonial regimes. She points out both implicitly and explicitly that most male authors and intellectuals left no room for an African feminine voice, but instead relegated the African woman to idealized symbols solidified within the literary imagination of the postcolonial era.[7]

The heroines considered here are sequestered ideologically by the environments in which they live. They strive to change them but fail because they are up against irreversible circumstances. Claire and Mireille commit violent acts to find release from the cumulation of sociocultural pressures and mores that push them to their limits. Their bodies and souls are caught up in the suffocating tutelage of societies which, although they try, they cannot change.

Losing oneself in madness is one way to find a release from the "mental structures of the group (or groups) to which the [heroine] is linked."[8] Nevertheless, even in their heroines' fits of rage, Chauvet and Bâ both make us aware that these protagonists act based on a series of choices they alone have made which ultimately aid or hinder their destinies. Though these women are victims of patriarchal structures, they are not blindly caught up in paths planned for them by men. Although Rose and Cécile, heroines of Chauvet's second and third novellas, do not survive the violence around them, they still do not face their deaths passively. At the end of both works, the heroines' deaths are used by the authors to proffer a statement on the universal, abject situations in which women can, and constantly do, find themselves. "In all cultures," Bâ exclaims, "social pressure shamelessly suffocates individual attempts at change. The woman is heavily burdened by mores and customs, in combination with mistaken and egoistic interpretations of different religions" and, I might add, ideologies.[9]

AMOUR, COLÈRE, ET FOLIE

Marie Chauvet's writing reflects her life in exile, imparting to readers her own introspection on, and critique of, Haiti's sociocultural and political collapse. Born in 1917[10] into the haute-bourgeoisie mulatto class of Haiti, Chauvet dedicated her life to describing the imbalance of Haitian class structures and how these encouraged the violent upheavals that eventually culminated into the repressive Duvalier regime which lasted almost thirty years (1957–1986).[11] Although Chauvet disguised "the political content of her novel by placing the [historic] events after the American occupation in 1939, her assault on the Duvalier regime was unmistakable and so shocking that it was blocked from distribution by French and Haitian authorities for twelve years following its publication."[12]

Chauvet's literary themes mirror those of many authors who live in exile because of persecution at home. However, what is unique about the author's writing, Yanick Lahens notes, is that she recognized from early on the importance of fostering a "vibrant national literature that [would] simultaneously give back Haiti to Haitians and the mother island to the diaspora, as well as expose all Haitians, 'those on the inside' as well as 'those on the outside' to [a] world [of] literature."[13] Spacial divisions between inside and outside are evident in the author's works, as Renée Larrier contends. Chauvet's protagonists, particularly Claire of *Amour,* "[locate themselves] on the periphery: invisible, lucid, dangerous, unmarried, childless"; she is powerful and positions herself as both a "spy and manipulator" on/of those around her.[14] Her novels also situate women within the larger sociocultural contexts of their society. Unlike many male Haitian authors of her time, Chauvet concentrated on delving into questions of identity not only for women but for Haiti, while recognizing that Haitian "identity has always been defined and lived through an Other, one [that is] exterior . . . hostile yet fascinating," and that "alienation shall always come with the quest for 'pure' identity."[15]

Chauvet's life and work were replete with turmoil and barbarous injustices. Born into the privileged mulatto class of the haute bourgeoisie of Haiti, the author enjoyed the intellectual and financial status her skin color and privileged place in society brought her. Her literary intellect was cultivated by the salons she attended, where she collaborated with several well-known poets, founding literary journals such as *Semences.* Chauvet and poets such as Antony Phelps cultivated the *Haïti littéraire* milieu and met with like-minds who formed groups such as the *Araignées du soir* [The Night Spiders]. Lahens suggests that these groups fostered the creation of a new literature—one influenced by writers of the *outside* and the exiled. From their outset, the groups were seen as a threat to the tyrannical government of the Duvaliers. As a result, many poets and novelists facing death fled across the globe. In the early 1960s, when Chauvet left for the United States, the importance of describing the "outside" in her writings became apparent. From abroad, she was more at liberty to study her brutal memories of Haiti and of Duvalier's repression as well as the conflicts inherent in Haitian culture: a culture constructed around the tenuous intricacies of skin color, class, and gender.[16]

Author of *La fille d'Haïti* (1954), *La Danse sur le volcan* (1957), and *Fonds-des-Nègres* (1961), all published prior to her 1968 triptych *Amour, Colère, et Folie*, Chauvet solidified in all of her writings a commitment to critiquing events in Haiti and the violent politics of Duvalier. Her novels continuously upset both her family and government officials.[17] All her works can be considered as acts of resistance wherein politics, race, and sexual repression are subtexts influencing the worlds of her heroines. *Amour, Colère, et Folie,* written in exile while in the United States, is a treatise of Chauvet's own investment in a resister's cause, personally as well as literarily. The author fled not only brutal repression, but also her husband, a highly ranked civil servant in the Duvalier regime. Although published in Paris in French by Editions Gallimard, the success of the collection of three short novels was limited due primarily to her family's censorship of the work. Her husband succeeded in buying up all unsold copies of the book from Gallimard and shutting them away until 1980, when the book was rereleased. Marie Chauvet died poor and forgotten in New York in 1975.[18] The collection stood for all that her family wanted to suppress: commentary on the exploitation of Haitians (by the French and the Americans), racial strife, violence, and the Duvalier regime's general dirty political practices. The collection is an allegory for the "tragic dimension of Haiti's national history,"[19] duly noted by Claire in the opening pages of *Amour*: "Nous nous exerçons à nous entr'égorger depuis l'Indépendance. Les griffes du peuple se sont mises à pousser et se sont acérées. La haine entre nous est née" [We have concentrated ourselves on slitting each other's throats since independence. The claws of the people have grown out and are sharp. The hate between us has been born].[20] The violence of the text, housed in the pure, raw words of the author, cause the reader intense anguish. We are caught up in the violence of the scenes and "once inside Chauvet's text [we feel] imprisoned."[21] Like the heroines, the reader experiences claustrophobic spaces, hemmed in by a society that is caught up in the throws of bestial violence from which there is no escape.[22]

Chauvet's triptych transgresses love, rage, and madness, binding the feminine characters within the boundaries of these three emotions. Each emotion provides a *toile de fond* for its respective story, yet all the heroines—Claire, Rose, Cécile—at some point encounter all three. Assessing to what extent these heroines transgress love, rage, and madness, as well as how sociocultural mores and politics confine them within barriers determined by class, race, and gender, is the objective of this chapter. The confinement of women within societal norms, as well as politics, their attempts to disobey these limits, and the subsequent results of these women's rebellion, is a central theme in Chauvet's novels. Yet, Chauvet's heroines do not passively sit by as victims and watch the world engulf them, as do Juletane and Cajou. Despite being caught up in the adverse situations (marginalized on the peripheries by their difference and defiance of social purviews) of the country and its politics, they do try to fight in their own fashion to change the tides of history, curb violence, and combat racial and class strife. They are much more active in their approach to survival in unpropitious situations than Cajou or Juletane. When we read the stories of Claire, Rose, and Cécile, we do not forget them. Within the confines of society, these heroines, particularly Claire and Rose, attempt to combat the dehumanizing effects of Duvalier and his Tontons Macoutes, prevalent every hour in their daily lives. They protect their bodies and their minds as much as they can in a world caught up in "the reality of madness and the madness of reality."[23]

Amour is the story of a bourgeois aristocrat, Claire, who, although of mulatto parents, is very dark: "Comme elle est différente de ses soeurs! A qui ressemble-t-elle?" [How she is different from her sisters! Whom does she resemble?] people remark as they adversely judge her skin tone for being "mal sortie" [cursed] from the beginning.[24] The protagonist is chastised for not having the right skin color for her class and is made to feel like an outsider from childhood. Unmarried and unwanted, considered "une vieille fille" at age thirty-nine, she lives a virgin's life in her family's house with her sisters Annette and Félicia, who, unlike the heroine, both possess the coveted "traits fins des blanches" [delicate features of white women], markers of the haute bourgeoisie.[25] Félicia is married to a white Frenchman, Jean Luze.[26] Claire lusts after her brother-in-law incessantly, living an unfulfilled fantasy locked away in her bedroom. Hiding in her room, she reads romance novels and masturbates while looking at pornographic postcards that she confesses to have bought from a shifty young man in Port-au Prince.[27] Claire suffers from vivid dreams during which she fantasizes about Jean Luze and experiences make-believe orgasms while also pretending to play roles she never could in reality. She admits that she is an old maid who is avid for love.[28]

Colère explores the rage of the Normil family, bourgeois landowners who have had to cope with the expropriation of their land by the invading "hommes en noir" [men in black]. Chauvet never names these invaders outright as Duvalier's Tontons Macoutes, preferring that the reader infer this fact through her allegorical descriptions. The ambiguity of these masked characters is unsettling, as they constantly crop up from nowhere throughout all three novels. The fact that they are not named turns Haiti's history into a universal one, symbolic for all the coercion and violence that has characterized many postcolonial regimes in the Afro-Caribbean diaspora.

The Normil's land becomes a prison as they hide behind the walls of their hacienda while being cordoned off inside with barbed wire. Rose, the family's only daughter, sells her body to a manipulative and evil lawyer who holds the fate of the family's land in his hands. He tells her that her father can regain the property if she will sleep with him for a month. The "Faustian pact" Rose makes with this devil results in her death.[29] Although she chooses to fight the phallocratic, dehumanizing forces that rain down on her body—figuratively and literally—she cannot, alone, conquer the prevailing evil in Haiti. Fighting to the last page, she succumbs finally to death out of sheer physical and mental fatigue, found by her brother who laments that she was killed by pure exhaustion.[30]

Folie, the last story in the triptych, is the tale of four poets hiding in a stinking hole that was once an apartment, trying to find a way to escape what they call the "devils"—the *loas*[31] dressed in black—who are trying to get them. Again, allegory is the prevalent qualifier of this tale, articulating the actual reality of the invasion of Duvalier's henchmen and their violence toward innocent people of all classes and races in Haiti during the 1960s. Simon (a white "Frenchman"), Jacques (black), and André and René (mulattos) make up the group of four poets whose only outlet in the face of the repression and violence that have overtaken their town are bottles of claret they drink daily in order to forget and *to not see* the reality of the madness around them. In the fashion of Samuel Beckett, Chauvet's concluding story reminds us of the absurdity that is found in the violent realms of savagery and tyranny. Once society is overtaken by violence, people are pushed to commit irrational acts. The author's theater of the absurd is heightened by the claustrophobic tensions (as created in *Amour* and *Colère*) she cultivates between the four poets who are sequestered inside the apartment. Their place is a festering den which offers no relief or way out except for one front exit which is blocked by a rotting corpse of indeterminate origin (they can't decide if it is a dog's or a man's). Decomposition outside as well as inside becomes a symbol for Haiti and her people, notes René the principal protagonist, who confesses that he has become used to terror and living "as a corpse."[32] Chauvet's message here reminds us that, in reality, human brutality reduces animals and men to the same inhumane state.[33]

As in *Amour* and *Colère*, Chauvet's *Folie* constructs an ominous, closed world where there is no possibility of exit. This claustrophobia creates ambiguous time frames and relationships between the characters. The author does not provide the reader with an explanation for how long the men have been entrapped. Again, particularly reminiscent of Beckett's *Waiting for Godot*, the last part of *Folie* is performed in theatrical form on the stage of a large village square out onto which the four *fous* emerge. On this metaphorical stage, the accused are surrounded by a crowd, the village priest, the prefect, and his various henchmen. Cécile, a mulatto woman who observes the square from her window, is sucked into a trap of rape and death. She is condemned only because she came to the aid of her maid who had been arrested for "having witnessed" René's outburst in the town's square (under Cécile's window) moments earlier. Chauvet's commentary on the senseless, absurd violence taking place on the square (an epitome of the island of Haiti) leads us down a path of no return. The characters are coerced to their deaths by firing squad simply because they dared to "BE" (a black maid, a mulatto lady, and a poet who seems "foreign"). They were simply people trying to go about their daily lives but who were condemned all the same.

Although all three stories send strong sociopolitical messages important to Chauvet, and each specifically demonstrates how violence and madness have been intertwined into the political turmoil that has characterized the politics of Haiti in the twentieth century, *Amour* and *Colère* best address the position of women, confinement, and madness (as it pertains to women) within the larger context of history and politics. For these reasons, I have opted to concentrate more on Claire and Rose, the first two heroines of Chauvet's collection. In these novellas, the author's principal objective is at work: to demonstrate that women, both psychologically and physically, attempt to resist repression as well as to counter "definitions of female vulnerability" that have been determined by the repressive regime of Duvalier's Haiti.[34] Even Cécile in *Folie,* who is much less developed as a character and seems at first to portray the sniveling vulnerability of the haute bourgeoisie that Chauvet loathes, in the end, as she faces the death squad's henchmen, prefers to die rather than to be raped and imprisoned.[35] The heroine's courage and strength attest to Chauvet's belief that women should not be afraid to engage the political, becoming active agents, even if it means dying as martyrs.

This chapter examines Chauvet's novels by comparing and contrasting varying degrees of madness, questions of identity and sexuality, as well as racial issues, in the context of women's sociocultural confinement. When assessing the influence of this confinement on the heroines, I draw again on the prevalent theme of position (for example the heroine's class and/or status) and positioning (her voice and how she uses it to challenge injustice) in terms of inside and outside sociocultural structures. The parameters of these two spaces are perpetually defined geographically, politically, racially, sexually, and linguistically. These demarcations are also based on the author's points of view and how she perceives the world around her in terms of classifications and categorizations of people, races, and genders. These classifications govern the actions of the heroines.

Classification of people based on skin color, gender, nationality, language, and class dictates the way Chauvet's characters cross boundaries, often leading them to act violently. "Classification is a social act," Thomas Szasz explains, and is responsible for psychological well- or ill-being, because being accepted as part of a group is one of man's most prevalent desires. "The classification of individuals or groups entails the participation of at least three different types of persons: classifier, classified, and a public called upon to accept or reject a particular classification."[36] The power to classify determines a certain amount of power for an individual or a group, depending on which is the strongest. As Thomas Szasz notes:

An individual may classify himself or others and, in turn, may be classified by others. In each case, the categorization proposed by the classifier may be accepted or rejected by others. To have one's classification of self or others accepted requires, in general, having a measure of power over others; this power may be intellectual (scientific) or political (coercive).[37]

With regard to Chauvet's work, we never lose sight of her efforts to rebel against classifications and the "regime of absolute evil and gratuitous violence" that various groups of people have caused in Haiti. Her pen is "profoundly rooted in the psychosocial reality of Haiti under Duvalier," and her writing never loses touch with the goal of exposing all facets of this reality to her readers.[38]

Chauvet's personal reality as an author writing from the outside looking *back in* on her society is illustrated through the actions of her female characters. The women in her stories are entrenched in realities constructed in terms of exile, marginalization, and insanity, rendering more evident the fact that "madness [is] a plea for understanding an alternate mode of communication . . . a protest against the repression of anti-social reactions."[39] Classifications and groupings of people by sexuality, class, and race dictate the parameters of the heroines' environments as well as the actions they take to survive from day to day. Claire is marginalized outside the normative/operative family structures in which she is expected to take part because she refuses to play the aristocrat, her birthright, as ordained by her society. Since her youth, she has been chastised for her dark skin color and, therefore, does not feel like she fits in with the rest of the family or her class. Consequently, she refuses marriage and her social milieu as well as the stereotypes of her gender, preferring to run the family property like a man. Although on the margins of bourgeois society and her own gender, Claire does not favor adopting the militant, nationalist rhetoric of underclass black male intellectuals who seek to overthrow the repressive regime. Rather, she sees rebellion as further undermining any possibility of unifying the country once Duvalier is overthrown. The protagonist's feelings about black nationalism echo Chauvet's own here. Claire at no time loses sight of her goal of finding the *other* in the selves of Haiti. Black nationalist movements would only isolate and exclude along racial lines, much like the race/class system had always done in her native island. A new form of all-inclusive nationalism had to be forged if Haiti were ever to free itself from the degradation caused by inequalities due to class and race.

Claire physically confines herself on the peripheries of her neighborhood and her family by seeking refuge in her room, preferring to "observe" from a window the events of the street below. Through the window she witnesses the constant insanity and absurdity of a country bound up in repression as it plays out in the streets. The window is also a physical marker dividing Claire's inside world from that of the outside. From this hidden space she witnesses prison warden Calédu's oppression and his treatment of the general populace of blacks and mulattos. She also observes Jean Luze, as well as her family, who moves as a fearful automaton living a superficial existence in an artificial setting. Chauvet's unnatural world is a reminder of the fragility of the human condition and how people fabricate trite, mechanical lives when faced with no way out of adverse situations. The author's characters are in denial, living fraudulent lives and false selves as they try to survive from day to day.

Rose, principal heroine of *Colère*, also acts on the marginalized peripheries of her class, attempting to keep herself and her family alive. Like Claire, Rose is dark, which puts her at odds with the mulatto social circle that surrounds her. However, the heroine is not daunted by adversity and takes action to ensure the well-being of her family. Chauvet's heroine counters misconceptions about feminine vulnerability in Haitian society, creating in Rose an accomplice to her father. This heroine proves to be stronger than he in scheming to guarantee the safeguarding of the family's property. When her father borrows money from his rich mistress in order to try to buy back the appropriated land from a manipulative lawyer supposedly handling their case, Rose takes matters into her own hands, agreeing, at all costs, to sacrifice herself in order to preserve their property. She is willing to do anything and go to any extreme.[40]

In her article on Chauvet's work, Janis Mayes explains that Rose's choice to act on behalf of her father's land overrides social norms rooted in the cultural practice known as *plaçage* (a practice wherein women have little say in the economic systems governing land wealth in Haiti). "Land is equated with male status and wealth" and "women are barred from its inheritance or its exchange."[41] Women's dependence on men for wealth and property assures their diminished position in society as passive subjects held at the mercy of patriarchal systems rendering evident that "the only socially recognized and validated representations of women's sexuality are those which conform to and accord with the expectations and desires of [men]."[42] Although, in the beginning, Rose acts as a dutiful daughter and "functions as an accomplice [to] this system," supporting her father in his efforts to "legally" buy back the land from the corrupt authorities, she does an about-face in the middle of the novel to actively take part in an "economic and social order" from which she would normally be barred.[43] Despite her father's protests, she alone decides to sell her body in exchange for transfer of the land back to her family. Rose overturns the passive image of Haitian women battered by Duvalier's violence by acting on her own behalf. She does not hide behind the males of her family to wait and see if the land will be returned, but rather insists on actively engaging the "established social norms that dictate that women should always remain on the peripheries of male-phallocentric power rooted in the land."[44] While her body is daily ravaged by the "gorilla," she plots the downfall of the evil elements in society that plague her family. Rose figuratively transforms herself into an animal to survive the bestiality around her, thus finding a mechanism to cope with the brutal situation with which she decides to engage. She survives by becoming what she defines as a stronger beast—a panther "ferociously veiled in false sweetness"—than the men around her. [45] Like Claire and Cécile, Rose "revolts against her oppression in order to survive, in order to create the possibility of new life."[46] Unfortunately, although fighting to the end, like Cécile, Rose dies in her efforts to combat the evil around her. The sociocultural norms based on phallocratic traditions, coupled with the brutality of a repressive regime, engulf these women. However, through their demise, Chauvet drives home the point that women are not passive players in history and that they, too, will go to great limits in order to preserve the dignity and honor of their families.

In *Amour,* the three principal characters—Claire, her brother-in-law Jean Luze, and the evil prison warden Calédu (whose name in creole means "somebody who beats hard")—are all peripheral agents performing in the margins of the established status quo.[47] Jean Luze, a white, French businessman, is both exploiter and idealist, operating both outside and inside Haitian bourgeois culture. On the one hand, he exercises his French business with impunity because he genuinely thinks that he has a right to capitalize on resources in Haiti, and on the other, he fully supports the uprisings of the lower classes and intellectuals who seek to put an end to the repressive brutality of the "men in black." Luze is the desired man of not only his mulatto wife Félicia but also her sisters, Annette (who actually has an affair with him) and Claire, who never lets him know how much she loves him. She confirms, nevertheless, that the attraction she feels for him drives her more crazy with each passing day.[48] Calédu, the antithesis of Luze, is an evil prison warden who is dark skinned like Claire (thus on one level making them the same because they both are outcasts and marginals leading liminal existences on the borders of the richer, highly valued mulatto culture). The warden strikes down his countrymen and women for no reason other than they are too rich, too poor, or too light skinned. He is insane with the power he exerts over people, particularly those of the Haitian aristocracy, whom he perceives as particularly deserving of his repression. These "Aristos," as he defines them, are incessantly the objects of his belligerence and his wrath.[49] He both detests Claire for her family's social status and desires her because she is an available woman and has wealth. To conquer her would mean conquering all that he detests about aristocratic mulattos, allowing him access to a class from which, historically, he has been banned because of his dark skin. Metaphorically, Calédu represents the violent repression of the Duvalier regime. Chauvet, through this vicious character, also examines the thin lines between brutality, power, and sexual prowess, all of which are present in the interaction between Claire and Calédu. Claire's fear of, as well as attraction to, Calédu is evidenced in an erotic dream she has one night. The dream explains both her repulsion from the violence he wantonly wields as well as her fascination with the power the warden possesses. He is the phallocentric epicenter she longs to be herself. However, Calédu also represents the brutal, masculine viciousness that reigns over the heroine and her country. For Claire he is repugnant. As the dream progresses she becomes aware of her powerlessness. The dream is a metaphor for the stifled and confined life she lives within the boundaries of bourgeois decorum: a life that renders her incapable of either fighting back or changing the tides of evil engulfing her family as well as Haitian society. The impotence that she feels rules her life surfaces in Claire's nightmare in a scene in which she struggles with the "phallus" of power that transforms into Calédu. The scene, as Lizabeth Paravisini-Gebert comments, "reinforces the images of rape, blood, and death as symbolic consequences of absolute power":[50]

Mon rêve d'hier soir me bouleverse encore: j'étais seule, debout en pleine lumière, au milieu d'une arène immense surmontée de gradins où gesticulait une foule terrifiante. . . . Je courais, honteuse de ma nudité, cherchant en vain un coin obscur pour m'y cacher . . . tout à coup je vis se dresser devant moi une statue de pierre. . . . La statue pourvue d'un phallus énorme tendu dans un spasme de voluptueuse souffrance était celle de Calédu. La statue s'anima et le phallus s'agita. . . . Je me jetai à ses pieds, à la fois soumise et révoltée. . . . C'était la foule qui poussait Calédu à m'assassiner. . . . [Son] arme s'enfonça doucement, profondément dans ma chair . . . décapitée, avec ma tête qui se balançait sur ma poitrine. Morte et vivant ma mort.

[My dream last night is still haunting me: I was alone, standing in full light, in the middle of an immense arena encircled by bleachers from which a terrifying crowd gesticulates. . . . I ran, embarrassed by my nakedness, looking in vain for an obscure corner in which to hide myself . . . all of a sudden I saw an enormous stone statue erect before me. . . . The statue, equipped with an enormous phallus held in a spasm of voluptuous suffering was Calédu's. The statue came alive and the phallus became excited. . . . I threw myself at its feet, both submissive and disgusted. . . . The crowd pushed Calédu to assassinate me. . . . (His) weapon thrust slowly, deeply into my flesh. . . . decapitated, with my head swinging on my chest. Dead and living my death.][51]

The phallus is both an instrument of rape and a weapon of destruction, making a connection, as Georges Bataille would contend, between "death and sexual excitement."[52] Surprisingly, in the closing scenes of the novel, it is Claire who kills Calédu, driving a knife through his flesh. Ironically, the knife she uses was given to her by Jean Luze. This knife, symbol of phallic power, is at once an object of desire as she strokes it, thinking of Jean Luze, and of fulfillment as she wields it, overpowering a man who would have killed her if she had not been armed and able to defend herself. The knife is impetus, a tool used to break out of the inner recesses of feminine vulnerability and suffocating bourgeois society into the outer realms of power.[53] Although she has been "co-opted . . . into the violence that characterizes the system," as Paravisini-Gebert notes, Claire also becomes "part of a process of liberating the masses." She thus sacrifices her own prospects (and also gives up her own vulnerability) in order to save those around her.[54] Once again, Chauvet writes an active role into history for her heroine.

Chauvet's novellas document the mental instability that occurs when her heroines attempt to transgress and challenge the boundaries of class and race. Claire Clamont's mental anguish stems from the perception that her skin color is not "claire" [light] enough, but rather too dark: "Claire a souffert de n'être pas à l'égale de ses soeurs, blanche et rose comme un lis" [Claire suffered not being equal with her sisters who are white and rose like a lily].[55] "A cette époque" [During this time] she admits, "j'étais, il est vrai, diminuée par la couleur foncée de ma peau." [I was, it is true, diminished by my dark skin color].[56] The heroine's difference from those of her class and the rest of her family was constantly noted by her father early on in her childhood. He both physically and mentally abused Claire because he considered his daughter a reminder of the dark African roots from which he had come— roots he wanted to forget and which he viewed as tainting his political aspirations. Throughout Claire's childhood, her father, crazed by political ambition, took his deficiencies out on her, attempting to mold Claire into something she couldn't be—male: "Pour m'endurcir et me faire payer sans doute ses espérances paternelles déçues, il décida brusquement de m'élever comme un garçon" [In order to make me tougher and to make me pay, obviously, for his disappointed paternal hopes, he decided abruptly to raise me as a boy].[57] She learns to cope by living a secret life, allowing no one access to her Self or her room.[58] Her dark skin relegates her to performing the duties of a domestic charged with directing household matters. Eventually she admits her life is reduced to that of an automaton where comfort can only be found in drunken sleep.[59] Claire's trauma over what she perceives as a truncated life hindered by skin color, the imperfections of gender, and the weakness of being in love with someone she cannot have bring to the forefront the intricate scenarios proposed almost twenty years before by Chauvet's Martinican counterpart, Mayotte Capécia. Yet, unlike Capécia's *Moi, je suis martiniquaise,* in which Mayotte feels that she needs a white man to have access to status, Claire (like Claire-Solange's love for Jacques in Lacascade's novel) desires Jean Luze not because he is white but *because he is a man*, nothing more. Although the tenuous role of color does play a part in Claire's own self-deprecated feelings, Jean Luze's white skin is not the reason she longs for his love. She is already part of the class presumed to have power in Haiti: thus "marrying white" would not gain her anything. Claire longs for, rather, what she feels should be rightfully hers; someone who will love her. The heroine explains Jean Luze's marriage to her sister Félicia as fulfilling his own desire to have a woman whom he can easily dominate; race and class have nothing to do with the relationship, a point that is obvious throughout Chauvet's novel. Unlike Claire's second sister, Annette, with whom Jean Luze has had an affair, but whom he considers to be nothing more than a "petite pute" [a little whore], and Claire, who challenges him intellectually, Félicia is neutral. As the heroine notes, Félicia is the most bland, the most insignificant of the three sisters, thus presenting no obstacles for the ambitious Luze.[60] Whereas the issue of color acts as a definitive factor in relations between men and women in novels such as Capécia's, for Chauvet, it is all but effaced as Claire remarks that Jean Luze only looks for women around whom he can "model his desire."[61] Reducing the amorous relationship between her sister and Luze to terms of male power and possession helps Claire console herself. Claire's desperation over not being able to find a man is due to the alienation of her social position, upbringing, and financial power, and not to her skin color. She is the "old maid," considered by her sisters Annette and Félicia to be the strongest and wisest but the poorest in terms of having the physical attraction to find a husband. What she perceives as her lack of attractiveness plays a role in the heroine's changing psychological state. Her aspirations, for the most part, are centered around being beautiful, which she determines will allow access to love, a husband, and having children, all of which are her ultimate desires.

Unfortunately, Claire's only hope of family is the fictitious one she creates in her mind when she is obligated to take care of Félicia's baby during her sister's hospitalization due to complications with her second pregnancy. Claire's embrace of this duty nurtures a make-believe role that allows her to feel as if she is able to possess some of Jean Luze's world. However, this illusion only succeeds in alienating her further from reality. Progressively, she turns inward as she realizes that Jean Luze, despite his recognition of her aid and his admiration, will never love her. She locks herself within her room and her thoughts. Like Juletane, Claire's marginalization because of her multifaceted difference (color, age, intellect), instead of weakening the heroine, makes her stronger and more calculating. It is exactly because of her alienation from the rest of the family that she becomes more aware of the world outside her window. Her attention to her surroundings links her to the sociopolitical events of the town, transforming her from passive to active player. She sees

> tout au bout de la grand-rue, dans cette ruelle misérable où s'élèvent les vieilles baraques branlantes, des mères pleuraient en regardant menotter leurs fils. . . . Les jours passent. La misère du peuple augmente. A chacun son lot. Notre égoïsme devient règle de vie. Nous nous enfonçons de plus en plus dans la lâcheté et la résignation.
>
> [to the end of the large street, in this miserable alleyway in which these tottering old houses stand, women crying as they watch their sons being handcuffed. . . . The days pass. The misery of the people increases. To each his luck. Our self-centeredness becomes the rule of life. We drive ourselves more and more into cowardice and resignation].[62]

Unlike Cajou and Juletane, whose malaise over their difference in the end causes them to self-destruct (literally and figuratively), Claire gathers strength from her position on the peripheries of her class and her family in order to fight phallocratic-authoritarian structures that are taking over around her. Not only does she take charge of the household because her sisters are too weak of spirit and intelligence to do it, she is "la femme experimentée qui a fait son choix, qui ne s'est pas mariée pour rester indépendante" [the experienced woman who has made her choice, who hasn't married in order to stay independent].[63] Claire's strength resides in this independent persona she has cultivated to face the solitude that her choices have left her: "C'est avec la révélation de la souffrance qu'on prend conscience de soi" [It is with the revelation of suffering that one becomes conscious of one's self].[64] Behind closed doors she is free to do what she likes, she plots and she watches: "Qui jamais se méfiera de moi? C'est là ma force" [Who has ever been afraid of me? There lies my power].[65] In her room Claire finds sexual solace in a world of illusional lovemaking, while imagining scenarios of fake motherhood using an old doll which she keeps hidden in her closet. Here too she writes in a journal, organizing an imaginary family made up of Jean Luze, his son, and herself: "Ma vie est si bien remplie! J'ai un fils et un homme. . . . Ma porte reste ouverte tout le jour à Jean Luze. Pourquoi aurais-je besoin d'un exutoire? Je vis pleinement" [My life is so full! I have a son and a man. . . . My door stays open all day for Jean Luze. Why would I need an outlet? I live fully].[66] The sexuality of Claire's inner sanctum becomes more and more apparent as Chauvet concludes her story. Claire "opens" both her spaces: those of her room and her body. Though she becomes neither wife nor mother, her desires are realized as she takes over Félicia's family when the latter no longer has the strength. So strong is Claire's desire to appropriate her sister's family that she finds herself plotting Félicia's death.[67] Although the heroine refrains from carrying out her fantasy, she becomes bitter. Her bitterness transforms her into an "être affamé que l'on tente sans assouvir sa faim" [a famished being whom one tempts without satisfying its hunger].[68] Vengeful, she claims that her destroyed possibilities of love have cumulated into a certain "mécontentement de soi" [dissatisfaction with herself] generating "le venin qui alimente la méchanceté" [the venom which nourishes meanness].[69] It is here in the last few pages of the book, as she sees her desires being quelled by the impossibility of fulfillment, that she declares she must take action in order to secure her future, throwing off "ce masque étouffant" [this suffocating mask] that she has worn for so long.[70]

Claire's domestic bitterness is embellished by the political violence raining down on them from outside her family's home. She increasingly views Calédu as the root of all evil. He is a killer who has murdered her friend Jane (a seamstress from the lower class) and her child. Divisions of class and of color are effaced, culminating in Claire's hate for Calédu: "J'écoute les cris . . . Ils sont tous là autour de moi et nous souffrons à l'unisson dans l'idée fixe d'une prochaine délivrance" [I hear the screams. . . . They are all around me and we suffer in unison in the fixed idea of timely deliverance].[71] Chauvet's message is one of the universal suffering of men and women, calling our attention to the artificial barriers which have divided people in Haiti and, in turn, bred violence and destruction.[72]

Between Claire's two worlds of love and hate—the domestic inner one and the political outer—she finds herself caressing Jean Luze's knife, lost in "rêveries atroces" [atrocious daydreams] in which she sees herself plunging the knife into Félicia's breast "sans une hésitation" [without hesitation].[73] This demented reverie overtakes her and threatens to engulf her total being. "J'ai la tête qui éclate" [My head is exploding] she admits as she seeks to "lutte contre l'horrible tentation" [fight against the terrible urge] to kill her sister. "J'ai l'impression d'avancer sous le fouet dans les flammes incandescentes d'un monde diabolique. . . . Je me sens perdue, comme égarée, au centre de la terre. . . . Je suis comme un animal qu'on tient en laisse et qui détourne la tête du chemin qu'il doit prendre" [I have the impression that I am going forward under the whip in the incandescent flames of a diabolical world. . . . I feel lost, lost, as if I've wandered to the center of the earth. . . . I am like an animal which one holds on a leash and which turns its head away from the path that it must take].[74]

Symbolic of phallic force of power, the knife furnishes Claire the strength to contemplate her next move as she asks herself whether or not she "est capable de tuer quelqu'un du premier coup" [is capable of killing someone with one stab].[75] In her deranged daydreaming she imagines her sister dead with the knife plunged into her body, the newspaper headlines announcing a suicide because Félicia couldn't decide whether or not to flee the violence in Haiti with her French husband.[76] In order to practice her technique, Claire kills the neighbor's cat, yet she is bothered by its final demise and wonders if she has enough strength to kill a human.[77] The knife is a catalyst that at first seems like it will aid the heroine in arranging her domestic world to her liking, but ultimately, in the concluding pages of the novel, she uses it to combat the layer of evils of the outside world. One night, as she looks at the agitated crowd of misfits, beggars, and the throngs of the lower classes who have begun a rebellion against the repression of Calédu and his henchmen, Claire's focus becomes clear. She sees herself as an instrument in finalizing restitution for the pain and the deaths of her fellow citizens. As she watches Calédu come up to the French doors of her dinning room from the streets below seeking refuge from the angry mob, she awaits hidden behind a curtain. "Je le guette et je l'attends" [I lie in wait for him, I await him]. As he enters, she plunges the dagger into his back, "une fois, deux fois, trois fois. Le sang gicle. . . . Je le vois partir en titubant et tomber de tout son long dans la rue, au beau milieu de la rigole. Les mendiants . . . comme des fous, se ruent sur son cadavre" [one, two, three times. The bloods spurts. . . . I see him go off tottering and falling all the way down the street in the middle of the crowd. The beggars . . . like crazy men, pounce on his corpse].[78]

The madness of Haiti's sociopolitical situation drive Claire to commit an act of violence, demonstrating that Chauvet's feminine heroines can break out of confining environments that usually keep them passive in order to fight against patriarchal, oppressive authority. Even if there seems to be no exit, women are able to re-create visions of their own selves despite the violence, brutality, and madness around them. Like Chauvet herself, the women of Haiti have played active parts in history and, like men, have stood up for what they believe. Yanick Lahens explains that Chauvet's novels open up the possibility of exploration of this "Other within ourselves" and provides another dimension to the daily life of women in Haiti calling upon those exiled and those still living on its shores to "conserve" history for everyone "who will come after."[79]

UN CHANT ÉCARLATE

Mariama Bâ finished her second novel, *Un Chant écarlate,* shortly before her untimely death in August 1981. The novel was published posthumously. Although the sum of Bâ's work consists of only two novels, *Un Chant écarlate* and the earlier *Une si longue lettre,* published in 1980, her writing has influenced African feminists and served to promote not only women's rights, but human rights as well in West Africa. Her work studies the female condition in Senegal with respect to sociopolitical and traditional arenas which mandate how women are expected to behave and conduct the business of their daily lives. Like Chauvet, Bâ positions her heroines in the "what if" sectors of society—those places on the outside where women are relegated to marginalized positions because they dared to go against the grain, to be something other than what is expected of them. Bâ's novels are more than testaments to the perseverance of women caught up in hopeless situations; they are condemnations of both men and women's insistence on "blind adherence to tradition and to an ideology" that has hindered the cultivation of humanism and equality in Africa.[80]

In *Un Chant écarlate,* madness is the cumulative result of suffocating traditionalism enmeshed in racial prejudice.[81] In Bâ's novel, the society and culture of Senegal form walls of a sociocultural prison, entrapping Mireille de La Vallée, a young, vibrant, white French woman who, in the wake of the 1968 French cultural revolution and decolonizing movements throughout West Africa, embraces the liberating Marxist-socialist ideals of equality between the sexes and the races popular among French and francophone youth at the time. She weds her young Senegalese lover, Ousmane Guèye, with the conviction that their love will overcome any racial and cultural barriers that might arise. Years before, as the daughter of a French diplomat living in Dakar, Mireille met Ousmane at the university. At that time, both shared equal visions of tolerance, equitable relations between the sexes, liberty, and social equality. It is only after Mireille is estranged from her parents (who were adamantly opposed to the marriage), converts to Islam, marries Ousmane in a mosque in Paris, and moves back to Senegal that the heroine slowly begins to see clearly the daunting odds she faces trying to survive in a foreign, extremely traditional society. Assimilation proves to be impossible because of the entrenched value system of traditional Senegal and Ousmane's family's hostility to mixed marriages. Particularly, Ousmane's mother, Yaye Khady, is revolted by the marriage, announcing to her husband that "Une Toubab ne peut être une vraie bru. Elle n'aura d'yeux que pour son homme" [A Toubab can't be a proper daughter-in-law. She'll only have eyes for her man].[82] Through the stoic yet unyielding mother, the author makes her point by condemning traditional practices which call on a daughter-in-law to take over the household work of her mother-in-law. For Yaye Khady, Mireille is depriving her of leisure in her old age: "Elle meritait une prompte relève. Beaucoup de femmes de son âge, à cause de la présence de leur belle-fille, n'avaient plus que le souci de se laisser vivre agréablement. Elles se mouvaient dans la paresse et l'encens. Leur bru les servait" [She deserved to be relieved soon. Many women of her age had nothing more to worry about than how to live out their lives agreeably, surrounded by praise and flattery, waited on by their daughters-in-law].[83] Moreover, Mireille cannot break the tight bonds of the traditional mother-son alliance that characterize Ousmane's relationship with his mother, a connection built on years of mutual understanding and common goals: "de fréquents tête à tête avaient tissé, entre la mère et le fils, une complicité qui les comblait" [Their frequent intimate conversations had woven an understanding between mother and son that made them both happy].[84] She finally realizes that the family's traditional values cannot be uprooted in order to embrace the utopian ideals Mireille thought Ousmane would share with her.

Bâ's commentary on the injustice of hard-line traditionalism is reverberated in the ideology of postcolonial African intellectuals of the day. These men promoted what Bâ defines, through the eyes of several of her protagonists, as covert "black racism" that did not open the floodgates of tolerance as once hoped, but sent a whole generation of young idealists into isolation and bigotry. The author condemns the postcolonial climate of Senegal as a refuge for African elitists who are little better than the colonialists whom they replaced.

Coupled with her commentary on the contemptible sociocultural climate of Senegal in the wake of colonialism, Bâ's message is one of a universalist feminism, what Alice Walker has defined as a *womanism*, demonstrating that any woman who makes the choice to give herself in selfless sacrifice for the benefit of a man risks tragedy. Yet, although Bâ's heroines are caught up in uncontrollable circumstances to which they eventually succumb (this is true for Ramatoulaye in *Une si longue lettre* and Mireille of *Un Chant écarlate*), they are not blind victims. Mireille, although free to leave Senegal and take her mulatto child with her, chooses to stay, resigned to never give in to the dominating patriarchal world of her father, nor the xenophobic society of her husband's family. Her choice leads her to opt to remain and try to negotiate her existence somewhere in between these two opposing worlds. Madness is a result of being kept out of her husband's world, even though in the beginning she wholeheartedly wanted to understand it. She chooses to stay in Dakar to brave reality, although this also means facing psychological torment. Equally detrimental is her hysteria at the end of the novel, which is precipitated, in part, by her refusal to return to the patriarchal, bourgeois, French world of her parents. Her pride and her will to adhere to the choices she has made in life keep her in Senegal. Analogous to Chauvet's work, Bâ similarly demonstrates that women—black and white—are often intertwined in the binds of stringent patriarchal power through which men dictate the behavior of women, suffocating them. In the same manner as Claire in Chauvet's novel, Mireille, alienated by her family, lashes out, changing the dynamics of her environment forever.

Shifting between outside and inside space, Mireille finds that she neither belongs nor is accepted in France or Senegal. She is "dislocated" and recognizes no sense of place with respect to one group. "To belong is not merely comforting, but an important ingredient of personal identity," writes Philip Rack in his seminal work *Race, Culture and Mental Disorder*.[85] Integration means reassurance about one's individuality and instills in one an "integrity of the self" as well as promotes assimilation into a group. As Rack explains further in his study, the idea of "home" is linked to "who I am."[86] As soon as an individual uproots from his/her place and group, the stress to the psyche becomes alarming. Bâ's novel pivots on the axis of home and dislocation as Mireille attempts to find her place somewhere in the middle of French and Senegalese cultures. Her novel depicts a heroine on "a quest for full participation in society and for a voice which [she may] call [her] own."[87] The work also demonstrates to what extent the will to belong can derail an individual's mental stability. Exile of the self is both physical and mental in the case of Mireille who, despite professing to be an individualist, being rational (she is a professor of philosophy specializing in existentialism), earning her own living as a teacher, and freely choosing to follow Ousmane to Senegal, is ultimately overpowered by her estrangement from her husband and from others on several different levels.

Bâ's work operates within many feminist spheres while positing several key questions in the novel. Why is belonging to a culture, a society, and a man so important to a woman's sense of self-worth? Why does Mireille allow herself (as do many women) to be engulfed by a man's domination and accept, as Ousmane tells her, that "en épousant un homme, on épouse aussi sa manière de vivre" [when you marry a man you also take on his lifestyle].[88] Why does marriage for a woman mean abandoning her identity, selfhood, and place, forcing herself to adhere to the patriarchal confines of her husband's sociocultural prison? These questions place the author's novel in the realm of the universal, offering Mireille as a feminine archetype who transgresses barriers of race, class, language, and nationality to elicit awareness about men's behavior toward women. For the questions she asks and the answers she provides, Bâ has been both criticized and heralded.

The societal, patriarchal constructs which make up human society, the author notes, affect all women in similar ways. Mireille is white, French, and suffers under her overbearing father, who sends her back to France once it is discovered she has a Senegalese boyfriend at the university. She is next obliged to wait until she is an adult and has her diploma and a job to break free of her father's tutelage. Education, however, as the author notes, does not protect a woman's liberty from the constraints of what men expect her to do. Mireille, once liberated, falls back into/under the purviews of patriarchal domination when she marries Ousmane. She gives up her own culture and religion and, subsequently, forces herself to stay with her husband even when he alienates her.

Bâ's commentary remains on a universal level when she introduces Ouleymatou, Ousmane's eventual second wife. Although this traditional, Senegalese, uneducated woman is the complete opposite of Mireille, she too falls into the trap of socio-patriarchal constructs that leave her little room for self-development, liberty, and the means to make an independent life. Sociocultural traditionalism plays out on two levels with regard to these two opposing heroines. Mireille is barred from acceptance by Ousmane's traditional family because of her otherness (this fact is incessantly made evident by Yaye Khady, Ousmane's mother).[89] On the other hand, Ouleymatou is imprisoned by the role she thinks she must play in order to live and survive in her society. First married off to an old man by her parents, she divorces him after he repeatedly beats her. She vows to do better in order to lift herself out of poverty and the hand she has been dealt. Unfortunately, she realizes, a better life for herself and for her family can only be achieved through a prosperous marriage. Her plotting and scheming to win the affections of Ousmane, even though she knows she will be his second wife, are done more for status and monetary gain than sheer love. Here, Ba's commentary on the difference between Western European, white individualism and African community and tribal-based worlds cannot be overlooked. Mireille, as a woman with an education, money, and her own profession, has the luxury of making a choice as to whom she wants to spend her life with. In contrast, Ouleymatou's winning over Ousmane (and her

subsequent total dependence on him) will mean financial security for herself and for her family as well as a move up on the social ladder within the
community. Her whole family will leave poverty through her marriage:
"Ousmane correspondait présentement à son idéal" [Ousmane now represented her ideal] and, remarks the author, "personne ne pouvait plus 'l'em-
prisonner'" [no one could hold her back anymore].[90]

Despite the differences in Mireille's and Ouleymatou's ways of structuring
their worlds with regard to Ousmane, for him, they are both reduced to feminine fantasy objects he arranges in his life in order to fulfill his sexual desire.
Again, Ba brings her commentary back to universals, stating that women, no
matter their ethnicity or background, are, in the end, repeatedly victims of
men and masculine prerogatives. Ousmane realizes that with Ouleymatou
he has "renoué avec lui-même" [he had restored his link with himself]. He
further observes that she is the "symbole double dans ma vie" [symbol of my
double life].[91] Through the black, African, feminine body, he reconnects with
his past, his true *Africanness*:

> Ouleymatou . . . Symbole de la femme noire qu'il devait affranchir, symbole de
> l'Afrique dont il était l'un des 'fils éclairés'. . . . Ouleymatou se confondait dans
> son esprit avec l'Afrique, 'une Afrique à réinstaller dans ses prérogatives, une
> Afrique à promouvoir.'
>
> [Ouleymatou . . . Symbol of the black woman, whom he had to emancipate,
> symbol of Africa, one of whose 'enlightened sons' he was. . . . In his mind he
> confused Ouleymatou with Africa, 'an Africa which has to be restored to its pre-
> rogatives, to be helped to evolve.'][92]

Bâ's disapproval of black intellectual movements' tendencies (such as that of
the Négritude poets) to promote the reinvention of an African consciousness
through the African feminine body is evident. As we read Ousmane's thoughts,
we are reminded of Négritude poet Léopold S. Senghor's earlier famous poem
Femme Noire (1945), which glorifies the rediscovery of Africa through the
body of the African woman:

> Femme nue, femme noire
> Vêtue de ta couleur qui est vie, de ta form qui est beauté! . . .
> Femme nue, femme obscure! . . .
> Je chante ta beauté qui passe, forme que je fixe dans l'éternel
> Avant que le destin jaloux ne te réduise en cendres pour nourrir
>   les racines de la vie.
>
> [Naked woman, black woman
> Robed in your color which is life, in your form which is beauty. . . .
> Naked woman, obscure woman. . . .
> I sing your beauty which passes, form which I fix in the Eternal
> Before jealous destiny reduces you to ashes to nourish
>   the roots of life.][93]

Social confinement for women is therefore drawn up within the parameters of, not only cultural constraints, but how men sexually symbolize women in their own lives. Ousmane's love for Mireille, he admits, was founded upon the attraction "de l'inconnu, le goût de l'originalité" [the unknown, a taste for originality], whereas Ouleymatou offers him a place to "reposer sa tête sur ses cuisses charnues" [rest his head on her plump thighs].[94] Neither Mireille nor Ouleymatou wins his devotion as an equal.

Mireille is left "isolée dans son monde" [cut off from her own people].[95] Her pride drives her to find out more about the double life she suspects her husband is living. Ousmane's younger sister, the only woman in his family to show Mireille any affection, leaves her a note denouncing her husband's actions and revealing all the details of his liaison with Ouleymatou. Mireille follows her husband and eventually finds out all that she needs to know. She learns the truth that her husband has a second wife and another child. The knowledge of Ousmane's double life leads Mireille to succumb to "une souffrance" that she incorporates "au rythme de sa vie" [in the rhythm of her existence].[96] She withdraws and becomes anorexic and depressive yet also galvanized in her conviction that she must take revenge. She has been hurt, but not broken,[97] and is resolved not to become a laughingstock in a "pays de l'égoïsme organisé [et] de veules commérances . . . [qui sont] l'ébranlement quotidien" [a country where self-interest is a way of life (and) where cowardly and spineless backbiting (is) the order of the day].[98] She decides to stay to fight:

> soutenue par un idéal . . . son amour et son orgueil conjugués rassemblaient les miettes d'un bonheur défunt pour les ériger en facteurs d'espérance. A la quête lucide de sa raison, à l'invitation au départ de sa conscience, ils refusaient de céder la plus minime part des domaines envahis. Pathétiquement, Mireille choisit de rester.
>
> [upheld by an ideal . . . her love and her pride together collected the crumbs of her dead happiness to build some elements of hope. While her reason still argued the pros and the cons, while her conscience told her she must leave, her love and pride refused to yield an inch of territory she had won. Pathetically Mireille chose to stay].[99]

Where would she go anyway, back to France? Mireille realizes that her father would delight in his "I told you so" and only insist on telling her "voilà ce qui arrive quand on piétine des traditions de dignité" [You see what happens when you disregard traditions of dignity].[100] As she holds her mulatto child in her arms she notes that her father is not all that different from Ousmane: "Et puis l'infidélité n'est point l'exclusivité des Noirs!" [black men are not the only ones who are unfaithful to their wives!]. Bâ again brings Mireille's story into the fold of a universalism providing a cheerless commentary on how women are expected to behave in societies where men have the most power.

"A quel moment la férocité de son tourment fit-elle basculer sa raison? [At what moment then, did her persistent agony spill over to flood her brain and drown her reason?],[101] the heroine, like the reader, never really is sure, but it is obvious that "Mireille était devenue folle" [Mireille had gone mad].[102]And it is this madness which becomes a blinding force that eventually pushes her to take a knife and stab her husband after she has killed her son with "des dizaines de comprimés dans l'eau d'une tasse" [a handful of sleeping tablets in a cup of water].[103] Ousmane's wounds are the metaphors for a million pains suffered by a woman who was not allowed "into" a society because of her difference. In the closing pages of the novel, Ousmane's wounds cry out in "un chant profond, écarlate d'espérances dispersées" [A scarlet song, the scarlet song of lost hopes].[104]

Ousmane is not fatally wounded and Mireille is taken charge of by the French Embassy (yet another patriarchal institution) in Dakar. Bâ's story ends in ambiguity, leaving the reader bound up in the perplexities of two cultures and two people who were not able to find the means to live with the foreignness of each other.

NOTES

1. See Renée Larrier whose study *Francophone Women Writers of Africa and the Caribbean* (Gainesville: University Press of Florida, 2000) defines these "objects" in a Foucauldien sense as being characteristic of women who figure in the works of African and Caribbean francophone authors.

2. Larrier, *Francophone Women,* 95.

3. Cixous, "The Laugh of the Medusa," 338.

4. Madeleine Cottenet-Hage, "Violence Libératoire/Violence Mutilatoire dans Amour de Marie Chauvet," *Francophonia* 6 (spring 1984): 17–28, 17.

5. Yanick Lahens, "L'apport de quatre romancières au roman moderne haïtien," *Notre Librairie,* 33 (January–April 1998): 26–36, 35.

6. Cixous, "The Laugh of the Medusa," 339.

7. Irène d'Almeida, *Francophone African Women Writers: Destroying the Emptiness of Silence* (Gainesville: University Press of Florida, 1994), 8.

8. Cottenet–Hage, "Violence," 17.

9. Mineke Shipper,"Mother Africa on a Pedestal: The Male Heritage in African Literature and Criticism," *African Literature Today* 15 (1987): 35–57, 46–47; as cited in Adele King's article "The Personal and the Political in the Work of Mariama Bâ," *Studies in 20th Century Literature* 18, no. 2 (summer 1994): 177–88, 180–81.

10. In my research I have come across two different birth dates for Marie Chauvet. Ronnie Scharfman cites 1919 in her article "Theorizing Terror: The Discourse of Violence in Marie Chauvet's Amour, colère et folie" in *Postcolonial Subjects,* ed. M. J. Green et al. (Minneapolis: University of Minnesota Press 1996) whereas Léon-François Hoffman indicates the date as 1917 in his anthology *Littératures francophones: Les Amériques* (Paris: Belin SUP, 1998).

11. In Clarisse Zimra's 1993 interview with Haitian author Yanick Lahens, the scholar explains that "outdated sexism, coupled with the self-censorship of intellectu-

als brutalized by years of tyranny" characterized most of Haiti's modern history. Duvalier was elected in 1957, which began a bloody regime, the duration of which did not come to an end until his son, Baby-Doc, was kicked out of office in 1986. In 1961, Stephen Alexis, returning from exile, sought to overthrow Duvalier but was subsequently murdered. This murder "unleashed the first waves of an increasingly brutal repression and the rise of the Tontons Macoutes," who are, incidentally, referred to constantly in Chauvet's works. It is noted by many scholars that the brutality of the Duvalier regime institutionalized an "amnesia" among the people of Haiti and certainly among authors and intellectuals. For most, writing from exile was the only means of escaping death and founding a literary voice. (See Zimra's "Haitian Literature after Duvalier: An Interview with Yanick Lahens," *Callaloo* 16, no. 1 (1993): 77–93. Rectifying this sociocultural as well as intellectual amnesia is still the task at hand for many Haitian authors living in exile at the present time. With Aristide's presidency, nothing has changed as far as violence is concerned according to Gérard Etienne, eminent Haitian author living in exile in Canada. I spoke at length with Etienne and his wife about Aristide's presidency and its hostility toward intellectuals at the annual Conseil International d'Etudes Francophones conference held in May 2001 in Portland, Maine. Considering Chauvet's as well as Etienne's work, Lahens's comments that the Haitian author is found somewhere "oscillating between mooring and escape" in his/her efforts to "lay down roots" while also seeking to "run away somewhere, anywhere, in order not to die asphyxiated" become concrete realities as I further my study of the works of this Haitian francophone author. See Zimra, "Haitian Literature," 82.

12. Laurie Lavine, "The Feminizing of the Trojan Horse: Marie Chauvet's Amour, colère et folie," *Women in French Studies* 2 (fall 1994): 9–18, 12. Renée Larrier notes that before Chauvet fled to New York "she had been criticized in certain circles for performing her own plays. Being an actress was not considered the "proper" profession for a member of her class, according to her daughter Erma Saint-Grégoire" (*Francophone Women Writers of Africa and the Caribbean* [Gainesville: University Press of Florida, 2000], 89).

13. Zimra "Haitian Literature," 80.

14. Larrier, *Francophone Women,* 95.

15. Larrier, *Francophone Women,* 80.

16. Larrier, *Francophone Women,* 82.

17. *Les Rapaces* (1986), an unfinished fifth novel, was published posthumously.

18. Scharfman, "Theorizing Terror," 229.

19. Scharfman, "Theorizing Terror," 233.

20. Maire Chauvet, *Amour, Colère, et Folie* (Paris: Gallimard, 1968), 14. My translation. All further translations of Chauvet's novels are my own.

21. Scharfman, "Theorizing Terror," 234.

22. See Scharfman's commentary on the violence of Chauvet's novel in "Theorizing Terror,"

23. Scharfman, "Theorizing Terror," 244.

24. Chauvet, *Amour,* 19.

25. Chauvet, *Amour,* 12.

26. Larrier notes the interesting choice of "Luze" as a name for Claire's male protagonist. "Luz etymologically translates as 'light'" and like "Claire" characterizes a protagonist who is seeking true "enlightenment, knowledge, and truth" in a world that has been darkened by violence, repression, and fear. (See Larrier, *Francophone Women,* 98).

27. Chauvet, *Amour*, 17.

28. Chauvet, *Amour*, 18.

29. Scharfman, "Theorizing Terror," 234.

30. Chauvet, *Amour*, 330.

31. Voodoo spirits that can be both good and evil.

32. Chauvet, *Amour*, 350.

33. Scharfman, "Theorizing Terror," 244.

34. Scharfman, "Theorizing Terror," 244.

35. Chauvet, *Amour*, 428.

36. Thomas Szasz, *Ideology and Insanity*, 53.

37. Szasz, *Ideology and Insanity*, 51–52.

38. Scharfman, "Theorizing Terror," 244.

39. Lillian Feder, *Madness in Literature* (Princeton, N.J.: Princeton University Press, 1980), 7.

40. Chauvet, *Amour*, 206.

41. Janis A. Mayes, "Mind-Body-Soul: Erzulie Embodied in Marie Chauvet's Amour, colère et folie,*" Journal of Caribbean Studies* 7, no. 1 (spring 1989): 81–89. For a discussion of *Colère*, the ideology of *plaçage* and women see page 85.

42. Elizabeth Grosz, *Volatile Bodies: Toward a Corporeal Feminism* (Bloomington: Indiana University Press, 1994), 202.

43. Mayes, "Mind-Body-Soul," 86.

44. Mayes, "Mind-Body-Soul," 86.

45. Chauvet, *Amour*, 293.

46. Mayes, "Mind-Body-Soul," 87.

47. Scharfman, "Theorizing Terror," 231.

48. Chauvet, *Amour*, 58.

49. Chauvet, *Amour*, 163.

50. Lizabeth Paravisini-Gebert, "The Alienation of Power: The Woman Writer and the Planter-Heroine in Caribbean Literature," in *The Woman, the Writer and Caribbean Society*, ed. Helen Pyne-Timothy (Los Angeles: University of California Press, 1998), 7.

51. Chauvet, *Amour*, 145.

52. Georges Bataille, *Erotism: Death and Sensuality* (San Francisco: City Lights, 1986), 11.

53. Calédu's character reemerges in the second and third novels as the "gorilla" lawyer who exploits and terrorizes the Normil family, seeking to repress them financially and sexually through his abuse of Rose in *Colère,* and as the prefect in *Folie* who is blinded by his zeal to kill those who are perceived as threats to the regime: women, mulattos, blacks, whites, those who speak French, in short, everyone.

54. Paravisini-Gebert, "Alienation of Power," 8.

55. Chauvet, *Amour*, 98.

56. Chauvet, *Amour*, 19.

57. Chauvet, *Amour*, 104.

58. Chauvet, *Amour*, 118.

59. Chauvet, *Amour*, 134.

60. Chauvet, *Amour*, 73.

61. Chauvet, *Amour*, 80.

62. Chauvet, *Amour*, 57.

63. Chauvet, *Amour*, 93.

64. Chauvet, *Amour*, 104.

65. Chauvet, *Amour*, 159.

66. Chauvet, *Amour*, 161.

67. Chauvet, *Amour*, 175.

68. Chauvet, *Amour*, 176.

69. Chauvet, *Amour*, 176.

70. Chauvet, *Amour*, 176.

71. Chauvet, *Amour*, 177.

72. Zimra, "Haitian Literature," 81.

73. Chauvet, *Amour*, 179.

74. Chauvet, *Amour*, 180.

75. Chauvet, *Amour*, 183.

76. Chauvet, *Amour*, 183

77. Chauvet, *Amour*, 183.

78. Chauvet, *Amour*, 186.

79. Lahens, "L'apport," 36.

80. Adele King, "The Personal and the Political in the Work of Mariama Bâ," *Studies in 20th Century Literature* 18, no. 2 (summer 1994): 177–88, 185.

81. Mariama Bâ, *Un Chant écarlate* (Dakar: Les Nouvelles Editions Africaines, 1981); translated by Dorothy Blair under the title *A Scarlet Song* (Essex, England: Longman, 1986).

82. Bâ, *Un Chant écarlate*, 101, 66.

83. Bâ, *Un Chant écarlate*, 111–112, 73.

84. Bâ, *Un Chant écarlate*, 15, 8.

85. Philip Rack, *Race, Culture and Mental Disorder* (London, Tavistock Publications, 1982), 55.

86. Bâ, *Un Chant écarlate*, 15, 8.

87. Glenn Fetzer, "Women's Search for Voice and the Problem of Knowing," *Baltimore College Language Association Publication* 35, (September 1991): 31–41, 31.

88. Bâ, *Un Chant écarlate*, 133, 87.

89. Bâ, *Un Chant écarlate*, 101, 66.

90. Bâ, *Un Chant écarlate*, 176, 115–116.

91. Bâ, *Un Chant écarlate*, 224–225, 148–149.

92. Bâ, *Un Chant écarlate*, 25, 149–150

93. Léopold Sédar Senghor, *Anthologie de la nouvelle poésie nègre et malgache de langue française.* (Paris: Quadrige/Puf, 1948), 151.

94. Bâ, *Un Chant écarlate*, 186, 123.

95. Bâ, *Un Chant écarlate*, 226, 150.

96. Bâ, *Un Chant écarlate*, 243, 163.

97. Bâ, *Un Chant écarlate*, 240, 160.

98. Bâ, *Un Chant écarlate*, 241, 161.

99. Bâ, *Un Chant écarlate*, 242, 162.

100. Bâ, *Un Chant écarlate*, 241, 161.

101. Bâ, *Un Chant écarlate*, 243, 163.

102. Bâ, *Un Chant écarlate*, 245, 165.

103. Bâ, *Un Chant écarlate*, 245, 164.

104. Bâ, *Un Chant écarlate*, 248, 166.

5

Rooms and Prisons, Sex and Sin

Places of Sequestration in Nina Bouraoui's *La Voyeuse Interdite* and Calixthe Beyala's *Tu t'appelleras Tanga*

> The fear of female self-determination is basic to the Muslim order and is closely linked to fear of fitna [chaos]. If women are not constrained, then men are faced with an irresistible sexual attraction that inevitably leads to . . . chaos by driving them to zina, illicit copulation.
>
> —Fatima Mernissi, *Beyond the Veil* (1987)

> [T]he prison seems to express in concrete terms the idea that the offence has injured, beyond the victim, society as a whole.
>
> —Michèle Foucault, *Discipline and Punish* (1975)

> What does it mean to use or to have one's body, time, and mind used solely for economic profit?
>
> —Phyllis Chesler, *Madness and Women* (1972)

Physical confinement and how it influences the mental stability of the heroines in the novels *La Voyeuse Interdite,* by Algerian Nina Bouraoui, and *Tu t'appelleras Tanga*, by Cameroonian Calixthe Beyala, are the subjects of this section. Both heroines in these novels are confined to rooms and prisons, the victims of sociocultural mores and male domination in societies where women have little power. Psychosis, thus, as Elizabeth Grosz contends, is the result of "social and sexual positions and behaviors appropriate to and expected from women" by the societies in which they live, and not because of inherent infirmity within the minds of the heroines themselves. Indeed, as Grosz points out, there is no "neutral" civilization when it comes to constraints placed on women, just varying degrees. In the two novels discussed here, "patriarchy is physically produced [through] . . . the constitution of women's bodies."[1] Nina Bouraoui's heroine, Fikria, is shut away behind closed doors because the ultraconservative Islamic fundamentalist environment in which she lives dictates that it be so. Tanga, a "woman-child," as she describes herself, is forced into prostitution by her mother and eventually thrown into prison, accused of making counterfeit money (so she wouldn't starve). Both women slip into madness. Fikria in particular blames her traditional society for her downfall.[2] The young Algerian woman contends that she is unable to change the tides of her fate. These novels illustrate extremes wherein societal norms, customs, family expectations, and the implications of poverty and destitution erode the rights of women. The authors of these novels also want us to understand the power of men over women as interpreters of religious views (as in the case of the *La Voyeuse interdite)* and as social regulators and exploiters of women's bodies (evident in *Tu t'appelleras Tanga*). In both cases, the feminine body becomes a vessel for madness as it sinks slowly into nothingness, buckling under the weight of oppression. Michel Foucault reminds us in *Discipline and Punish* that "the body as object and target of power" is forever present in the master/slave dialectic wherein "reigns the notion of 'docility'" because the body "that is docile . . . may be subjected, used, transformed and improved."[3] These novels exemplify that the feminine body may be used to gain status and wealth, evident in Bouraoui's novel, or to make a point and set an example, as Beyala's work suggests. In both instances, the female body is considered in need of being physically contained because it is perceived to be a threat, volatile, and hostile to the social order.

LA VOYEUSE INTERDITE

In 1991, twenty-five-year-old, Algerian-French Nina Bouraoui published a harrowing novel, *La Voyeuse Interdite*. The author tells the story of Fikria, a young Algerian woman sequestered in her room, whose every move is watched by her Islamic fundamentalist father. This young girl has only one window from which to observe the outside world.[4] Bouraoui describes a hyper-phallicized world situated in Algiers, Algeria, sometime in the early 1970s. All elements contained in this world are aimed at destroying any possibility of feminine liberty. Liberty is but an illusion for women, Fikria observes, as day after day she watches the street below where men roam free and women are hunted and shamed for daring to venture outside.[5]

In order to comprehend the hyper-phallicized space of Nina Bouraoui's novel, it is imperative to understand the sexualized space of traditional Muslim societies where inside, interior domains are viewed as feminine, and outside, exterior as masculine. Fatima Mernissi, Moroccan feminist and scholar, explains that this spacial division is at the heart of traditional Islamic social structures and is founded on the belief that women are synonymous with "disorder or chaos—*fitna*" because of their sexual prowess. Mernissi further contends that "In societies in which seclusion and surveillance of women prevail, the implicit concept of female sexuality is active . . . [it is thought that women's] sexual capacity is greater than men's."[6] Because of the perceived threat of inciting chaos within society and because it is believed they possess the power to drive men insane with lust, women must be contained behind closed doors, constantly watched, preferably by men who are able to create social structures to curtail any feminine misbehavior. Therefore, "preventing women from showing themselves unveiled, expresses men's fear of losing control over their minds, falling prey to *fitna* whenever they are confronted with a non-veiled woman."[7] It is the premise of the possible transgression of gendered boundaries that sets the tone for Bouraoui's book about a young woman whose father, upon her first signs of puberty, stops looking at her, locks her within the confines of their home, and proceeds to seek out a suitable husband for her. Even the winter, interior garden terrace of the house, once a nice sunny place, is walled in so that men in the streets can no longer spy on Fikria and her sisters, Zohr and Leyla.[8]

The themes in Bouraoui's novel deconstruct the power associated with the action of "spying." Normally, the act of gazing is described in Western discourse as defining power in sexual terms, affording the voyeur/voyeuse the possibility of *possessing* the object of the gaze (that which is desired). As Martin Jay remarks, "The non reciprocity between look and eye, between being and the subject and object of the gaze, is in fact related to a fundamental struggle for power. For the one who casts the look is always subject and the one who is its target is always turned into an object."[9] However, because of the segregated gendered spaces designated by the traditional Islamic values depicted in this work, the privileged space of the voyeuse as one who is able to objectify the object of her gaze is truncated. Fikria is unable to benefit from gazing and the sexual power it connotes because *le regard absolu* is curtailed by strict Islamic gendered spaces. She can exist only on the inside, interior space of the weaker feminine domain, whereas outside space connotes prowess and masculine domination.[10] Fikria cannot objectify anyone or anything existing in the outside world because she cannot physically penetrate this forbidden space. Turning the tables on the subject/object dialectic of the voyeuse's world, Fikria's gaze, instead of desiring, is filled with pity and horror as she spends most of her time observing the degradation that women suffer when they hazard going outside into the hostile, male-dominated street. Her gaze is empty and she feels no sexual attraction to the men on the street. In fact, she is repulsed by the men who lurk under her window and is crazed with empathy for the suffering women who have risked the hostility of public space.

Although the novel focuses on the demise of one woman's mental health as she is caught up in the throes of sociocultural abjection and isolation, Nina Bouraoui is also quick to indicate how traditional Muslim gendered spaces and hyper-phallocratic social structures also contribute to adversely influencing the lives of men. Fikria's father is ridiculed for his lack of male progeny:

> Mâle parmi les femelles, il engendra que trois corps au sexe béant. Honte à lui! Où va-t-il se cacher pendant la journée? . . . Pauvre papa! Dans la rue, les voisins le montrent du doigt, les platanes s'esclaffent, les murs rigolent, la famille se moque, les petites filles meurent d'insouciance et les hommes s'étreignent pour se consoler. . . . Affublé d'un pénis, il doit prouver. Toujours prouver!

> [The male amongst females: the best he'll ever do is engender three bodies with gaping sex. Shame on him! Where's he going to hide all day long. . . . Poor Daddy! In the street the neighbors point at him, the plane trees shriek with laughter, the walls snicker, the family pokes fun, little girls die from carelessness and the men embrace each other to console themselves. . . . Rigged with a penis he has to prove something. To always be proving!][11]

Driven by the social parameters, which also construct her father's domain of mores, and confining traditions that he is forced to respect, he too is condemned to live a truncated existence. We are not privileged to truly know this man, who is obligated by the ultra Islamist sector to fulfill irrational actions and uphold an unyielding, cruel demeanor. However, Bouraoui leads us to believe that perhaps he wasn't always bent under the weight of the religious doctrines ruling fundamentalist Algeria. Only recently did he adopt the stringent attributions of an Islamicist: beards, facial hair, and dress.[12] Facial hair (beards and mustaches) is synonymous with hard-line Islamic fundamentalism and is part of the necessary components of masculine authority in orthodox circles. Fikria's father's adoption of stringent religiosity coincides with her own launch into pubescent femininity, marking definitively their respective spaces and forbidding any transgressions. Fikria observes that she sees the changes in her father's behavior toward her when the first signs of her menstruation cycles occur. He becomes cold, ceases to talk to her, and then locks her away:

> Je sais maintenant. Je sais qu'il ne me donnera jamais ce plaisir que j'invente avec peine dans mes mutilations volontaires. Je ne demandais pas grand-chose! Un baiser, une caresse, un sourire. . . . Non. Il a préféré me laisser à la solitude. Effroyable solitude qui donne aux plus faibles l'envie de mourir.

> [Now I know. I know that he will never give me this pleasure I painfully invent in my voluntary mutilations. I wasn't asking for anything major: a kiss, a caress,

a smile. . . . No. He preferred leaving me to solitude. The dreadful solitude that makes the weakest want to die.][13]

The only female presence in the street below Fikria is the little girls who attempt to play and who have not yet been marked by the adolescence that seals their fate. Yet, these young innocents are also victims of the dangers of outside male space. Fikria's fate is determined and her mental stability markedly in decline as a result of one of the most gruesome scenes of the novel, when a young girl is run over by a bus in the street below. Bouraoui metaphorically alludes to the entrapment of women in closed spaces, as the little girl lies literally encased in the asphalt of the street. This accident is a lesson taught to those women who venture out and dare to "exist" in the male, outside realm:

Les pneus à l'odeur caoutchouteuse font trembler les murs de ma demeure. Un frisson s'engouffre dans les anneaux de ma colonne vertébrale. Je fais un tour sur moi-même en imaginant le pire. Une autre petite fille a dû se faire écraser. Les bras en croix, la jupe relevée, elle gémissait sous la mécanique de fer plus lourde que le ventre de sa mère . . . une fillette est emprisonnée dans l'asphalte.

[The smelly rubber tires make the walls of my house tremble. A shiver disappears into the rings of my spine. I do a job on myself imagining the worst. Another little girl must have been run over. Her arms crossed, her skirt lifted, she was groaning beneath the iron machinery so much heavier than her mother's stomach. . . . A little girl is imprisoned in the asphalt.][14]

As Fikria watches the macabre scene below, her father observes her from the doorway. This is their last encounter before he decides her fate by marrying her off to an older man. Metaphorically, like the little girl trapped between asphalt and metal, Fikria is caught in the in-between space of the door and her room, hemmed in on all sides by the masculine perimeters which impede her freedom. She describes her father, standing in the doorway observing her, as a vulture, waiting to prey upon her, selling her to another man.[15] She is alone with him, yet separated from him by "La loi, la religion, nos sexes et notre haine" [Law, religion, our sexes, and our hate].[16] Her future is decided as the door closes behind him, shutting her away forever.[17] From this time forward her "mutilations volontaires" [voluntary mutilations] become more frequent as she awaits her inevitable marriage and, thus, another set of walls to close around her.[18]

Ourdhia, the family's maid, is the only woman in the novel who circulates freely outside the home. Yet, as Fikria observes, this freedom is located in what she describes as an unreal, yet benevolent, world. It is a world of the Imaginary.[19] Ourdhia is free because she is from another place about which only Fikria can dream. Ourdhia is an "étrangère" whom Fikria's mother does not consider to be a woman because she is black, a "nomade," from the

South, "the desert."[20] Ourdhia's otherness and refusal to kowtow to the repressive traditional milieu (she rejects covering her head or staying indoors) render the street more accessible to her. Unfortunately, as Fikria observes from her window, although different, the maid's liberty is but an illusion and she is not spared the abjection and violence of the men who lurk outside:

> [E]lle avait le droit de quitter la prison. . . . Ourdhia ne couvrait jamais sa tête, uniquement ses épaules: premières marques d'un corps parfait pouvant attiser le désir de ces hommes toujours en rut. . . . Un morveux lui lança une pierre, un autre, plus courageux, lui cracha en pleine figure, deux jeunes hommes faisaient courir leur mains répugnantes sur son beau corps.

> [She alone had the right to leave the prison. . . . Ourdhia never covered her head, only her shoulders: first signs of a perfect body able to stir up the desires of these men who were always in heat. . . . A snotty-nosed kid threw a rock at her, another, more courageous, spit right in her face, two young men let their disgusting hands run over her beautiful body.][21]

Ourdhia eventually leaves because of the hostility of the streets, dominated by masculine depravity and lechery, and because Fikria's father rapes her. She simply packs her things and melts back into the desert, the privileged action of a woman-nomad not bound by the purviews of Bouraoui's intensely sequestered spaces. Ourdhia, because of her difference, finds a means to leave. This nomadic life offers a counterpoint to the sequestered, amputated existence of the young girl who seeks refuge in her friendship with the outsider. Ourdhia for Fikria represents liberty and freedom and is a woman who has profited from "choice, knowledge of truth, and movement."[22] Yet, the maid's life does not, according to Bouraoui, offer a heartening alternative for women living sequestered in the Maghreb. Although free to move about in the street, for city dwellers, Ourdhia is spurned because of her dark skin color and her nomadic life and, therefore, forced to live on the margins of urban society. The author alludes to Algeria's ongoing policy to make sedentary the nomadic populations who still are present in the country. In Bouraoui's world, otherness and difference are a double-edged sword synonymous with liberty as well as marginalization. Since independence in 1962, nomadic tribes have been viewed as counterproductive to creating a sedentary, socialist, communal, and unified society.

The disappearance of Ourdhia launches Fikria's descent into madness. The maid was the only source of affection the young woman had ever known. With her departure, Fikria returns to her gazing, an observer of a mad world, locked in her feminine space, kept out of the streets and away from contact with others. She is a commentator without an audience noting, "Comment ne pas s'ennuyer dans un pays musulman quand on est une fille musulmane?" [How not to be bored in a Muslim country when one is a Muslim girl].[23]

There are many layers of different prisons in Bouraoui's novel, each influencing the mental state of the young heroine. Vivid, horror-laden words crisscross the pages of the work, exposing these prisons from the heroine's point of view. Physical prisons in this novel abound, as Bouraoui leads us from Fikria's cell to her father's house, to the street, and then to a deformed city locked away in a country that is phallicized and a city (Algiers) that she describes as a "vaste asile psychiatrique" [vast psychiatric asylum] where men and women will be forever separated by religion.[24] Not only is Fikria encased in her room, her "cellule mortuaire" [mortuary cell],[25] "la chambre des mille et une peines" [the room of one thousand and one pains],[26] her house also is a masculinized fortress, a "temple de l'austerité" [temple of austerity],[27] built by the heroine's grandfather and fortified by her father and his devotion to Islam and the Koran, whose "premiers sourates . . . sont gravées sur les portes" [the first suras of the Koran are engraved on the doors] as a religious beacon under which all the inhabitants of the house are placed under surveillance.[28] Fikria is sheathed in her father's law as well as the physical confines he and his forefathers have built to shut the gynaeceum—this den of females—within its walls. He is her jailor and the reason for her self-mutilations: "Mon père a été le déclencheur de ma violence. Le responsable que j'accuse!" [My father has been the trigger of my violence, the responsible party whom I hereby accuse].[29] It is he who locks her away, he who plays with her fate, sells her to the highest bidder, and burns a cigarette into her lips.[30] Her body and mind are coerced into accepting the fate of a woman caught in the fetters of traditional Islam.

As Fikria moves from commenting on the sickness reigning both in the exterior and interior spaces of her prison, her "cloisons . . . d'exil" [partitions . . . of exile][31] become increasingly deformed. She slips more frequently in and out of dreamlike ravings and declares: "Je me renverse dans un autre moi" [I reverse myself into another me].[32] This "moi" is a Self transformed by insanity and capable of inflicting self-mutilations, swinging Fikria back and forth between the living and the dead. She wonders: "Etais-je morte ou semiconsciente? Je ne sais plus" [Was I dead or half-conscious? I no longer know].[33] Days and nights are plagued with jarring dreams which become indiscernible from reality. The desire to end her existence leads to frequent outbursts of violence where she hurls her body against the window of her room in despair: "une jeune fille hysterique . . . une victime" [a hysterical girl . . . a victim].[34] Her ravings lead her to realize, and even fantasize about, destroying her virginity with a coat hanger. This act would result in her suicide and, in turn, defy and topple her father's and family's honor. However, her self-preservation is too great; she stops herself at the last minute from committing this ultimate abuse. Out of solidarity with other women who are cloistered, she resigns herself to go through with the wedding.

Her body, "LA souillure" [THE filth], as her father calls it, is also a prison that Fikria blames as being "le pire des traîtres" [the worst of traitors].[35] It is this feminine body that has condemned her to a life of sequestration. Her body is so disdainful that she imagines how she might die in order to rid herself of it: "Je m'invente des maladies mortelles, poumons incandescents, cerveau en forme de vase, intestins biliaires" [I invent deadly illnesses for myself, burning lungs, a muddled brain, pitted intestines, and biliary nausea].[36] In Bouraoui's novel, the feminine body is castrated, devoid of any power, lacking and hindered by bodies "[qui nous] rappelaient [notre] faiblesse . . . [un] sexe amputé" [that reminded (us) of our weakness . . . (our) amputated sex].[37] Even motherhood—the ultimate sacrifice of a woman's body—is debased if it cannot bring forth male life. Fikria's mother grieves over her inability to give birth to a boy, blaming herself for bringing into the world three daughters. This unnamed mother desires power, a penis, Fikria exclaims, that would give her status and position, respect in a society that is frustrated sexually and morally.[38]

Feminine bodies in Bouraoui's world are heavy hindrances, prisons of flesh. The women in Fikria's family are encumbered by the sheer weight of their bodies. Breasts, buttocks, thighs, stomachs become appendages of torment for Fikria, her mother, and her sisters.[39] The author describes the feminine body throughout her novel as oscillating between two extremes: first, as a white, infirm, and fat mass unable to breath because of lack of light and exercise. This body is full of a "graisse dévastatrice" [devastating fat][40] which is unsatisfied, left to fester in "cellulite et amertume" [cellulite and bitterness].[41] Tant K, accomplice to Fikria's parents' endeavors to marry the heroine off, embodies this feminine form; her "chair dégoulinante s'étale fièrement sur les coussins" [oozing flesh proudly spreads out on the cushions].[42] Contrastingly, Bouraoui's second version of the feminine body is one that is wasted and controlled. Zhor, Fikria's older sister, hones and tames her physical appearance in order to hide its budding femininity. Anorexic, Zohr wraps her breasts tightly in bandages, refusing to eat, hoping her starved state will render her eventually androgynous, eliminating all traces of her feminine form: "Zohr est faible. Zohr est malade. Personne ne la voit. Personne ne l'entend s'acharner comme une démente sur ses ongles et ses phalanges" [Zohr is weak. Zohr is sick. Nobody sees her. Nobody hears her going after her nails and fingers like a nutcase].[43]

In this extremely religious, fundamentalist world, the feminine body is not only sequestered, it is also expected to remain pure and intact until marriage. Before Fikria's marriage, her body and genitalia are inspected by other women to make sure that she is a pure virgin; a nubile adolescent, ripe and perfect, who meets the requirements of her future husband—this "inconnu," as she defines him. Fikria is also expected to fulfill the demands, the "l'orgueil, l'espoir et l'attente de la famille" [the pride, hope, and the expectation of the family].[44] The protagonist's sexuality is coveted by the women who attend to her before her marriage. Her duty is to further the progeny of her future husband and bring prosperity to her family. All rights to her own selfhood are eliminated and her identity is crushed. Fikria is destined to be, simply, a reproducing machine. The rest of her, she exclaims, has been "décédée depuis longtemps de l'intérieur, desséchée de l'extérieur" [deceased for a long time inside, dried out on the outside].[45]

Marriage, for the heroine, is a coffin in which she is nailed shut. She accepts the fact that "la tradition est une dame vengeresse contre qui je ne peux lutter" [tradition is a vengeful lady against whom I cannot fight].[46] Adhering to tradition and the popular slogan of young cloistered women, Bouraoui tells us that "Une femme musulmane quitte sa maison deux fois: pour son mariage et pour son enterrement. Ainsi en a décidé la tradition!" [A Muslim woman leaves her house twice: for her marriage and for her funeral. Or so tradition had decreed].[47] In the closing pages, as Fikria is swept away from one coffin to another, her memory and her very being melt into nothingness: "Comme un animal qui desquame je leur laissai en cadeau ma première peau, mon être et ma respiration" [Like a shedding animal, I left them my first skin as a present, my being and my breath].[48]

Many scholars of francophone fiction have wondered if Bouraoui's world of feminine horror is real or imaginary. Even Fikria, at one point, wonders whether or not her life "is real or unreal?" Reality or fiction? Yet, in terms of clarifying the world of extreme feminine abjection, Bouraoui's novel, although at times criticized for its hyperbolic constructions, nevertheless draws our attention to the plight of women in ultraorthodox milieus. Her work emphasizes the importance, in Fikria's words, of exposing *the story*: "l'important est l'histoire. Se faire une histoire avant de regarder le vrai. Réelle, irréelle, qu'importe!" [What matters is the story. To make a story for oneself before looking around at what's true. Real, unreal, what's the big deal!].[49] Through Fikria we comprehend that the reality of the story lies in the "danse grotesque" that a woman must perform between "la folie et le désespoir" [madness and despair].[50]

TU T'APPELLERAS TANGA

"Donne ta main, et mon histoire naîtra dans tes veines" [Give me your hand and my story will be born in your veins],[51] Tanga tells Anna-Claude as they both languish in a prison cell in an unnamed African country, the former a seventeen-year-old, black, African teenager, the latter a white, Jewish-French woman from Paris. Calixthe Beyala opens a world of feminine abjection that teaches us the universalisms possible when considering the feminine condition. Madness, marginalization, violence, death, poverty, racism, motherhood, infanticide know no difference of color, ethnicity, or nationality: "Je vais mourir, femme. Les blancs meurent aussi, tu sais? Plonger dans la mort comme dans la vie. Sans visa, sans passeport" [I am going to die, woman. White people die as well you know? To dive into death as you do into life. Without a visa, without a passport].[52] The commonalities of the female condition make up the central message of the work of controversial Cameroonian author Calixthe Beyala.[53] Author of twelve novels whose primary aim has been to expose the deplorable conditions in which women and children have had to live in both Africa and Europe, Beyala champions the rights of these two groups demanding a universal humanism for all. Physical and mental violence inflicted on women is never restricted to one race or one country. As Beyala's two heroines demonstrate, madness is possible for any woman whose body and mind have been tortured and brutalized enough to make her want to give up, to expunge herself; "Partir vers des lieux sans terre ni ciel" [Leave for places that have neither earth nor heaven].[54]

As in Nina Bouraoui's novel, Beyala paints a portrait of a prison that takes on many forms. These forms range from the concrete cell in which Tanga and Anna-Claude find themselves, to the sociocultural prison that is constituted through the wills of men, violence, and death in a country that leaves little opportunity for women to follow their dreams. Like Fikria, Tanga and Anna-Claude have been locked away by men who wield overbearing brutal authority over them (lovers have made both women false promises, Tanga's father has raped her). Tanga is accused of having worked with counterfeiters, laundering fake money, and Anna-Claude of political activism (she denounced the government for having kidnapped and killed children from the school where she taught). In prison they share stories. Tanga is slowly dying and her last wish is to give up her identity—her story—to *transfer it* to Anna-Claude "jusqu'à [quand elle devient] sa propre histoire" [until it becomes her own story].[55] Anna-Claude will become Tanga: "Alors, entre en moi. Mon secret s'illuminera . . . il faut que la blanche en toi meure. Donne-moi la main, désormais tu seras moi. Tu auras dix-sept saisons, tu seras noire, tu t'appelleras Tanga" [Well, then, enter into me. My secret will be illuminated. But first, the white woman in you must die. Give me your hand; from now on you shall be me. You shall be seventeen seasons old; you shall be black; your name shall be Tanga].[56]

With the fluid transference that takes place between the heroines, Beyala's story proposes another conception of the feminine body that relies on an idea of essence rather than solid corporeality. For the author, women's *essence* is found beyond the body; her physicality is not essentially made up of skin and bone but is, as philosopher Elizabeth Grosz contends, "open-ended, [a] pliable set of significations, capable of being rewritten, reconstituted, in quite other terms than those which [constitute its physical make up]."[57] Certain critics have faulted Beyala for what seems like a "sell out" to white hegemony. The author is accused of divesting a black woman of her identity and right to subjectivity by effectively turning her into a white woman. However, I contend that these critics fail to consider the larger, universal message of Beyala's story: that women are able to connect and transgress the boundaries of race and corporeality in order to survive. Tanga becomes Anna-Claude, but Anna-Claude, in the end, becomes Tanga, her own identity evaporating as Tanga's soul inhabits the white shell that is left once Anna-Claude's departs. Individual identity is melded to create one woman who will continue to exist and to fight against the madness, violence, and abjection that have engulfed both heroines. Beyala's novel is an example of a new brand of feminism, as Juliana Makuchi Nfati-Abbeyni notes:

> Black women/feminist critics [seek] to posit the problematic of womanhood as seen through their own "I"/"Eyes" by positioning themselves and the works that are the object of their critique at the center of their discursive practices. By so doing, they have brought the lives of black women to the forefront either by rejecting the position of "Other" ascribed to them by dominant discourses or by claiming their "Otherness" as a weapon of resistance against those hegemonic discourses.[58]

Both Anna-Claude and Tanga claim their otherness as a means of survival. Although both suffer mental instability, they do resist to some extent the patriarchal structures that are imposed upon them. Anna-Claude continues to live in her dreamworld in Paris and, eventually, acts within it to follow the unreal, fabricated lover she has invented for herself. Tanga, although victimized by her father, mother, and prostitution, is able, in the end, to escape into a world she has fashioned on her own terms. She adopts a young boy, Mala (a twelve-year-old orphan), renounces her life as a prostitute, and finally leaves her family. Beyala's work thus becomes a story about two women who both have been "othered" and cast out by their respective societies. However, this marginalized state leads them to ultimately find, even when locked away in a cell, a world that they are able to share because their life experiences have been so similar. The cell becomes a reflective space allowing a dialogue to emerge from this otherness—the marginalization—that brought them to be imprisoned. Race, class, and nationalities are relegated to secondary positions as Beyala's story becomes a treatise to women's capacity to survive in hopeless situations. Despite their imprisonment and their ultimate demise, these women's stories persevere and are passed on to others.

What are the prisons in this novel? And what role does madness play in the deaths of the protagonists? Although both women, in a sense, die in the prison cell (Tanga physically and Anna-Claude mentally, since she loses her self, her *essence*, in becoming Tanga), the story remains "an indictment of human depravity in African urban slums, of patriarchal society as a whole; one that condones child abuse/slavery/prostitution; a society in which women and children are the Other."[59] As Nfati-Abbeyni suggests, Beyala's novel is a commentary on the process of "othering," not only of women but of groups that have no power. Her heroines are relegated to depraved milieus where they must make hopeless choices in order to survive. Like Fikria, Tanga and Anna-Claude realize that their concrete cell, the four walls that close in on them, are but one form of prison. In fact, they have been prisoners all their lives, caught up in alienation, living in the margins in countries whose very systems swallow up the defenseless and the helpless: "Que dire dans un pays où tout, même l'air, est prison?" [what is there to say in a country where everything, even the air, is a prison?].[60]

Calixthe Beyala's work has been considered from many angles; however, little study has been accorded to the role of madness in forming the aforementioned prisons which eventually engulf both heroines. Insanity is what propels Anna-Claude, a Jewish-French high school philosophy teacher who suffers from paranoid interludes, to embark for Africa. In France "sur les murs de son appartement à Paris elle dessinait des figures menaçantes pour exorciser le mal de vivre" [On the walls of her Paris apartment, she would draw menacing faces to exorcise the pain of living],[61] while she "passait ses jours de congé à concocter des gâteaux d'anniversaire pour les démons qui avaient persécuté son repos. . . . Folle, elle l'était vraiment" [She would spend her free days concocting birthday cakes for the demons who hunted down her repose. . . . She really was mad].[62] And yet, curiously, Anna-Claude's madness also acts as a catalyst, propelling her to invent an African husband, Ousmane, who, she eventually claims, has made her pregnant. Fluctuating between lucid and insane worlds, she sets out on a quest to find the fictitious Ousmane. Her flight tears down geographical frontiers, while opening up the deranged parts of her mind: "De cette folie qui questionnait sans jamais répondre, de celle qui créait le temps et l'arrêtait, de celle qui se réclamait de tous les lieux du monde où l'homme abolira les frontières. Les frontières demeuraient, la folie demeurait" [The kind of madness which asked questions without ever replying, which created time and stopped it, claimed kinship with every place in the world where man abolished frontiers. The frontiers remained, her madness continued].[63] Anna-Claude's madness launches her on a trip to Africa (the pretense being to find her fictitious lover, Ousmane) where she obtains a teaching job in a high school near a small town, located in an unnamed West African, francophone country. She dedicates her time to improving the welfare of hundreds of faceless children. In Africa, many of her students disappear, she doesn't understand why, and her pleas fall on deaf ears. Subsequently, she buys a placard on which she writes "Où sont nos enfants? Égorgés par un boucher!" [Where are our children? Strangled by a Butcher!][64] and marches day after day until she is thrown into prison for being "crazy," a "subversive and uncontrollable," element.[65] Incarcerated, talking to herself, slipping in and out of lucidity, she awaits her fate. Not until Tanga arrives, bleeding and half dead, does Anna-Claude find the will to take the younger girl's hand, allowing her story to enter her mind.

Through the narrative of Tanga's story, we emerge from the walls of the prison cell to explore other milieus of insanity which in their own manners are also prisons from which there is little opportunity of escape. These obsequious spaces in Tanga's world are situated between two extremes; one is lodged in reality and the other in the world of dreams. One space is occupied by the "femme" and one by the "fillette," marking the duality in which the protagonist lives. She is neither woman nor child and her reality is so horrifying that often it takes on supernatural qualities. We repeatedly wonder if we haven't, in fact, entered a world of nightmares. Indeed, as the novel progresses, readers are privy more and more to the irrational acts that Tanga must perform in order to survive. It is perhaps only her insanity that allows her to cope with an endless progression of sordid scenes. She observes and wanders aimlessly, experiencing events and places in streets where she states "je marche sans connaître ma destination" [I walk without having a sense of where I'm going]. People encircle her and "commentent les couleurs de la folie qui [la] pourchasse" [comment on the hue of the particular madness which pursues (her)], yet nothing can bring her out of her profound stupor.[66]

Like Fikria in Nina Bouraoui's novel, Tanga searches for some semblance of normalcy in a very abnormal world. Equally, Tanga realizes the impossibility of this task. The violence that rules both interior and exterior spaces leaves no room for dreams. Robbed of her childhood by the father who raped her (making her pregnant) and the subsequent verbal and physical abuse by her mother, Tanga will never overcome the "souffrance" she has endured and which she states will last "jusqu'au jour de . . . ma mort" [until the day of . . . my own death].[67] Death, she admits, will be her only means of attaining peace.

Tanga's reality is made up of a family that inflicts such physical and mental trauma on her body and soul that she becomes fused in between being a woman and being a child, a "femme-fillette" [a woman-girl child]. Her father's sexual abuse, followed by her mother's insistence that Tanga prostitute herself to earn money for them all, leads her to disregard her body as but an appendage of her soul, "an-Other, that is, not-I."[68] "J'amenais mon corps au carrefour des vies. Je le plaçais sous la lumière. . . . Je ne sentais rien, je n'éprouvais rien. Mon corps à mon insu s'était peu à peu transformé en chair de pierre" [I brought my body to the crossroads of other lives. I put it underneath the light. . . . I felt nothing; I had no feelings, no sensations. Little by little my body had turned from flesh to stone].[69] This body, figuratively made of stone, is subjugated by men and brutalized by other women, most seriously by her mother who forces Tanga to undergo a clitoridectomy, which she feels will prepare the girl for men and the prostitution market.[70] Mutilation of body parts in order to allow men easier access to female sexuality further locks the prison door of Tanga's world. She is now considered a "woman" according to tribal ritual and therefore accepted into a patriarchal construction that gives men power over her body. The young girl's mother has also contributed to the traditional structures that ensure the continuing domination of women:

> Tanga's experience shows how women within patriarchy are built into the ladder of power struggles in such a way that they become accomplices with that very control of power and sexuality that men have claimed for themselves. Tanga's mother quietly looks the other way at her daughter's rape and pregnancy and jubilates at her clitoridectomy.[71]

The monstrous family structure which fetters Tanga also fosters her dreams of an ideal life "où une nouvelle vie [existe] où j'offrirais la mère à un enfant qui en aurait besoin, d'autres enfants encore, l'homme, la maison, le chien, la pie au bout du pré. Est-ce trop demander?" [where a new life (exists) in which I'd offer to be a mother to the child that needs one,—to other children as well—a man, the house, the dog, the magpie at the end of the meadow. Is that too much to ask?].[72] In the violent world Beyala paints, yes, it is too much to ask. Tanga will never fulfill her desires, such men as in her dreams do not exist. She rejects the love offered by Cul-de-jatte (which is translated in the English version of the novel as "Lame-leg," but which in actuality literally means a legless cripple), a man who professes that he does love her and wants to have a son. However, she cannot fulfill his wishes and remarks: "Je ne veux pas prêter mon ventre à l'éclosion d'une vie. Tant d'enfants traînent par la ville! Je déteste alimenter les statistiques" [I do not want to lend my womb to the unfurling of a life. So many children already loiter in the streets! I despise feeding the statistics].[73] In order to completely reject the possibility of ever physically becoming a mother, Tanga mutilates her womb, rendering her body lifeless and unfeeling; she becomes simply a "bête de somme" [beast of burden].[74] As a result of this mutilation, Tanga's physicality becomes imperceptible to her, lifeless, an inanimate object, detached: "j'ai l'impression d'être immatérielle, une ombre presque. Je veux assister à la mise en péril du corps par le corps. Détruire. Saccager. J'invoque la déflagration qui va apporter l'anéantissement" [I feel like I'm lightweight, ethereal, almost a shadow. I want to witness the body's endangering of the body. To destroy. To pillage. I call upon the explosion that will bring annihilation].[75] It is this becoming imperceptible, this self-annihilation, that frees Tanga ultimately from the abject corporeality that she has endured. But what does becoming imperceptible mean? Deleuze and Guattari in *A Thousand Plateaus* define the realm of the imperceptible as a positive space which allows the marginalized "to go unnoticed . . . to be a stranger . . . eliminate all that is waste, death and superfluity." They state further that such a becoming ensures that "by process of elimination, one is no longer anything more than an abstract line, or a piece in a puzzle that is itself abstract." When one becomes imperceptible one becomes a pure line of abstraction, a communicating body that "[slips] between things and [grows] in the midst of things," one is free.[76] It is this letting go of her body, this flowing into Anna-Claude that allows Tanga to continue to exist on another plane, another plateau; she becomes a pure feminine essence: "Son corps s'absente, dépasse son ombre. Plus de sexe. Plus de seins. Plus de nez. Le vide. Seule la bouche dessine une étrange litanie, indépendante. ACCUMULER DES SILENCES/ACCUMULER DES SILENCES/ L'ILLUSION C'EST MOI/LA FOLIE, C'EST MOI" [Her body absents itself, overtakes its shadow. No sex. No breasts. No nose. The void. Her mouth alone forms a strange independent litany. ACCUMULATE SILENCES/ ACCUMULATE SILENCES/ I AM ILLUSION/ I AM MADNESS].[77]

Calixthe Beyala's novel ends with two women fused through their feminine essence by madness. The heroine now exists as a woman with a white shell and a black soul. When Tanga's mother comes to the prison to inquire as to the whereabouts of her daughter, Anna-Claude confronts her stating, "vous nous avez tuées, madame" [you have killed us both, Madame].[78] These words are ambiguous. In physical terms, Tanga has disappeared and Anna-Claude stands in her place, yet the white woman's mind has gone, replaced by Tanga's. If, as Rousseau argued in the eighteenth century, that man is whole only in terms of the mind/body connection, then the person that Tanga's mother finds before her isn't subjectively a person. Yet if we view Tanga's and Anna-Claude's transference as a fusion into each other through the catalyst of madness, or, as Shoshana Felman would contend, a melding through "madness as [an] impasse" to another plane of existence, then Beyala's story takes on new contours. The author's goal was not to delve into the individual hardships of either Tanga or Anna-Claude, but to expose the commonalities of women's lives across the globe. The cold, harsh reality is that Calixthe Beyala sheds a light onto the female condition that, once again, recalls the words of Elisabeth Mudimbé-Boyi, who claims that "madness functions as a metaphor of the female condition and [women's] alienation."[79]

NOTES

1. Elizabeth Grosz, *Volatile Bodies: Toward a Corporeal Feminism* (Bloomington: Indiana University Press, 1994), 60.

2. Nina Bouraoui, *La Voyeuse Interdite* (Paris: Gallimard, 1991), 126; translated by Melissa Marcus under the title *Forbidden Vision* (Barrytown, N.Y.: Station Hill, 1995), 91.

3. Michel Foucault, *Discipline and Punish* (New York: Vintage, 1979), 136.

4. Curiously, whereas the French title evokes the idea that the girl is "physically" forbidden to engage in the act of looking (voyeuse means "female voyeur"), the title in English suggests that it is the vision that is curtailed, not the young girl. I can only speculate on why the translator deformed the meaning.

5. Bouraoui, *La Voyeuse*, 56, 36.

6. Fatima Mernissi, *Beyond the Veil: Male-Female Dynamics in Modern Muslim Society* (Bloomington: Indiana University Press, 1987), 30–31.

7. Mernissi, *Beyond the Veil*, 31.

8. Bouraoui, *La Voyeuse*, 25, 16

9. Martin Jay, *Downcast Eyes: The Denigration of Vision in Twentieth-Century French Thought* (Berkeley: University of California Press, 1994), 288.

10. Jay, *Downcast Eyes*, 91. Consult his work also for an in-depth explanation of the power associated with the "regard absolu."

11. Bouraoui, *La Voyeuse*, 93, 65.

12. Bouraoui, *La Voyeuse*, 93, 66.

13. Bouraoui, *La Voyeuse*, 95–96, 67.

14. Bouraoui, *La Voyeuse*, 90–91, 63–64.

15. Bouraoui, *La Voyeuse*, 91, 64.

16. Bouraoui, *La Voyeuse*, 92, 65

17. Bouraoui, *La Voyeuse*, 95, 67.

18. Bouraoui, *La Voyeuse*, 95, 67.

19. Bouraoui, *La Voyeuse*, 52, 36.

20. Bouraoui, *La Voyeuse*, 57, 39.

21. Bouraoui, *La Voyeuse*, 56–57, 39–40.

22. Inge E. Boer, "The World Beyond Our Window: Nomads, Traveling Theories and the Function of Boundaries," *Parallax* 3 (September 1996): 7–26, 11.

23. Bouraoui, *La Voyeuse*, 64, 46.

24. Bouraoui, *La Voyeuse*, 21, 13.

25. Bouraoui, *La Voyeuse*, 88, 46.

26. Bouraoui, *La Voyeuse*, 139, 100.

27. Bouraoui, *La Voyeuse*, 63, 44.

28. Bouraoui, *La Voyeuse*, 23, 15.

29. Bouraoui, *La Voyeuse*, 66, 47.

30. Bouraoui, *La Voyeuse*, 67, 48.

31. Bouraoui, *La Voyeuse*, 88, 62.

32. Bouraoui, *La Voyeuse*, 88, 62.

33. Bouraoui, *La Voyeuse*, 109, 79.

34. Bouraoui, *La Voyeuse*, 119, 85.

35. Bouraoui, *La Voyeuse*, 61, 42.

36. Bouraoui, *La Voyeuse*, 64, 44.

37. Bouraoui, *La Voyeuse*, 42–43, 29.

38. Bouraoui, *La Voyeuse*, 42, 28.

39. Bouraoui, *La Voyeuse*, 43, 28–29.

40. Bouraoui, *La Voyeuse*, 80, 56.

41. Bouraoui, *La Voyeuse*, 130, 93.

42. Bouraoui, *La Voyeuse*, 79–80, 56.

43. Bouraoui, *La Voyeuse*, 131, 94.

44. Bouraoui, *La Voyeuse*, 116, 84.

45. Bouraoui, *La Voyeuse*, 132, 95.

46. Bouraoui, *La Voyeuse*, 126, 91.

47. Bouraoui, *La Voyeuse*, 124, 89–90.

48. Bouraoui, *La Voyeuse*, 139, 100.

49. Bouraoui, *La Voyeuse*, 10–11, 4.

50. Bouraoui, *La Voyeuse*, 130, 94.

51. Calixthe Beyala, *Tu t'appelleras Tanga* (Paris: Stock, 1988), 14; translated by Marjolijn de Jager under the title *Your Name Shall Be Tanga* (Portsmouth, N.H.: Heinemann, 1996), 7.

52. Beyala, *Tanga*, 5, 1.

53. In 1995, Beyala was accused by the French newspaper *Le Canard Enchaîné* (11 January 1995) of having plagiarized several pages from the well-known novel by Howard Buten *When I Was 5 I killed Myself* (1981) in order to embellish her own work, *Le Petit Prince de Belleville* (1992). She was found guilty by a Parisian court. See also the follow-up article in *Le Canard Enchaîné* (18 January 1995) in which Beyala denies the accusation.

54. Beyala, *Tanga*, 5, 1.

55. Beyala, *Tanga*, 14, 8.

56. Beyala, *Tanga*, 14, 7.

57. Grosz, *Volatile Bodies*, 60.

58. Juliana Makuchi Nfah-Abbenyi, "Calixthe Beyala's 'femme-fillette': Womanhood and the politics of (M)othering," in *The Politics of (M)othering: Womanhood, Identity, and Resistance in African Literature*, ed. Obioma Nnaemeka (New York: Routledge, 1997): 101–113, 101.

59. Nfah-Abbenyi, *Calixthe*, 101–102.

60. Beyala, *Tanga*, 96, 68.

61. Beyala, *Tanga*, 7, 2.

62. Beyala, *Tanga*, 8, 3.

63. Beyala, *Tanga*, 8, 3.

64. Beyala, *Tanga*, 12, 6.

65. Beyala, *Tanga*, 12, 6.

66. Beyala, *Tanga*, 166–67, 120–21.

67. Beyala, *Tanga*, 46, 30.

68. Nfah-Abbenyi, *Calixthe*, 103.

69. Beyala, *Tanga*, 15, 8. This passage is also cited in Nfah-Abbenyi's work to explain this loss of "I," which is discussed at length in her article (103).

70. Nfah-Abbenyi, *Calixthe*, 104.

71. Nfah-Abbenyi, *Calixthe*, 105.

72. Beyala, *Tanga*, 91, 64.

73. Beyala, *Tanga*, 166, 120.

74. Beyala, *Tanga*, 94, 66.

75. Beyala, *Tanga*, 131, 94.

76. Deleuze and Guattari, *A Thousand Plateaus*, 279–280.

77. Beyala, *Tanga*, 175, 127. Author's emphasis.

78. Beyala, *Tanga*, 190, 137.

79. Mudimbé-Boyi, "*Narrative 'Je(ux)'*," 137.

STATE III

RECONCILIATION: FEMININE UTOPIAS

A l'heure actuelle, dans notre pays, une femme qui écrit vaut son pesant de poudre.

[In our country at the present time, a woman writer is worth her weight in gunpowder.]

—Kateb Yacine, introduction to *La Grotte éclatée* (1979)

Le cheval ne doit pas te conduire, c'est toi qui dois conduire ton cheval.

[The horse mustn't ride you, you must ride it.]

—Simone Schwarz-Bart, *Pluie et Vent sur Télumée Miracle* (1972)

Introduction to State III

If madness truly is the "impasse" to another plane of existence, as Shoshana Felman contends, then what do women do once they get there? What is this other plane, this plateau? Is it a plane of consistency, as Deleuze and Guattari suggest, which comes about after "absolute deterritorialization" from the norm where there are "no longer forms or substances, content or expression" that would curtail a woman's development?[1] What do women do who do survive madness and/or the hurdles of marginalization within their own societies? Like heroine Gagneseri in the 1997 film *Tableau Ferraille*, who sets out in a boat with no precise destination, women writing from Africa and the Caribbean are wondering what will be their destinies.

Francophone women's writing considered in this section offers us a look at the destinations of heroines who "arrive" at what Elisabeth Mudimbé-Boyi defines as the realm of the "unsayable."[2] Protagonists in the novels *La Grotte éclatée, Et pourtant le ciel était bleu, Pluie et vent sur Télumée Miracle,* and *Douceurs du bercail* enter the *vel*, an arena of public agency where they become monsters instead of angels. They are women who take the lead with voices that comment, argue, and disagree with prevailing norms. These women throw off the veils of debilitating madness and victimhood to reach their final destinations: new platforms where speech takes place and from which women are able to write their own h(er)stories.

Maryse Condé suggests that "for each and every writer, writing is both a constructive and destructive urge, a possibility for growth and for change. We write to build ourselves word by word, to forge our unique identity. With the help of our imagination and our mastery of the word, we replace the world we live in with a utopia."[3] It is exactly this utopia that I suggest is open for those women francophone authors who drive madness away to arrive at the other side of the feminine psyche. These women are finally able to engage in open dialogues in public spaces, establishing themselves as equal voices in society and culture.

In the following novels, each heroine portrayed has experienced a moment of insanity which alters the course of her life. However, she perseveres, conquering her madness to forge a new identity for herself, her own utopia. In certain instances this utopia is a new form of family or nation constructed on the heroine's own terms. It is a world that is shaped to counter the effects of pain, war, and revolution, as in the case of Yamina Mechakra's *La Grotte Eclatée* and Hajer Djilani's *Et pourtant le ciel était bleu,* or racism and xenophobia, as depicted in Aminata Sow Fall's *Douceurs du bercail.* Yet in all circumstances the heroines in these novels, while temporarily suffering from the torment and alienation of the "female condition," as defined by Mudimbé-Boyi, are able to find happiness in other terms that do not always conform to the status quo. In every case the heroine is left alone to combat masculine tutelage, while working outside patriarchal systems. Ideas of family and motherhood are construed within alternative paradigms in order to favor these women's search for subjecthood and well-being. Nations and cultures become something that these women contribute to, but are not duped by. In the works discussed in this section, women have reconciled themselves to living on the borders of the norm in order to, in Virginia Woolf's words, find a "room of one's own."

NOTES

1. Gilles Deleuze and Félix Guattari, *A Thousand Plateaus*, 70.
2. Elisabeth Mudimbé-Boyi, "*Narrative '(Je)ux,*'" 137; (see note 60, chapter 2).
3. Maryse Condé, "Language and Power," *College Language Association Journal* 39, no. 1 (September 1995): 18–25, 19.

6

War, Revolution, and Family Matters
Yamina Mechakra's *La Grotte éclatée* and Hajer Djilani's *Et Pourtant le ciel était bleu*

> If a feminine vanguard does not continue the daily fight against stupid prejudices and shameless privileges, then this hope will remain—and for how many generations yet to come?—an illusion.
>
> —Fadéla M'Rabet, *Les Algériennes* (1967)

Fifteen years separate the novels of Algerian Yamina Mechakra's *La Grotte Eclatée* (1979) and Tunisian Hajer Djilani's *Et Pourtant le ciel était bleu* (1994).[1] However, within both novels are embedded certain similarities which are striking, demonstrating the fact that women have been (and continue to be) pawns as they are caught in the middle of war, violence, family expectations, and the constraints of motherhood. Both novels are by women from the Maghreb. These works draw attention to the uniqueness of the social constructions of this region, notably the gendered spaces that are maintained even in times of war, when women are called upon to take up arms and enter into what is traditionally masculine space. Both Mechakra's unnamed heroine and Djilani's Chems are condemned by the traditional societies in which they live for fighting for freedom and a cause. Thus, as scholar Zineb Ali-Benali remarks, these authors signify the certainty that

> [i]n our Maghrebian societies, a woman who speaks and writes her voice in outside space, in the public space reserved for men, provokes scandal. Her discourse is inadmissible, and what's more: inconceivable. What it disturbs is the social foundation which is supposed to stay unchangeable: the separation of the sexes and the sequestration of women.[2]

In both novels war breaks down the sociocultural traditions binding women in the secluded areas of traditional Islamic societies, thus provoking "the inconceivable" to which Ali-Benali alludes: women disturbing the "social foundations" of their societies. Mechakra's novel, in particular, reminds us of Frantz Fanon's commentary in *A Dying Colonialism* (1959), on Algerian women who participated in the revolution of independence (1954–1962) and thus disrupted their traditional society: "Each time she ventures [out], the Algerian woman must achieve a victory over herself, over her childish fears," and these fears encompass not only what she has to do in the way of violent acts, but it also includes the fear of overturning the taboos that have been placed on and instilled in her.[3]

Chems, of Djilani's novel, is a Tunisian doctor who embarks with a group of colleagues from Tunis to aid the people of Iraq during the American-Iraqi war in 1990. Although she is an emancipated young woman who puts her life on the line to aid the victims of the war, she still finds herself viewing the violent conflict as the impetus that allows her to "[run] toward [a] place, [where] the taboos are forgotten."[4] Djilani's character breaks down gender barriers by taking an active, militant role, performing just as many operations on the battlefront as her male counterparts. In addition to these feats of heroine-ism, Chems also enjoys a sexual freedom she has never known before. She notes that her liaison with Salah, an Iraqi doctor, in the throes of war, could never have taken place in a traditional Muslim society which forbids sexual relationships before marriage.[5] War for both Mechakra's and Djilani's heroines becomes not only a determinant for reflection on themselves as women and their roles in their respective societies; it also propels them to tear down the gendered boundaries of traditional Muslim society. Algerian women, in particular authors such as Yamina Mechakra and Assia Djebar, have been militant activists for years. These women set out to change traditions both through the themes of their novels and as speakers championing human rights. Their efforts remain examples of how dangerous public speech in the Maghreb can be for women. Speaking publicly always leads women to revolution, thus marking the fact that, as Algerian author Hédi Bouraoui notes, "[both women and speech are] the two most oppressed and muzzled elements of society. . . . [R]evolution and change can [only] be accomplished through them."[6]

Entering into the public sphere where they speak their minds and become *visible*, throwing off their veils and taking up arms, has meant that these heroines counter age-old accepted mores associated with women as the keepers of tradition in the Maghreb. These novels question the assumption that women must act as the social glue for families and societies caught in the transition from colonialism to independence. Within this transitory space, women often find themselves relegated to ambiguous positions.[7] Certainly, this transitory space is true for women in Algeria where, as Fanon points out, they were and have been synonymous with nation, purity, and providing the *real* core of the Algerian nation-state. "The Algerian woman does not need emancipation. She is already free because she takes part in the liberation of her country of which she is the soul, the heart, and the glory," an author states in a 1959 issue of *El Moudjahid*, the Front de la Libération Nationale's famous newspaper.[8] Women were expected to fight and "overcome all timidity, all awkwardness," while passing bombs and taking up arms against the European colonizer.[9] Yet, once the revolution was won, according to scholar Marnia Lazreg, Algerian women were "headed for an uncertain future" due to "having radically upset the value system that had hitherto governed gender relations by stepping out of their usual home-centered social roles and into the world of urban and rural guerrilla warfare."[10] Positioning themselves on the outside of traditional society meant women had to construct a new corporeal reality that no longer gave way to the symbolic unknown. Once colonialism was thwarted, women in Algeria, as well as in other parts of the Maghreb, now were compelled to fight new battles in order to situate themselves inside the new postcolonial nation-state.

LA GROTTE ÉCLATÉE

In 1979 Yamina Mechakra published her first novel, *La Grotte éclatée*.[11] Although the author herself was only four at the time of the outbreak of the war of independence, her rendition of the events of the revolution and its bloodshed take on the contours of an eyewitness, firsthand account. Well-known Algerian author Kateb Yacine, friend and ally of the younger Mechakra, reveals in his introduction to *La Grotte éclatée* that its autobiographical nature is due to her having seen, at a very young age, a dissected corpse, wantonly thrown to the street. This event, coupled with the torture of her father during the war, solidified her resolve to write.[12] These insane incidents of terror and violence, associated with the war years of her youth, remained vivid images in Mechakra's mind and figure prominently in her novel. The prose, like the life of the heroine it describes, is disjointed and difficult to read (both on a thematic and textual level). The novel takes the form of a journal and a poem, written by a young woman caught up in the upheaval of revolution, war, bloodshed, and madness. Through the events depicted in the novel, the reader becomes acutely aware of the sacrifices made both mentally and physically by Algerian women not only during the war, but long after independence was won.

The solidifying theme of Mechakra's work is the idea that women are the source of a nation and the foundation of the independent nation-state. Like Fanon, Mechakra saw women's participation in the war as providing the cornerstone of the new Algerian nation. However, unlike the young psychiatrist who died before the revolution was over, Mechakra, writing seventeen years

after the war's end, views women as providing the new nation-state with future generations of Algerian youth who will uphold the idea of nation and
family as synonymous necessities for the benefit of the collective good. In a
sense, for Mechakra, the nation cannot exist without the power of the family: the two are inextricably linked. It is the nation-state, born out of war and
revolution, which will, in turn, give birth to an egalitarian utopia enjoyed by
men and women.

Mechakra's work is a study of the family dynamics of a postrevolutionary
society and how these dynamics were cultivated into the symbol of the Algerian family-nation. The notion of the family-nation has been an essential
component in the politics of the Front de la Libération Nationale's (FLN) one-
party system and served in 1962 and thereafter (certainly in the 1970s, at least
according to the Party's view) to unite the Algerian people at the beginning
of the postcolonial era. The family takes on both mythical and symbolical proportions as it provides the grounding centerpiece of this novel of revolution
written by a young woman—too young to have, in reality, fought for the
maquis. Despite the fact that she wrote the novel in 1979, Mechakra succeeds
in capturing the horrors lived by the maquis as seen by a young woman
fighter for the *moujabdine*. Considering the novel twenty-three years after it
was published, we are left wondering if the national Algerian family (synonymous for the nation and the people), envisaged by the author as a positive road for Algerians to take toward an idyllic socialist state, was ever possible. A socialist utopia will never be established in a country that has been
repeatedly torn by civil war and Islamic fundamentalism, both of which in the
last fifteen years have particularly victimized women.

In my analysis of Mechakra's novel, I seek to explore how traditional gendered spaces, the madness of war and violence, and the context of the revolutionary family (both real and metaphorical) are used by her heroine to
build a new reality for herself in postcolonial Algeria. What constitutes a family? And why is family (both traditional and atypical) such a necessary component in the heroine's struggle against the insanity of war? How is the Algerian family a symbol for the nation-state family, an idea that was so dear
to the rebels of the revolution and the subsequent governments seeking to
rebuild Algeria? For Mechakra, these questions are answered within the ideology set forth by Boumediene, Algeria's second postcolonial president.[13]
The family would serve as a model not only to illustrate the ideal Marxist society (thought to be the supreme ideology on which to found a modern nation) but also to ensure the continuation of the Algerian people, fostering a
strong sense of unity among them.

Mechakra's novel is constructed on two principal axes, the first being
women's roles in society (traditional and nontraditional) on which the
heroine frequently comments. For the author, there are definitive charac-
teristics associated with women who fall into either group. Mechakra ex-

plores the development of her heroine's identity by placing her in a nontraditional realm as a very atypical Algerian woman: she is an orphan, has no family, no name, no ties to a community, and is totally marginalized on the fringes of society:

> Ramassée dans la Souika constantinoise je fus ballottée d'orphelinat en orphelinat, de famille en famille charitable. Très jeune je connus le mépris de la pitié des nomdotés, très jeune je pris goût à mon sort et dégustais mon indépendance, ma vie sans attache . . . j'aimais personne. Chez les uns on m'appelait Marie ou Judith, chez les autres Fatma. Je portais mes prénoms comme des robes et mes saints comme des couronnes.

> [Found in the Souk of Constantine I was shuffled from one orphanage to another, from one charitable family to another. At a very young age, I knew the disdain and pity of families with names, at a very young age I liked who I was and enjoyed my independence, my life without attachment. . . . I didn't like anyone. Some called me Marie or Judith, others Fatma. I wore my first names like dresses and my saints like crowns.][14]

Her marginalization by those "with names," as well as her life without any family attachment, makes the heroine a perfect candidate for the maquis. Within the violent milieu of the rebels' camp, she at last feels she belongs because there are no traditional rules governing this revolutionary space. War becomes liberating even though she suffers from temporary madness and loneliness. In the end, as she recovers physically and mentally in a Tunisian hospital, she is victorious in the knowledge that, even as a new mother, abandoned, alone, and without the privilege of family ties, she will contribute to building the new Algerian nation-state. She stands metaphorically before a tabula rasa on which to construct a decolonized and untraditional, new, postcolonial Algerian identity.

The second axis of Mechakra's work scrutinizes the ideology of the family as a symbol for a new nation caught up in reconstruction. What will constitute this new family and nation? How will it succeed in reclaiming traditional and historical roots denied it during the colonial era, while including new ideologies of equality and national identity? Although Mechakra writes at a time when these ideologies were taking form, slogans sung by freedom fighters such as "L'Algérie est mon pays, l'Arabe est ma langue, l'Islam est ma religion" [Algeria is my country, Arabic is my language, Islam is my religion] proved later to have dire repercussions for women. One wonders if Mechakra had waited ten years later to write her novel what her words would be. Already, in 1979, when we read between the lines of *La Grotte éclatée*, imposing questions arise. What future would the Marxist family offer women in the new Algerian Republic of the new society? What would be women's ultimate place and role? And where would women ground their identity—in traditionalism or modernity?

Yamina Mechakra situates her story in 1955, a year after the first Algerian bombs exploded, launching the revolution against the French colonizers. The novel is a web of disjointed prose and poetry recounting vague information imparted to readers through bits and pieces of the heroine's memories concerning her origins, family, and the war. As stipulated above, she has no name. Her mother, manipulated by a man who promised her the moon but left once she became pregnant, is also but a somber memory in the mind of the young heroine. The protagonist's mother abandoned her with Catholic nuns in a convent, leaving her nameless with no family and no means by which to root herself in traditional Algerian culture. Later, this absence of family facilitates the heroine's ability to cut ties with the convent and leave for the mountains and the maquis just as the revolution is taking form: "j'étais heureuse de n'appartenir à aucune communauté, m'inventais des hommes et un pays aussi libres que moi" [I was content not to be a part of any community, inventing for myself people and a country as free as me].[15] Her flight to the maquis marks the beginning of her identity quest. As an orphan in a society where family is the root of society, she is an outcast: "moi, je suis née de père et de mère inconnus dans un creux de l'humide et vieille Constantine" [I was born of unknown parents in a corner of old, humid Constantine].[16]

Lack of family and social ties allows her access to spaces not often frequented by women. Yet at what price? As she transgresses the highly masculinized sphere of the maquis, she is forced to do away with every feminine characteristic that could mark her as weak (as a woman). She shaves her head and becomes physically androgynous, preferring to "ressembler à un authentique pirate des montagnes" [resemble an authentic pirate of the mountains], so that she will easily integrate into the maquis' camp high in the Aurès mountains.[17] Once she wipes away her feminine attributes, she more easily is accepted into the realm of the male maquis. These men become her family: "Là, sur une frontière morte . . . je rencontrai des frères venus de tous les coins d'Algérie, des frères venus d'outre-mer tuer l'oppression. Là, j'avais épousé mon peuple" [There on a dead frontier. . . . I met brothers who had come from all corners of Algeria, brothers from abroad who came to kill oppression].[18] This larger, extended male family, found in the mountains, is made up of Salah (a young, wounded twelve-year-old boy), old Kouider (the patriarch of the group, who has already survived World War II, fighting the Germans for the "colons"), and several assistants who help take care of the maimed and dying, hidden away in a cave in the high mountains. Although, in the beginning, the heroine plays the role of a man, often fighting outside the cave, she is quickly relegated to performing more nurturing, feminine tasks which include taking care of the wounded, hidden inside the cavern.

The heroine masks her femininity, supposedly helping to create an androgynous space inside the cave. However, ironically, the cavern becomes a metaphorical (almost mythical) uterus that is sometimes a generator of life, or a space in which life lingers in its last moments. In the cave, the young woman remarks that its occupiers "vie en dehors du temps . . . sans fiche d'état civil, sans nom, sans prénom" [live outside time . . . without national identity papers, without family or first names].[19] The cave is where she "vivais clandestinement sous terre. J'étais un hors-la-loi" [clandestinely lives underground. I was an outlaw].[20] It is in this peripheral, marginalized space, devoid of real time, where individual identity is obliterated as a result of the horrors associated with war, death, and madness. As a uterine symbol, this cavern also plays a role in providing a place where, although human death is ever present, life is occasionally brought forth. Within the cave, the young heroine meets her future husband, Arris. In the expanse of two paragraphs, she marries and loses him, claiming he "mourut de ses blessures" [died from his wounds].[21] Some moments of pleasure terminate in death and war. Yet from this brief liaison she becomes pregnant. The cave provides a milieu from which she enters a new phase of her life and her identity: motherhood. She alone establishes family ties through a son to whom she gives the name Arris (both the first name of her dead husband as well as the name of the village of the maquis). On a symbolic note, the protagonist becomes a contributor to the new, larger family of the national Algerian community on the eve of Algerian independence. Unique in its composition, her family is one formed by her own volition and not held accountable to patriarchal regimes and the family names of men. Mechakra's family is founded on matriarchy, a new alternative she recommends for the burgeoning Algerian nation: "L'enfant qui va naître aura un nom; il aura une place parmi nous: c'est le fruit d'une prostitution légale. [Mais aussi] [m]on enfant n'aura pas de nom: j'ignore le nom de son père qui, aux yeux des autres, justifiera mon existence. Mon enfant aura droit aux rêves de sa mère" [The child who will be born will have a name; he'll have a place among us: he is the fruit of legal prostitution. (But also) (m)y child will not have a name: I don't know the surname of his father who, in the eyes of others, will justify my existence. My child will have the right to his mother's dreams].[22]

Her husband's death is followed by the explosion of the cave by French troops.[23] From the shattered cave, the young heroine and her son emerge, wounded but alive. All other maquis who were with her are killed. Here, Mechakra reveals a symbol not only for the renaissance of her heroine but also for hope for a new kind of family for her liberated country. The mother-son link, divested of masculine presence, posits a new utopian conception of the idea of a mother-nation, cleansed of the colonization and patriarchal traditionalism that relegated women to a milieu devoid of speech and agency. Nonetheless, on a more negative note, the price of this utopia has been enormous. In a Tunisian psychiatric hospital, the young heroine slips in and out of madness. Her son was blinded by the attack and she has lost an arm. Insanity offers a temporary refuge from the war and allows the heroine to "leave a world that has become insane with violence and death."[24]

In addition to the author's unusual mother-son dyad, which proposes a new view of motherhood, as well as a new family dynamic, Mechakra's novel offers insight into the "family-State" symbol which is (and was in 1962) the foundation of the Algerian Republic. The revolution, as well as the Marxist ideology (posited immediately afterward by the FLN in an effort to build a new egalitarian society), theoretically should have changed the status of Algerian women. Psychologically, during the conflict, Algerians experienced a transformation with respect to traditional relationships between men and women. For the first time in Algerian history, both fought side by side for the same thing: Liberty. However, as Marnia Lazreg writes in her study *The Eloquence of Silence: Algerian Women in Question*:

> [m]ore than men, [women's] participation in the war entailed greater personal sacrifices and dangers . . . [because] women risked loss of the protection and safety of their homes and families and the possibility of good marriage and family life . . . [as well as] the omnipresent danger of rape.[25]

Simultaneously, the struggle for independence in Algeria also generated a movement for feminine emancipation. For a fleeting moment, Algerian women hoped that this evolution would bring about profound changes in societal mores (certainly on an ideological level) and eventually furnish the basis for a new, postcolonial, egalitarian society. Unfortunately, as the end of the war drew nearer, the Front de la Libération Nationale's rhetoric became increasingly masculinized.

The FLN's reliance on phallocratic ideology as well as its increasing alliances with the powerful *ulemas* (ultra-Islamists) divided men and women on many levels.[26] Certainly conceptualization of how the new nation would be formed and the roles that women, particularly, would take with regard to the nation and the state were constantly at the forefront of Algerian politics. Men and women had conflicting views on what nationalism and patriotism would mean for the budding country. In Algeria, as in other newly independent African countries, nationalist and patriotic ideologies took on different meanings according to which gender was considering them. Typically, nationalism is defined by the singular politics of a group which seeks to establish supreme authority on sovereign territory. Patriotism, on the other hand, is a sentiment shared by the people of a nation who seek to establish a community which is both social and political at the same time. In order to establish a new nation, it is necessary to have an equilibrium between these two concepts. The men and women of the FLN during the war knew that a mutual investment in these two ideologies would ensure not only a new brand of postcolonial politics, but also guarantee the loyalty of all toward Algerian culture and society. In her book *Sexuality and War*, Evelyn Accad remarks that the word "patriotism" is "intertwined with fe-

male and male images—*patria* as mother earth to whom loyalty is a con-
genital duty, *pater* as the father who commands loyalty at once gentle and
appropriate—while nationalism is a kind of imperialist ideology that im-
poses uniformity on geographic areas that may be infinitely extended."[27]

Throughout Mechakra's novel there are clear definitions made by the
characters in terms of their duties to the patria as a symbol of mother earth.
Both female and male ideologies mix within the generating space of the
cave—the inner sanctum of the earth mother. Unfortunately, at the end of
the novel, it is nationalism in the guise of a hyper-patriarchal framework
that wins out, supplanting the idea that attachment to the earth as a symbol for the foundation of a utopia would be equally profitable for men and
women. Nationalist patriarchy in the end provides the rhetoric and the ideology for recapturing lost identity. Nationalism and state building became
the exclusive affair of men, upheld by the need to harmonize and unify Algerian culture and society into a strong, nation-state. French historian
Gérard Noiriel explains that a true, strong state exerts "power over a space
that coincides with the limits of national territory and therefore affect[s] the
population living within those boundaries . . . the state intervenes in nation
formation essentially by destroying traditional oral cultures through indus-
trialization and replacing them with a centralized, written culture spread
throughout the national territory."[28]

Where women thought that they had fought (in the name of patriotism,
the love of country) to restore and heal the lands of Algeria (the colonial-
raped mother earth—*terre-mère*), the FLN countered by increasingly favoring a more masculinized Marxist politics to found its new political system.
This system allowed no place for nostalgic references to tribal lands or pro-
visos for the birth of new women's roles in postcolonial society. The postcolonial Algerian state would be built through a "bond that unites members
of a national community [in order to form] collective representations." The
principal strength of the new Algerian state would rely on this state being
"seen as the agent that creates and spreads national images and symbols."[29]
Unity among the Algerian people became the principal rallying point of FLN
ideology, thus renouncing any possibility of individualism and recourse to
individual family/tribal ties with the land. At the heart of FLN ideology, Algerian land is reconquered, but traditionalism is refashioned as a means only
to found a collective identity lost under French colonial occupation. Concerning this ideology, which promoted only one view of nationhood and
revolution, that of a national, collective identity, Benjamin Stora writes,

[it was important] to drain all convictions . . . putting off particular interests for
later. This conception of a unified society, "guided" by a unique party, fostered
a particular vision of the nation. After independence, an undecomposable
block, the nation is seen as a solid and unified entity.[30]

Algerian nationalism at the end of the war, and henceforth, would be linked to symbolic family traditionalism wherein men and women would have specific roles determined by gender in order to uphold the larger national goals which stipulate "the restoration of the sovereign, democratic, and social Algerian state within the framework of Islamic principles."[31] There is no place within this schemata for claims to equality or individual attachment to the land (*patria*—mother earth) as the only foundation of the new society. Women thought they had fought for change in their social status not only in terms of the nation but also within family and tribal organizations. Unfortunately, their claims to the land, to new social structures, and to equality were lost, as Marnia Lazreg maintains: the "language of the revolution that extolled the woman fighter who became 'free' the moment she joined the movement gave way to the language of immutable gender inequality."[32] Women's agency, thus, was "managed" by the FLN-Marxist-nationalist power structure. As Anne McClintock states, in the case of Algerian women freedom fighters: "Feminist agency . . . [was] contained by and subordinated to nationalist agency."[33]

In Mechakra's work, repudiation of the phallo/autocratic FLN rhetoric in favor of an individual woman's quest to bond with her land is most evident. Her propensity for equality, as well as loyalty to the pater and devotion to the patria, is continually noticeable throughout the novel. For the heroine, love of *la terre* is the only genitor possible for a new Algerian family as well as a new political system for the nation. Devotion to mother earth and fatherland are contained in the eternal confusion centered around the word "Arris." ARRIS (written in capital letters) refers to a village high in the Aurès mountains. The heroine shares a particular bond with the village since it is a magical place to which she will go once independence has been won: "Quand viendra l'indépendance, nous nous irons là-bas à ARRIS" [When independence comes, we will go there, to ARRIS], she tells her son:[34]

> Je murmurerai ta chanson, Arris, à notre fils quand il aura tes yeux pour me comprendre et mes lèvres pour te nommer. Je vieillirai, mon amour à l'ombre de ta mémoire et sur chaque ride jaillissant de mon corps, j'inscrirai ton nom et ma jeunesse. Arris, mon amour, aujourd'hui charogne puante et que j'aime, demain terre riche en phosphore où danse un feu follet.
>
> [I will whisper your song, Arris, to our son when he has your eyes to understand me with, and my lips to name you. I will grow old, my love, in the shadow of your memory and on each wrinkle sprouting forth from my body, I will inscribe your name and my youth. Arris, my love, today a beloved stinking carcass, tomorrow earth rich in phosphorous where a will-o'-the-wisp will dance].[35]

In these paragraphs, "patria" (the love of mother earth, the homeland) and "pater" (the love of son, father, heritage, family, and national identity) are unified in an ideology that links the protagonist to a man, the land, and the nation. For Yamina Mechakra, the new Algerian people will be born from the land, tribe, and family and from the new Algerian nation: "Arris, mon fils, tu étais ma révolte. A toi aujourd'hui mon enfant. Je dis ton père mort, sur ses lèvres mon amour. . . . Je dis ARRIS mon pays et ses moissons/AR-RIS mes ancêtres et mon honneur/ARRIS mon amour et ma demeure" [Ar-ris, my son, you were my revolt. To you, today, my child. I pronounce your dead father, on his lips my love. . . . I say ARRIS my country and its har-vests/ARRIS my ancestors and my honor/ARRIS my love and my home].[36]

The author notes that ancient, tribal family values, as well as those of the new Marxist state, must coexist in harmony in order to ensure the well-being of postcolonial Algeria as well as the women who are its citizens. The attachment to both the land and the nation is, for the protagonist, as well as for the author, the only solution for founding an equilibrium for the country after more than a hundred years of colonialism and eight years of war (both displaced tribes, decimated villages, and scattered thousands of people). Al-gerian independence for Mechakra must be more than the politics of the FLN. A true, new nation must be conceived by men and women who will work to build a utopia. At the end of the story, in the wake of independence, the wounded heroine, holding her blind son, leaves the Tunisian mental hospital where she has convalesced. She has no possessions and is left abandoned and alone on 4 June 1962. She returns to the Algerian-Tunisian border, stop-ping at ARRIS. Taking off her shoes, she walks on the scorched, rocky earth, symbolically rooting herself on and within Algeria:

Je laissai tomber mon bras puis je me déchaussais. De mes pieds couverts de cratères du napalm, mes pieds nus et carbonisés, je foulai avec douceur la terre brûlante de mon pays. Je fis un pas, puis un autre, puis encore un autre. Les cail-loux me déchiraient la peau, les ronces m'égratignaient, j'eus soif, j'eus mal à la tête et m'évanouis.

[I let my arm fall and then took off my shoes. With my feet covered in craters of na-palm, my naked and charred feet, I walked softly upon the scorched earth of my country. I took a step, and then another, and then still another. The rocks shredded my skin, the brambles scratched me, I was thirsty, I had a headache and I fainted].[37]

On the edge of the frontier of Algeria she finds her peace and her identity. A lone tree marks the place of the exploded cave where she lost her friends, comrades, and husband. The freestanding tree "était l'unique quelque chose qui avait poussé dans ma mémoire quand ma grotte mou-rut, il était l'unique quelque chose qui me parlât encore de mes amis" [was the only single thing that had grown in my memory when I was in my dy-ing cave, it was the only single thing that still spoke to me of my friends].[38] On this tree she hangs her belt, reminding the knowledgeable reader of the Algerian women's tradition of hanging a belt on a sacred tree in order to bring forth life, to give birth. As scholar Zineb Ali-Benali points out in her article on Mechakra's work, this ritual allows a woman to "make a pact with underground forces, germinating forces. She will come back, at the birth of a child, to manifest her recognition of the forces of Nature. She will bring food which will be shared and eaten under the tree."[39] This pact links woman, nature, and birth in an all-encompassing harmony that cannot be broken. As she hangs her belt on the tree, this nameless heroine at last, symbolically, roots herself in the post-independence destiny of Algeria.

Within the schemata of patria-pater-motherhood and war, Mechakra's work becomes more than a war journal; it is a testament to women who founded their Algerian identity in the land and not the rhetoric of nationalist ideology which, in the end, rewarded them with very little. The author pays homage to a woman who had to fight like a man on the bloody battlefields of revolution. Her vision encompassed the creation of a utopia that would redefine the ideology of nationhood, motherhood, and feminine identity for Algerian women. She, like so many Algerian women who fought for freedom, asks "Nous avons l'indépendance, mais que reste-t-il de moi?" [We have independence, but what is left of me?].[40]

ET POURTANT LE CIEL ÉTAIT BLEU

Tunisian Hajer Djilani's first novel presents a woman in a strong central role.[41] The work also posits the larger political conflicts of the Gulf War, the effects of violence and bloodshed on the heroine, and deep-seated sociocultural beliefs that are often detrimental to women's independence in traditional Islamic societies. Djilani's 1994 work examines Arab/Muslim-Western relationships, studies the contentions of international politics between East and West, and exposes the internal oppositions among the Iraqi people. Djilani's literary voice not only engages the questions centered around women's roles in war, it also postulates some very interesting, more global questions that concern Arab-Islamic politics in general and how women's identity is defined within them. The author's novel is little known, but truly fosters a platform for women's agency in the Maghreb and, indeed, throughout the Muslim world.[42] Like Mechakra, Djilani seeks to determine if, through war, women can connect with a deeper sense of their selves as well as their sexuality. Can, out of the madness of war, women find emancipated identity? Are sexuality and war, as Evelyn Accad suggests, "indissolubly linked," and does the intersection of the two lead women to better understand themselves in relation to "nationalism, feminism, violence, love, and power as they relate to the body, the partner, the family . . . religion, and pacifism [?]"[43] Considering both Mechakra and Djilani's novels in terms of these topics and within the realm of Mudimbé-Boyi's "unsayable" as a metaphor for the female condition, I propose that the madness of war for these heroines becomes the impetus for their own truer sense of their identities. Through violence, these protagonists find a manner to express a new form of feminine existence, or as Juliette Flower Maccannell contends, a *feminine essence*. Like Mechakra's heroine, at the end of her novel, Djilani's Chems perseveres with her sanity and her body intact. The author leaves her heroine metaphorically on the edge of a new conception of womanhood that she would never have experienced if she had not encountered changes in herself (made out of necessity) due to witnessing war and death.

The events surrounding the Gulf War are reviewed through the eyes of the heroine who feels compelled to act to counter the ongoing suffering in Iraq in 1991. The young woman uproots herself from Tunis in order to fly to Baghdad as a member of a team of Tunisian doctors offering humanitarian medical aid. The story is told through both Chems' personal journal entries and letters to her family. The third person voice of the author also contributes to the weaving of an intricate dialogue that reflects the personal relationships between the characters, as well as political commentary on the actions of Iraq and, more generally, on the state of politics in the Arab world. Underlying these three important textual layers are the author's subtle views on the status of Muslim women, primarily in Iraq. As she implies, women bear the brunt of the horrors of war, famine, death, and poverty. In times of war, they and their children are the most vulnerable, as Accad notes:

Most of the police, most of the prison wardens, and most all the generals, admirals, bureaucrats and politicians who control the apparatus of coercion and collective violence are men. . . . Violence is not just an expression; it is a part of the process that divides different masculinities from each other. There is violence within masculinity; it is constitutive.[44]

Chems, like the author who invents her character, does not take sides in the political conflict. Like the government of her native country, Tunisia, she remains neutral throughout the novel.[45] The young woman's sole aim is to offer her medical training as a humanitarian gesture to the people of Iraq who are the constant targets of indiscriminate bombs and gunfire. Her direct confrontation with the war force her to question the actions of humanity as a whole. Chems' desire to fathom incomprehensible acts of violence is aligned with her own quest of self-knowledge. It is her aspiration to answer these questions that activates her decision to remain in Iraq and travel still closer to the front lines of the war, long after her Tunisian colleagues decide to abandon their efforts because of the escalating danger. Her personal quest for self-knowledge coincides with her efforts to reconcile the absurdity of the conflict with her own place in the world as a woman, doctor, and member of the Muslim world; "en tant que femme et sur cette terre qui a vu jaillir en l'homme l'étincelle de sa grandeur et de sa permanence . . . j'espère qu'un jour le monde abolira la violence, la mort de l'homme par l'homme, la mort de l'enfant, la mort de l'innocence" [as a woman and person on this earth who has seen gush forth from man the spark of his grandeur. . . . I hope that one day the world will abolish violence . . . the death of man by man, the death of children, the death of innocence].[46]

It is the insanity and senselessness of war, Chems' headlong flight directly into it, and her efforts to combat its destruction that jettison all the past taboos and restrictions she has been taught. She, like Mechakra's heroine, is left with a tabula rasa on which to construct a new place "a-centered" from what is normally acceptable: "Elle court vers ce lieu, les tabous sont abolis, les interdits ont explosé à la mesure des bombes" [She runs towards this place, the taboos are forgotten, the forbidden exploded like bombs]."[47] It is this propulsion into an uncharted space ruled by horror, pain, and suffering as well as self-discovery that allows Chems to explore her own inner self, love, and the power of loving a man she has only just met: "Elle court vers la chambre d'un homme qu'elle connaît à peine, elle, dont les parents se sont vus pour la première fois le soir des noces" [She runs toward the room of a man she hardly knows, she, whose parents saw each other for the first time on their wedding night].[48] Salah is an Iraqi doctor who is disdainful of war and, like Chems, seeks only the good for humanity as a whole.[49] As she falls more and more in love with him, Chems realizes that she must reach a place of peace in order to love and be loved. This place lies beyond the borders of conflict and does not contain any rules of convention. However, it is a space where she and Salah must mediate their differences. Even though they speak the same language, they are worlds apart. Salah, already widowed once (his pregnant wife, Mériam, was the victim of a bomb), hesitates to embrace love, which Chems offers him. However, each realizes it is precisely this space of turmoil—of war, bombs, and destitution—that draws them together, allowing them to mediate their differences and their pasts. Chems writes in her journal that existing only for the present makes it easier to require no tradition, no past, and no sense of future in order to survive. Her path is left open for union with Salah as war and the sexual consent of the two lovers create an equilibrium in which they enjoy no boundaries and no preconditions: "Si le bonheur existe, il a le goût de ce matin. . . . Pardon ma mère, pour les tabous volés en éclats, j'ai fait offrande à Salah de ce que j'avais de plus cher, j'ai fait offrande à Salah de ma vie" [If happiness exists, it tastes like this morning. . . . Mother please forgive me for the stolen taboos, I offered to Salah the most dear thing I have, I offered Salah my life]."[50]

Within their space of freedom there are no restrictions, but there are also many hindrances. Chems becomes pregnant by Salah, thus complicating her situation and her work. Their equilibrium becomes tenuous and fragile. It is eventually shattered when the heroine becomes a victim of the war. Hurtling herself upon a child in order to shield him from an exploding bomb, Chems is severely wounded; "Le tireur ne l'a pas ratée. Sur le bitume défoncé et poussièreux, elle gît, corolle blanche, les yeux mi-clos, un sourire aux lèvres, une tache rouge lentement colore sa blouse, pourtant, le ciel était bleu!" [The sniper didn't miss. On the dusty, warped asphalt, she was hit, a white corolla, eyes half closed, a smile on her lips, a red stain slowly coloring her shirt, yet, the sky was so blue].[51] Paralyzed by the fear that Chems will die on the operating table, Salah asks his close friend Farès to save her. The bullet is successfully removed and she lives. She is a heroine and a saint for the village people, particularly for the women whom she has struggled to save from death, even at the cost of risking her own life. Despite her and Salah's renown for their healing capacities, and although they are supported wholeheartedly and held in esteem as "miracle workers" by the villagers, the doctors are asked to leave by the Iraqi military which finds their popularity too disruptive. The villagers, who demand to know Chems' health status, threaten to storm the hospital in order to catch a glimpse of her and thus be reassured of her continuation among them. Nevertheless, because she is not Iraqi, she is forced to leave by Iraqi officials' pressure to expel foreigners, despite Salah's protests. They hastily marry before she sets out in an ambulance for Baghdad. Once again, Chems takes flight, leaving one place of territorialization for another. In her last journal entry, on 5 April 1991, as she leaves for Tunis, she writes to Salah, who stays, "Ma vie, c'est toi [My life is yours]."[52] Out of the pain, suffering, and the madness of war she has endured, caught up as both player and victim of the Gulf conflict, she discovers a self she has never known. Although the fate of her relationship with Salah is left in ambiguity, at the end of her journey Chems has found the key to her question "Qui suis-je?" Who am I? She discovers the answer in the very multiplicity of her being as she completes her long journey from Tunis to Iraq back to Tunis. Despite her separation from her lover, the novel ends on a positive note. Chems finds, as she closes this long nomadic circle through the insanity of war, that her true self is not rooted in a single, stagnant persona, but is one that is manifold: woman, doctor, lover, wife, mother, and survivor. Like Mechakra, Djilani roots her story in the perseverance of womanhood.

NOTES

1. A version of this section on Hajer Djilani's novel first appeared in my book *Nomadic Voices of Exile: Feminine Identity in Francophone Literature of the Maghreb* (Athens: Ohio University Press, 1999). See pages 189–204.

2. Zineb Ali-Benali "Dires de la folie: dires de la liberté. Discours de la folie dans la littérature des femmes en Algérie," *Bulletin of Francophone Africa* 7 (spring 1995): 9–25, 9.

3. Frantz Fanon, *A Dying Colonialism* (New York: Grove Press, 1965), 52.

4. Hajer Djilani, *Et pourtant le ciel était bleu. . . . Roman* (Sidi Bou Saïd, Tunisia: Editions Techniques Spécialisées, 1994), 67.

5. Djilani, *Le ciel était bleu*, 67.

6. Marie-Blanche Tahon, "Women Novelists and Women in the Struggle for Algeria's National Liberation (1957–1980)," *Research in African Literatures* 2 (summer 1992): 39–49, 39.

7. Tahon, "Women Novelists," 40.

8. Marnia Lazreg, *The Eloquence of Silence: Algerian Women in Question* (New York: Routledge, 1994), 130.

9. Fanon, *Colonialism*, 59.

10. Lazreg, *Eloquence of Silence*, 119.

11. Mechakra published a second novel in 1999 entitled *Arris* (Paris: Marsa Editions). This second work is a continuation of *La Grotte éclatée,* delving further into the story of the mother and child dyad of her first novel. There is very little information available on Mechakra's life. She was born in 1950 and, in 1973, began writing *La Grotte eclatée* while a student of psychiatry at the university of Algiers. In Algiers she met Kateb Yacine before leaving for Rome and Paris. According to an article in French on the Internet, in 1997 Mechakra (a practicing psychiatrist at the time), while treating a young boy, was inspired by her notes kept on his status to begin working on *Arris*, the name of the heroine-mother's son in *La Grotte éclatée*. (See Rachid Mokhtari's article "Yamina Mechakra," www.lematin-dz.com/les_gens/yamina_mechakra.htm).

12. Kateb Yacine's preface "Les Enfants de la Kahina" to Yamina Mechakra's *La Grotte Eclatée* (Algiers: Editions SNED, 1979), 7.

13. In a coup d'état in 1965, Houari Boumediene deposed Ahmed Ben Bella. Boumediene constructed a new government which he led until his death from a rare blood disorder in 1978.

14. Yamina Mechakra, *La Grotte éclatée*, 33. All translations of Mechakra's novel are my own.

15. Mechakra, *La Grotte éclatée*, 34.

16. Mechakra, *La Grotte éclatée*, 29.

17. Mechakra, *La Grotte éclatée*, 26.

18. Mechakra, *La Grotte éclatée*, 29.

19. Mechakra, *La Grotte éclatée*, 34.

20. Mechakra, *La Grotte éclatée*, 34.

21. Mechakra, *La Grotte éclatée*, 69.

22. Mechakra, *La Grotte éclatée*, 69–70.

23. Mechakra's description of French troops exploding the cave is reminiscent of the "enfumades" carried out by the French armies of the 1830s during the conquest of Algeria. Reference to these horrid acts occurs in several places in the novel. "Des jeunes filles, la peau noircie de charbon, ne rient plus à Guelma" [young girls, with carbon blackened skin, do not laugh anymore at Guelma] (112), is but one example. In the 1830s, as General Bugeaud's troops hunted down Algerians and massacred hundreds in villages across Algeria, people fled to caves in the Aurès mountains. In order to eradicate these people, the French army would either smoke them out in order to massacre them or burn them alive in the caves.

24. Zineb Ali-Benali, "Dires de la folie: dires de la liberté. Discours de la folie dans la littérature des femmes en Algérie," *Bulletin of Francophone Africa* 7 (1995): 9–25, 14–15.

25. Lazreg, *Eloquence of Silence*, 119.

26. It should be noted that, at the outset, the FLN sought to form a government based on a "Western ideology of socialism as the engine for rapid development," however, the Islamists had always been highly organized and repeatedly forced their way into government policy making (Martin Stone, *The Agony of Algeria* [New York: Columbia University Press, 1997], 148–150).

27. Evelyn Accad, *Sexuality and War: Literary Masks of the Middle East* (New York: New York University Press, 1990), 15.

28. Gérard Noiriel, *The French Melting Pot: Immigration, Citizenship, and National Identity* (Minneapolis: University of Minnesota Press, 1996), xvi.

29. Noiriel, *French Melting Pot*, xvi.

30. Benjamin Stora, *La Gangrène et l'oubli: La mémoire de la guerre d'Algérie* (Paris: La Découverte, 1991), 171. My translation.

31. John Ruedy, *Modern Algeria: The Origins and Development of a Nation* (Bloomington: Indiana University Press, 1992),159.

32. Lazreg, *Eloquence of Silence*, 132.

33. Anne McClintock, *Imperial Leather: Race, Gender, and Sexuality in the Colonial Contest* (New York: Routledge, 1995), 367.

34. Mechakra, *La Grotte éclatée*, 137.

35. Mechakra, *La Grotte éclatée*, 142.

36. Mechakra, *La Grotte éclatée*, 172.

37. Mechakra, *La Grotte éclatée*, 170.

38. Mechakra, *La Grotte éclatée*, 171.

39. Ali-Benali, *Dires de la folie*, 19.

40. Danièle Djamila Amrane-Minne, *Des Femmes dans la guerre d'Algérie* (Paris: Editions Karthala, 1994), 108.

41. Parts of my analysis of Hajer Djilani's work *Et Pourtant le ciel était bleu . . .* appeared in my book *Nomadic Voices of Exile*, reprinted here with kind permission of the publisher.

42. To my knowledge, I am the only Francophone scholar to have written on Hajer Djilani's works (she has written two: *Hamza*, 1996, and this one). I first met the author in 1997 at the Colloque International: Le Maghreb à la croisée des cultures held in Hammamet, Tunisia, 15–21 June 1997.

43. Evelyn Accad, *Sexuality and War*, 2–3.

44. Accad, *Sexuality and War*, 32.

45. Although Tunisia upheld the general resolutions of the League of Arab Nations' Convention 3 August 1990 held in Cairo to condemn the "Iraqi aggression" against Kuwait and the immediate withdrawal of Iraqi troops from the area, the Tunisian government refused to support foreign intervention and declined any involvement of its own military forces. This policy was supported by President Zine El Abidine Ben Ali's "Address to the Tunisian People at Carthage," 11 August 1990 wherein he stated: "Tunisia, both as a State and as a people, enjoying excellent relations with both Iraq and Kuwait, and in view of her national and historical duty, refuses to ratify *faits accomplis* or side with one party or another" (*Tunisia and the Gulf Crisis: A Constant Commitment to International Legality*, a collection of speeches and *Acts on the Gulf War* published by the Tunisian government (Tunis:1990: 68–69).

46. Djilani, *Le ciel était bleu*, 265. All translations of Djilani's novel are my own.

47. Djilani, *Le ciel était bleu*, 67.
48. Djilani, *Le ciel était bleu*, 67.
49. Djilani, *Le ciel était bleu*, 101.
50. Djilani, *Le ciel était bleu*, 181.
51. Djilani, *Le ciel était bleu*, 289.
52. Djilani, *Le ciel était bleu*, 330.

7

Feminine Voices and H(er)stories

Simone Schwarz-Bart's *Pluie et Vent sur
Télumée Miracle* and Aminata Sow Fall's
Douceurs du bercail

> Today more than ever, changing our minds—changing the mind—is a
> woman's prerogative.
>
> —Shoshana Felman, *Women and Madness* (1991)

Guadeloupian Simone Schwarz-Bart's 1972 novel *Pluie et vent sur Télumée
Miracle* and Senegalese Aminata Sow Fall's work *Douceurs du bercail*
(1998), although written by women from different regions of the francophone world, share many similarities. Both novels pay homage to women
who have endured hardships and hurdles and who have at last made peace
with their own identities as well as with the environments in which they
live. I choose to analyze these two novels at the end of my study as proof
that women can fall into pits of insanity and still crawl out in order to survive and persevere, eventually constructing an environment more favorable
to their well-being than what they knew before. These are stories wherein
the heroines come to terms with the complications associated with being female in traditional cultures. They also seek to address questions about their
own feminine identity with regard to their larger communities. In the end,
after a series of arduous sacrifices, these heroines are able to locate and
profit from a rich sense of spirituality that enhances their own lives as well
as those of others.

As critics of their own societies, who constantly seek ways to improve
women's futures, these authors' heroines—Télumée (*Pluie et vent*) and Asta
(*Douceurs*)—reflect on the female condition within the whole of humanity.
Both Schwarz-Bart and Sow Fall seek to build more fruitful relationships
with their cultures as women and individualists, while striving to understand

their own identities as housed within contemporary humanity. Although the novelists are from different backgrounds, there are many similarities in the feminine voices that explore the abject realms of madness, racism, xenophobia, and death. Indeed, as these novels demonstrate, out of abjection is born a feminine resolve to create a better society for both women and men. This volition, as Télumée remarks, leads women to convince themselves to "ride the horse, and not let it ride [them]," a frequent maxim throughout Schwarz-Bart's novel. It is evident in both works that each author endeavors to flush out a "fresh vision of humanity" that will allow their heroines to find an inner peace.[1] Both Télumée's and Asta's recognition of the unique singularity of their individual Selves is achieved through their relationships with others and their realization of the importance of "a much larger, collective identity" in their own lives.[2] This investment into the collective—the greater good—particularly evident in Schwarz-Bart's and Sow Fall's writing, also indicates a growing trend among the younger generations of francophone women authors to search for feminine identity beyond postcolonial issues on which earlier writers concentrated. As Nicki Hitchcott observes: "Sometimes violent, sometimes lyrical, the texts [of contemporary francophone women authors] mix registers as well as genres, moving away from . . . univocal autobiographical narratives [to create] a multiplicity of voices that reflect the multifaceted nature of African female subjectivity."[3] This subjectivity demands to know and seeks answers to the question, Where are we going and how will we get there?

PLUIE ET VENT SUR TÉLUMÉE MIRACLE

Few contemporary francophone novelists have attained the poetic beauty and facility of blending the surreal with the real and the historical with the mythical as has Simone Schwarz-Bart. *Pluie et vent sur Télumée Miracle* is the author's first novel after *Un Plat de porc aux bananes vertes* (1967), coauthored with her husband, the well-known French author André Schwarz-Bart. *Pluie et vent* traces three generations of women of the Lougandor family and their struggles to survive on the island of Guadeloupe sometime between the nineteenth and twentieth centuries. Each generation suffers from the memories of slavery and the realities of poverty endured by the black population on the island. Heartache, violence, death as well as the "legacy of humiliation" of the cane fields are constant denominators in the lives of Minerva, great-grandmother and matriarch, Télumée's grandmother Toussine, known as "Queen without a Name," Victory, who eventually abandons her daughter, and Télumée, the main voice of the novel.[4]

In Schwarz-Bart's world the "search for identity [is] both personal and collective":[5] personal in the sense that Télumée must constantly redefine who she is as men in her life fail her, poverty wields its head at every turn, and starvation, violence, and death are forever at her door, and collective because identity is also very much a part of the heroine's as well as the author's own self-searching, prompting both to ask the ever present question: How do "peoples uprooted from traditional communities and forced into exile and slavery" come to terms with their lost origins in order to, hopefully, one day redefine their identity?[6]

This Guadeloupian author's novel, for the past twenty-two years, has continually been hailed as one of the most beautiful and poetic in the francophone canon. Scholars have analyzed the work's many themes and scrutinized its text in the classroom to the delight of students of francophone literature who find the novel rewarding to read on many levels.[7] The plethora of scholarly articles on all of Schwarz-Bart's novels and plays attest to the rich thematic elements contained within them that are incessantly being discovered. Indeed, one is overcome by the variety of contexts in which to analyze *Pluie et vent*. However, I feel the most relevant aspect of the novel for the study at hand here is, again, how the heroine is able to overcome the servile spaces that constantly threaten her and which are often lodged in the dark recesses of insanity. Télumée is marked by a particular historical, collective madness that the author contends is inherent in the West Indian environment and forever ready to terrorize all who live there (women as well as men): "Lorsque, durant les longs jours bleus et chauds, la folie antillaise se met à tournoyer dans l'air au-dessus des bourgs, des mornes et des plateaux, une angoisse s'empare des hommes à l'idée de la fatalité qui plane au-dessus d'eux" [When, in the long hot blue days, the madness of the West Indies starts to swirl around in the air above the villages, bluffs, and plateaus, men are seized with dread at the thought of the fate hovering over them].[8] The madness which is caught up in the fate of many, the heroine notes, is housed both in the realms of the real and imaginary. Some succumb and are caught in its talons, and others, like Télumée, find the knowledge to identify the three paths that will adversely influence their lives if they embark down them: "voir la beauté du monde, et dire qu'il est laid, se lever de grand matin pour faire ce dont on est incapable, et donner libre cours à ses songes" [to see beauty of the world and call it ugly, to get up early to do what is impossible, and to let oneself get carried away by dreams].[9] The author's primary message is that life is always ready to engulf a woman in insanity and she must be ready to confront it and to know that "le cheval ne doit pas te conduire, c'est toi qui dois conduire le cheval" [the horse mustn't ride you, you must ride it], as Télumée remarks on numerous occasions.[10] Schwarz-Bart's novel is an odyssey which recounts the perseverence of the women of the Lougandor family who, as Maryse Condé contends, possess a "grand superiority . . . that resides in their capacity to withstand sadness, madness and the absurdity of the world without giving up."[11]

Where is madness located? Schwarz-Bart tells us that it is continually present in both real and unreal milieus of island life. Place-names, for example, are no-man's lands representing loss of identity, of self, and of spiritual hope. Fond-Zombi (meaning literarily Zombi depths), La Folie (madness), and L'Abandonnée (the Abandoned) are the names of the rural villages which house the former slaves of Guadeloupe who are so destitute they call themselves "la confrérie des Déplacés" [the Brotherhood of the Displaced]. These people live in constant uncertainty and are disparaged the knowledge that their destinies are ominous and foreboding.[12] The villages of Schwarz-Bart's novel are the places where "the dishonor and physical and spiritual displacement suffered by [Télumée's] ancestors leave psychological and social scars and interiorized, but no less damaging, shackles."[13] These pitiful spaces are historically linked to murder and violence. They are synonymous with slavery, a legacy that constantly haunts the protagonist even after its disappearance (at least officially) from the islands. Yet, although the white man's plantations are no more, the author tells us that slavery is still manifest in many forms. Despite the disappearance of white slave owners on the island, the heroine still feels the weight of slavery's legacy in Guadeloupian society, particularly in the cane fields (now owned by white corporations) which remain like vast wounds on the island's surface. The fields continually engulf those who are forced to work in them. Although workers work for wages, the effects of the cane are the same: broken backs and despair that are relieved only in rum and absinthe. Slavery thus is still a yoke around the necks of the people of the island: "Savons-nous ce que nous charrions dans nos veines, nous les nègres de Guadeloupe? . . . la malédiction qu'il faut pour être maître, et celle qu'il faut pour être esclave" [Do we know what we carry in our veins, we Negroes of Guadeloupe—the curse of being a master, the curse of being a slave].[14] Can one shed the yoke, the burden of so many years of history—a history that seems to repeat itself? On several occasions Télumée feels that she cannot escape this burden she defines as inescapable, her precipice. It is something inevitable, that is approaching. The cane fields and the slavery associated with them are part of not only her people's history, but her own as well; it is a legacy that will repeat and not go away.[15] The cane fields wait for her like an abyss opening up to nowhere, a *Beyond* that holds no positive future if she cannot redefine her identity and overcome the legacy of enslavement still present on her island. Schwarz-Bart, here, draws on the history of the "plantation [as] prima facie evidence . . . the fundamental component in a history of exploitative relationships between the plantation and Carribean masses." The disdainful relationship Télumée endures with everything associated with the cane fields indicates that this place is still a "locus" of history that "denotes a recognition of the plantation as the crucible for the oppressive socio-political and economic structures that bind both men and women in a post-slavery plantation order."[16] Certainly, the most horrible psycho-historical scars still present among those of the island community in the novel are the cane fields in which Télumée refuses to work until circumstances force her to do so. To avoid the cane, she lives on wild fruit which makes her sick and gives her hallucinations.[17] When Télumée finally does go "into" the cane, this "heart of malediction," with the other "haggard ghosts" who work there, the fields psychologically take their toll on her.[18] The cane cutters' toil is excruciating, their arms and legs are torn by the cane prickles. It is because of the cane that Télumée temporarily loses her mind, slipping into a state where she runs aground, her "voilier s'était enlisé dans les sables" [ship had run into the sand].[19] An insanity like no other takes hold of her, pushing her toward a bestiality—*a becoming-animal*—that risks totally effacing her identity. As she "grovels" in the cane, she feels a transformation coming over her. She is now a beast, so altered that "la mère des hommes elle-même ne me reconnaîtrait plus" [even the mother of men wouldn't know me].[20] The cane fields for Télumée wrench away her identity and force her to accept what she defines as the "yoke"; the "affliction" of history which has always told slaves "voilà où un nègre doit se trouver" [this is where a Negro ought to be].[21]

Death in Schwarz-Bart's novel is synonymous with an impending void. The thin line between madness and death is constantly present within the communities of La Folie, Font-Zombie, and L'Abandonnée and still higher in the mountains where the "Égarés" [the Strayed]—those who have lost their souls—live. Within these high forests of Schwarz-Bart's novel is a middle space trapped between the living and dead. It is a space of metamorphosis, but where evil is still very strong.[22] In Télumée's own life this impending void opens up and threatens to engulf her. Darkness, the unknown, death all are synonymous with what lies on the other side of the "Bridge of Beyond"; a place that nearly takes the heroine's mind and life after she is beaten by her once beloved husband Elie, who subsequently leaves her for another woman:

> Et puis, parvenue au pont de l'Autre Bord, je me suis sentie lasse et me suis assise sur une motte de terre, tout contre la butée du pont, et j'ai pleuré. . . . Je n'ai pas le souvenir des jours qui suivirent. Je sus plus tard qu'on me vit assise sur une pierre, le lendemain matin. . . . Je restai là plusieurs semaines, sans bouger, ne distinguant même plus le jour d'avec la nuit. Reine Sans Nom me donnait à manger et me rentrait le soir venu. . . . Lorsqu'on me parlait je restais muette, et l'on disait que la parole m'était devenue la chose la plus étrangère du monde. Trois semaines s'écoulèrent ainsi. Pour ne pas faiblir devant moi, Reine Sans Nom partait pour la première fois lancer son chagrin en pleine rue . . . mon enfant, mon enfant, sa tête est partie, partie.
>
> [When I came to the Bridge of Beyond, I felt tired, and sat down on a mound by the support of the bridge and wept. . . . I have no memory of the days that

followed. I learned later that I was found next morning sitting on a stone. . . . I
stayed there several weeks without moving, no longer even able to tell day
from night. Queen Without a Name fed me and brought me in at night. . . .
When anyone spoke to me I was silent; they said that of all the things in the
world speech had become the most alien to me. Three weeks went by like this.
So as not to weaken in front of me, Queen Without a Name went, for the first
time, to speak her grief in the street: 'My child, my child, her mind has gone,
her mind has gone'].[23]

So intense is the draw of insanity, Télumée risks losing all tangible presence.
Her very sense of self begins to float away. Schwarz-Bart's lessons tell us that
loss of self is always a possibility when women give too much to others, particularly to men. As Elie beats Télumée more frequently because of his own
discontentment with life which he soaks in rum and then absinthe, she no-
tices slowly that "maintenant aucun fil ne reliait plus ma case aux autres
cases" [now there (was) no longer any thread linking my cabin to the others];
the marginalized violent world in which she lives with Elie has cut her off
from her community which before had always given her strength.[24] Her husband whittles away so much of her identity that she begins to fade:

je m'allongeais à même le sol et m'efforçais de dissoudre ma chair, je m'emplis-
sais de bulles et tout à coup je me sentais légère, une jambe m'abandonnait puis
un bras, ma tête et mon corps entier se dissipaient dans l'air et je planais, je sur-
volais Fond-Zombi de si haut qu'il ne m'apparaissait plus que comme un grain
de pollen dans l'espace.

[I would lie on the ground and try to dissolve my flesh: I would fill myself with
bubbles and suddenly go light—a leg would be no longer there, then an arm,
my head and whole body faded into the air, and I was floating so high over
Fond-Zombi it looked no bigger than a speck of pollen in space].[25]

Schwarz-Bart's recurring theme of the disappearance of identity threatens
Télumée with every relationship she has, forcing the heroine to realize that a
woman's effacement is always a possibility when she loves a man too much.
When a woman loves, she risks renouncing her identity forever, dispersing
her being into nothingness. Télumée's devotion to Elie causes the heroine an
almost total loss of selfhood, a becoming-imperceptible. Only at the very last
moment does she wake up to alter the destiny that seemingly was mapped
out for her by evil forces that haunt the island. She, in the end, does take her
horse by the reins. This glimpse, this quasi-entrance into the realm of nothingness where she almost lost her total physical presence, encourages
Télumée to start her life over, to obliterate all that Deleuze and Guattari define as "waste, death, and superfluity, complaint and grievance, unsatisfied
desire, defense or pleading, everything that roots each of us . . . in ourselves
. . . ."[26] Through perseverence, the heroine crosses the Bridge of Beyond to
the other side of imperceptibility in order to catch "the dawn of the world,"

and a new beginning.[27] Télumée's resolve to return from the abyss of madness is due to, she admits, the strong ties she has with her community:

> Ce qui me remit pour de bon, ce furent toutes ces visites, toutes les attentions et les petits présents dont on m'honora lorsque ma tête revint d'où elle était partie. La folie est une maladie contagieuse, aussi ma guérison était celle de tous et ma victoire, la preuve que le nègre a sept fiels et ne désarme pas comme ça, à la première alerte . . . ces rires, ces marques d'attention contribuaient à me remettre en selle, à me faire tenir en main les brides de mon cheval.
>
> [What really cured me were all the visits, all the attentions and little gifts people honored me with when my mind came back from wherever it had been. Madness is contagious, and so my cure was everyone's, and my victory the proof that a Negro has seven spleens and doesn't give up just like that at the first sign of trouble . . . this laughter, these marks of attention, helped to lift me back in the saddle, to hold my horse's bridle with a firm grip.][28]

Upon her emergence from madness the heroine realizes that, although she departed from her community for a while, when she returned the bonds that tie her with it are stronger than she had ever thought. Her house is linked to others in Font-Zombi like a "réseau d'une toile d'araignée, dont les fils se croisaient" [like a spider's web, with the threads intersecting].[29] From others, she draws her strength, perceiving that selfhood does not lie elsewhere but is, rather, rooted "in the human heart . . . [where there is no] supernatural Logos" but instead the power of a woman's will to overcome adversity and find the good that lies within humanity.[30] In the closing pages of the novel, Télumée alludes to the connections that link her not only to those of the island, but also to a larger human continuum: "Comme je me suis débattue, d'autres se débattront, et pour bien longtemps encore, les gens connaîtront même lune et même soleil, et ils regarderont les mêmes étoiles . . . je mourrai là, comme je suis, debout, dans mon petit jardin, quelle joie! . . ." [As I struggled others will struggle, and for a long time yet people will know the same sun and moon; they will look at the same stars. . . . I shall die here, where I am, standing in my little garden. What happiness!].[31] Out of the Brotherhood of the Displaced emerges a solid, rooted community, a small utopia in which the heroine finds hope for not only her own story, but those of others.

DOUCEURS DU BERCAIL

In 1976 Aminata Sow Fall[32] helped break the gender barrier in Senegal by publishing *Le Revenant*, the first major novel written in French by a Senegalese woman.[33] Sow Fall has been writing for over two decades. Her recent novel *Douceurs du bercail,* published in 1998, explores the situation of not only African women, but also a variety of sociocultural issues, the most important of which are the economic difficulties faced by the Senegalese people (particularly women) at home and the racism that is often waged against them in Europe.

Thematically, *Douceurs du bercail* is noteworthy for all of the issues raised above, however, the most significant is that it is Sow Fall's first novel promoting the concerns of women through a female protagonist. Up to the point of its publication, Sow Fall had been criticized for "the apparent absence of female perspective in texts that . . . seem to privilege the traditional point of view [of men]."[34] However, I contend that the author's dearth of feminine voices is due to her larger, more humanist agenda. Issues of consumerism, tensions between Europe and Africa, poverty, and the dehumanization of African peoples and people of color are what most concern the author. In an interview, Aminata Sow Fall remarks that "people are becoming dehumanized because of money," and it is this process of dehumanization that she wishes to address.[35] In view of her more global project to analyze questions and issues surrounding what the word "humanism" means, Sow Fall has rarely promoted purely feminist ideologies. Like many African women, the author has been suspicious of the word "feminism," at least in the European sense, and, on one occasion, was taken aback when placed in a feminist camp, exclaiming "Féministe? Moi?"[36] In conjunction with many of her counterparts, Sow Fall has recognized "the need to address the issues of exclusion, exploitation, and the multiple colonizations faced by women" in Africa rather than use of feminism as the only "productive ground for struggle" for women in her homeland.[37] Sow Fall is more genuinely interested in the failure of systems in contemporary Africa, be they political, cultural, and/or social,[38] and how these failures must be cured by a symbiosis of "political responsibility" between African leaders and the people they lead.[39] Therefore, Asta Diop, heroine of *Douceurs du bercail,* is not only a strong feminine archetype who stands by her responsibility to her country and her people, she is a critic of the myths that surround both Europe and Africa. These myths, she contends, have led people down paths of racism, intolerance, and injustice. In situating Asta between two cultures, as Sow Fall does throughout the novel, a dialogue is fostered, focusing commentary on these subjects as well as others. Her ultimate goal is to "hold a mirror up to society" (both African and European) in order to find solutions to better the lives of human beings.[40] One of the images she challenges is how African immigrants are perceived in Europe, notably France. From the first few pages of her novel, immigration and the lack of humanism present within the immigrant's world are principal topics.

Asta Diop is an accomplished divorcee and single mother, traveling to Paris to attend "la Conférence sur l'Ordre Economique Mondial" [Conference on the Economic World Order]. Knowing the stringent bureaucratic hurdles foreigners must face when entering France, Asta has made sure every possible paper pertaining to her visit is *en règle*:

Elle fouille dans son sac et laisse tomber dans les mains de l'un des policiers tout un paquet de papiers. Non seulement le passeport et le billet d'avion, mais aussi la carte professionnelle, le certificat de résidence (cité baobab no. 1022-Dakar, Sénégal), l'extrait de casier judiciaire, le certificat de nationalité et l'ordre de mission en trois exemplaires. Elle y ajoute, dépliée, la lettre officielle par laquelle l'organisme qui l'emploie est invité à envoyer un représentant à la Conférence sur l'Ordre Economique Mondial. Il y est mentionné que tous les frais de transport et de séjour seront pris en charge par les organisateurs.

[She fished in her handbag for a parcel of papers which she placed in the hands of one of the passport officers. Not only the passport and the airplane ticket, but also her professional identity card, certificate of residence (public housing project "Baobab" no. 1022-Dakar, Senegal), a copy of her police record, a national identity card and assignment papers in triplicate. She adds the official letter of the organization inviting her to the Conference on the Economic World Order. Mentioned is the fact that all transportation and lodging costs are to be paid by the organizers.][41]

Despite the plethora of papers, the passport control officer still has the audacity to ask her, "Qu'êtes vous venue faire?" [What did you come here for?].[42] In his eyes, Asta is nothing more than another *immigrée* seeking asylum in France. It neither occurs to him, nor is it even a consideration, that she might be happy in her own country and want to go back even after he questions her about her return ticket:

–Vous restez combien de temps?
–Une semaine.
–Réservation retour?
–C'est fait. . . . C'est ok sur le billet.
–Réservation hôtel?
–C'est fait. . . . Par les organisateurs de la conférence. C'est indiqué dans la lettre.

["How long are you staying?"
"One week."
"And your return trip?"
"It's made . . . it's all okayed on the ticket."
"Hotel reservation?"
"It's made . . . by the conference organizers. It's all in the letter."][43]

Reading of Asta's confrontation with the white French authorities, we are reminded of Frantz Fanon's words, "I move slowly in the world, accustomed now to seek no longer for upheaval. I progress by crawling. And already I am being dissected under white eyes, the only real eyes. I am fixed . . . I am laid bare."[44] Because she protests against the passport official's aggressive attitude toward her, Asta is subjected to a strip search by a woman in uniform whose "mains gantées lui balaient toutes les parties du corps, passent sous le soutien-gorge, descendent jusqu'aux genoux, remontent sous la jupe. Asta frissonne de dégoût. Elle a le sentiment qu'on la brise" [gloved hands swept all over her body, passing even under her bra, descending down to her knees, going up her skirt. Asta shivers with disgust. She feels as if she is broken].[45] Yet, the most humiliating aspect of the strip search occurs when Asta "réalise qu'une main insolente bifurque et cherche à forcer un passage fermé. Asta serre les jambes. La main insiste" [realizes that a despicable hand goes astray and seeks to penetrate a closed passage. Asta squeezes her legs shut. The hand insists]. It is here where she defends herself, "Jamais!" [Never] she screams.[46] A rage washes over her as she seizes the neck of the female officer between her hands. Asta is blinded by temporary madness due to the humiliation she has endured. The heroine remembers nothing after the incident until she wakes up (she fainted from the sheer humiliation of her ordeal), handcuffed and forced to sit on the floor of the deportation detention center which the detainees have named "layover." It is here where "des noirs, des métis et des arabes pour la plupart tous attendent d'être expulsés vers leurs pays d'origine" [blacks, mulattos and Arabs, for the most part, all wait for expulsion to their country of origin].[47] In this ominous space Asta connects with a global voice that sheds light on the inadequacies of modern human life in the non-European world. These inadequacies lead all the characters to reflect upon not only the racism they have experienced in Europe (as workers and as people of color), but also the injustices they have endured in the everyday life of their homelands.

What sets Sow Fall's novel apart as a major contribution to contemporary feminine francophone writing is that her work depicts an individual woman's humiliation and how it is turned into a positive catalyst for social change. In the novel, Asta's story becomes a national sensation in France and Senegal. Her "incident"—her moment of madness—ends up as a headline in local Parisian papers and in Senegal, benefitting not only the people with whom she passes a week in the Parisian airport detention center, but also people back home because the event fosters dialogue on the difficult lives of immigrants in France. Sow Fall's characters, Yakham, Dianor, Babou, and Séga, fellow deportees, help reinstate Asta's dignity through their conversations concerning race, immigration, and contemporary social issues both in Europe and at home. She discovers through their stories that the lives of others from her country have been as painful as her own. Yakham, who came to France to try his luck, figures he has nothing to lose since he lost his chance to attend a highly selective foreign university because his acceptance letter was never delivered simply because he lived in a slum area where postmen feared to go.[48] Missing his chance to further his education, he leaves for France, accepting out of necessity the lowest paid jobs he can find in the bowels of Les Halles, the central market of Paris. Here he "porter sur [ses] frêles épaules des quartiers de viande lourds à vous briser la colonne vertébrale" [transported meat on his frail shoulders so heavy that it would break your spine].[49] Dianor, an artist, offers the next story telling the others that he was obliged to live with six other men in a one-room apartment in the Foyer du Quartier de la Gare "avec une population cinq fois supérieure à sa capacité, [et] des conditions sanitaires exécrables défiant toute norme d'hygiène, de salubrité et de simple décence" [with a population five times greater than its capacity (and) sanitary conditions that defy all regulations on hygiene, salubrity and simple decency].[50]

The airport's deportation center becomes a forum for discussing the sociocultural and political situations of immigrants in France and the general welfare of people in Senegal and other regions of Africa. Sow Fall plays devil's advocate on a variety of fronts. On the one hand, she condemns France's political policies toward people of color where "le racisme gagne bel et bien du terrain!" [racism is winning ground],[51] while on the other, she takes to task modern day Senegal which has become unbalanced by materialism and the ever present, huge socioeconomic gap that has been created between those who have and those who don't. On another level, the author's goal is also to dispel the misconceptions of her fellow Senegalese that Africa is a wasteland when juxtaposed to France (perceived as the summit of perfection). "Quand on vient ici [en France], on croit toujours aller au Paradis" [When we come here (to France), we always believe it will be Paradise], Yakham remarks at one point. Yet he follows up this observation by affirming the cold reality that he ended up heeding "les conseils de [son] cousin: ne pas [s']aventurer à chercher ailleurs que dans les 'boulots durs' dont les gens d'ici ne veulent pas: bâtiment, enlèvement d'ordures, manutention dans les marchés hebdomadaires ou dans les halles. Tout le reste était risqué à cause des papiers" [the advice of (his) cousin: don't look anywhere except for jobs that are hard and which the people here don't want: construction, waste collection, handling daily produce in open air or covered markets].[52]

France is not Paradise and Africa is not a heart of darkness where intellectual thought processes are held at bay by famine, drought, and poverty. For Sow Fall, Africa and its people share the same kind of hopes and fears as the rest of the world. Evidence of considering humanity with all its trials and tribulations—a humanity extracted from the parameters of racism and xenophobia—is summed up by Anne, who is a white Frenchwoman and a close friend to Asta. Anne asks two rhetorical questions which serve as central themes for the rest of the novel: "Comment exister en cette époque de paradoxes où la misère physique ou morale étale ses plaies dans le ventre même des temples de l'abondance!" [How to exist in this era of paradoxes where physical or moral misery opens wounds in the stomach even of temples of abundance], and How can modern society promote "Tolérance" and uphold ideals such as "Tous les hommes—Sont égaux—Non au racisme—Oui à l'amour—Entre les peuples—Au-delà des races—Et des croyances" [All men—Are equal—No to racism—Yes to love—Between people—Beyond race—And religious beliefs(?)], slogans for which Anne adamantly fought twenty-five years previously and which continue to be relevant today. Anne and Asta both agree that humanity must remain vigilant because all human beings, regardless of color, are confronted more frequently with "la fracture sociale . . . l'avenir bouché des générations actuelles . . . [et] la pauvreté" [fractured society . . . a truncated future for contemporary generations of today . . . and poverty].[53]

A place *beyond race*, Anne asserts, is an *au-delà*, a milieu where racial and gender differences are nullified and the pain of human suffering is lifted. Anne's words mirror Sow Fall's utopian message which promotes the concept of this *au-delà* as a paradise on Earth in Africa. This paradise is, indeed, created by Asta and her companions years after her incident in the Parisian airport. Asta's farm, Naatangue (Wolof for "happiness, abundance and peace"), becomes a sanctuary for her fellow deportees from France. The heroine finds money through financial organizations to fund her project, a lifelong dream that brings "l'ineffable bonheur" [ineffable happiness] because it allows one to "sentir la terre, de communier avec elle quand, de son sein, jaillit la vie, la nourriture qui donne vie et consistance" [smell the earth, to communicate with her when from her breast gushes forth life; food that gives life and sustenance].[54] Naatangue is a place that will convince others that "le Paradis n'est pas forcément ailleurs" [Paradise is not necessarily somewhere else].[55]

In the closing pages of the novel, Naatangue is "in effervescence." Men, women and children from all over the region come together to help celebrate the first true harvest of Asta's farm worked by *Waa Reewu Takh*, "those who come from concrete cities."[56] Almost ten years have elapsed since Asta's incident at the airport where madness overtook her for a brief moment and changed the course of her life. Despite endless hurdles and obstacles due to not only lack of money and resources, but also to the neighboring villagers who originally viewed the newcomers with "un oeil méfiant" [a skeptical eye], Asta succeeds in bringing together her friends whose unique force of knowing nothing of the earth, but nevertheless feeling a strong attachment to it, enables their success.[57] The villagers discover that, like themselves, these urban-misfits-turned-farmers seek to "régénérer tout ce qui pousse" [regenerate all that grows], while also planting other crops from "autres cultures, d'autres espèces pour enrichir le site" [other cultures, other species in order to enrich the site].[58] Symbolically, Sow Fall alludes to a global human connection that can be forged even among people who come from different backgrounds. Working the earth convinces Asta and her compatriots of their "détermination à ne jamais se laisser aller au découragement et au doute" [determination to never give in to discouragement and doubt].[59] Their farm products labeled as "douceurs du bercail" (sweetness of the fold) are sold "partout dans le pays et ailleurs" [everywhere in the country and other places] promoting "l'idée d'une terre généreuse et hospitalière capable de donner plus qu'on lui a offert" [the idea of a generous and hospitable earth capable of giving more than what was offered it].[60]

Sow Fall's novel is a lesson in the strength of the human spirit, as well as a testament to one woman's capacity to construct a world according to a *woman's desire,* as a *free female subject* who lives her life according to a *woman's way.*[61] The author's heroine finds peace on the margins of society, in a space she constructs for herself after a moment of insanity that almost jeopardized her confidence in humanity. Asta's space, like that of Télumée's (and unlike that of Juletane's or Fikria's), is pregnant with tranquility and spirituality, found in her own country. Asta has reached her "potential," something Sow Fall declares that all women have and should put to use in order to take their place of merit in society.[62] Naatangue is not only synonymous with a place of celebration for the life it gives forth to the heroine and the band of misfits from the airport detention center; it is also a statement about the power of humanity to conquer the ills of racism, abjection, poverty, and despair.

The novels of Simon Schwarz-Bart and Aminata Sow Fall are legacies to the perseverence of women as well as homages to these women's dedication to promoting the well-being of humanity. Both authors show us that the female condition is, indeed, part of the larger *condition humaine,* an investment in the lives of others no matter their race, religion, or nationality. These women fight against the dehumanization that is ever present in modern society, ready to engulf both men and women in senseless madness.

Although madness takes many forms depending on the heroines studied in this section, it never effaces these protagonists' own sense of self. Whether the author is Algerian or Senegalese, Cameroonian or Tunisian, for her heroine who has experienced and survived the world "between health and illness, between reason and madness" there will always be "the pronoun I."[63] This "I" is something of which Chems, Mechakra's protagonist, Asta, and Télumée, despite overwhelming odds, never lose sight. To know the "I," the essence of being in the world, is a grounding force for these women. Although they are threatened with effacement for a short time, eventually they re-inscribe a stronger selfhood in a space each has fashioned according to her own set of parameters. As Michel Foucault would contend, madness has acted in these novels as a conduit through which pass "all those words deprived of language whose muffled rumbling, for an attentive ear, [rise] up from the depths of history, [to create a new] language which speaks by itself."[64]

NOTES

1. Kitzie McKinney, "Second Vision: Antillean Versions of the Quest in Two Novels by Simone-Schwarz-Bart," *French Review* 62, no. 4 (March 1989): 650–660, 651.

2. Nicki Hitchcott, *Women Writers in Francophone Africa* (Oxford: Berg Press, 2000), 50.

3. Hitchcott, *Women Writers,* 27.

4. Bridget Jones, introduction to *The Bridge of Beyond* (translation of *Pluie et vent sur Télumée Miracle*) (Portsmouth, N.H.: Heinemann, 1982): iv-xviii, vii.

5. McKinney, "Second Vision," 650.

6. Mckinney, "Second Vision," 650.

7. I have taught this novel numerous times and have always been rewarded by my students' intense reverence for it. Such positive results attest to the novel's timeless pertinence to the perseverance of women, as well as its capacity to generate other debates and discussions around the topics of slavery, racism, and poverty in the developing world.

8. Simone Schwarz-Bart, *Pluie et vent sur Télumée Miracle* (Paris: Seuil, 1972), 40; translated by Barbara Bray under the title *The Bridge of Beyond* (Portsmouth, N.H.: Heinemann, 1982), 23.

9. Schwarz-Bart, *Pluie et vent,* 51, 30.

10. Schwarz-Bart, *Pluie et vent,* 79, 51.

11. Condé, *La Parole,* 15.

12. Schwarz-Bart, *Pluie et vent,* 187, 128.

13. McKinney, "Second Vision," 651.

14. Schwarz-Bart, *Pluie et vent,* 162, 111.

15. Schwarz-Bart, *Pluie et vent,* 144, 98.

16. Lizabeth Paravisini-Gebert, "The Alienation of Power," in *The Woman, the Writer and Caribbean Society,* ed. H. Pyne-Timothy (Los Angeles: University of California Press, 1998): 3–10, 5.

17. Schwarz-Bart, *Pluie et vent,* 195, 133.

18. Schwarz-Bart, *Pluie et vent,* 198, 136.

19. Schwarz-Bart, *Pluie et vent,* 203, 139.

20. Schwarz-Bart, *Pluie et vent,* 200, 137.

21. Schwarz-Bart, *Pluie et vent,* 201, 138.

22. Schwarz-Bart, *Pluie et vent,* 157, 107.

23. Schwarz-Bart, *Pluie et vent,* 166, 113–114.

24. Schwarz-Bart, *Pluie et vent,* 153, 104.

25. Schwarz-Bart, *Pluie et vent,* 153, 104.

26. Deleuze and Guattari, *A Thousand Plateaus,* 279.

27. Deleuze and Guattari, *A Thousand Plateaus,* 280.

28. Schwarz-Bart, *Pluie et vent,* 169, 115.

29. Schwarz-Bart, *Pluie et vent,* 127, 85.

30. McKinney, "Second Vision," 654.

31. Schwarz-Bart, *Pluie et vent,* 248–9, 172–3.

32. The following pages on Sow Fall's work were first published in my article "Writing New H(er)stories for Francophone Women of Africa and the Caribbean," *World Literature Today* (winter 2001): 40–50.

33. Two other women of notable importance writing in the 1970s were Aoua Kéita (*Femme d'Afrique: La Vie d'Aoua Kéita racontée par elle-même* [Paris: Présence Africaine, 1975] and Nafissatou Diallo (*De Tilène au plateau: Une Enfance dakaroise*

[Dakar: Nouvelles Editions Africaines, 1975]). Their works were more autobiographical in scope. (See Christopher Miller, *Theories of Africans,* 250).

34. Hitchcott, *Women Writers,* 89.

35. Hitchcott, *Women Writers,* 90.

36. Irène Assiba d'Almeida, *Francophone African Women Writers: Destroying the Emptiness of Silence* (Gainesville: University Press of Florida, 1994), 12.

37. D'Almeida, *Francophone Writers,* 12.

38. D'Almeida, *Francophone Writers,* 144.

39. D'Almeida, *Francophone Writers,* 125.

40. Françoise Pfaff, "Aminata Sow Fall: L'écriture au féminin," *Notre Librairie* 81 (1985): 135–138, 136.

41. Aminata Sow Fall, *Douceurs du bercail* (Abidjan: Nouvelles Editions Ivoiriennes, 1998), 15–16. All translations of the author's work are my own.

42. Sow Fall, *Douceurs,* 16.

43. Sow Fall, *Douceurs,* 18. The author also states in her novel that her protagonist Asta does not tell the officials that she is really staying at her French friend Anne's apartment during the conference. If the truth were known, Anne would be responsible for obtaining a "certificat d'hébergement visé par l'autorité municipale . . . portant des mentions très précises sur la surface de l'appartement" [a certificate of residence stamped by the municipal authorities . . . mentioning very precisely the size of the apartment](19). Sow Fall here alludes to the stringent French *Loi Debré* which was adopted in 1997 to curtail the harboring of immigrants (illegal or otherwise) for indefinite amounts of time in French homes. The law has been met with much opposition by human rights groups, to no avail.

44. Frantz Fanon, *Black Skin, White Masks* (New York: Grove Press, 1967), 116.

45. Sow Fall, *Douceurs,* 27.

46. Sow Fall, *Douceurs,* 27.

47. Sow Fall, *Douceurs,* 38.

48. Sow Fall, *Douceurs,* 98.

49. Sow Fall, *Douceurs,* 101.

50. Sow Fall, *Douceurs,* 125.

51. Sow Fall, *Douceurs,* 101.

52. Sow Fall, *Douceurs,* 101.

53. Sow Fall, *Douceurs,* 148–149.

54. Sow Fall, *Douceurs,* 200.

55. Sow Fall, *Douceurs,* 201.

56. Sow Fall, *Douceurs,* 203.

57. Sow Fall, *Douceurs,* 204–105.

58. Sow Fall, *Douceurs,* 205–6.

59. Sow Fall, *Douceurs,* 210.

60. Sow Fall, *Douceurs,* 217.

61. Juliet F. Maccannell, *Hysteric's Guide,* xiv–xv. Terms in italics are Maccannell's.

62. See Françoise Pfaff's interview in *"Aminata Sow Fall."*

63. Shoshana Felman, *Writing and Madness* (Ithaca, N.Y.: Cornell University Press, 1994), 66–67.

64. Felman, *Writing and Madness,* 41, citing Foucault's *Histoire de la folie.*

Epilogue
Transgressing Boundaries, Reconstructing Stories

Elle sera de jaspe et de corail
Elle sera de souffle et de feu.

[She will be of jasper and coral
She will be of breath and fire.]

—Werewere Liking, *Elle sera de jaspe et de corail* (1983)

The title of Malika Mokeddem's most recent novel, *N'zid*, in Arabic means "I will continue" as well as "I am born."[1] The novel focuses on a young Algerian woman, Nora, who wakes up on a boat floating aimlessly on the Mediterranean sea, unable to remember her name or why she is there. She is a woman lost between two shores, the East and the West, an Algerian who speaks French, but who desperately seeks to find and return to her true country. Where does her destiny lie? In Algeria, a country torn by civil war and Islamic fundamentalism? Or in France, her country of exile? Nora is a woman caught between two lovers, without family, without a past and, in her state of amnesia, not sure of her future. She is a nomad who sails the seas without home or native land:

"N'zid?": "Je continue?," et aussi: "Je nais." Elle aime la sonorité de ce mot, n'zid. Elle aime l'ambivalence qui l'inscrit entre commencement et poursuite. Elle aime cette dissonance, essence même de son identité. "N'zid," elle aime la voix qui la reconnaît de cette langue, elle qui croyait que son physique n'était nulle part. "N'zid" . . . il faut d'abord être de quelque part pour se sentir étrangère ailleurs.

[N'zid: I continue?, and also, I am born. She liked the sonority of this word, n'zid. She liked its ambivalence inserted between beginning and continuation. She liked this dissonance, the very essence of her identity. "N'zid," she liked the

181

voice that recognized her in this language, she, who believed that her physical being was from nowhere. "N'zid" . . . one had to be from somewhere in order to feel foreign in other places.][2]

Nora recovers from her amnesia and rediscovers her name, but realizes that the only way to "continue" (physically and mentally) is to nomadically wander freely across the seas and the deserts which lie before her. What Nora teaches us about feminine identity is that francophone women from the Afro-Caribbean diaspora are still seeking the essence of their being, somewhere in the in-between spaces of cultures and societies. Nora refuses to be a prisoner anywhere and will never be dominated by any single man or any set of cultural mores. Mokeddem leaves her heroine in flux, drifting in an uncertain space on the edge of self-discovery. This space is liberating and thrilling, foreboding and full of trepidation, yet it is the space of contemporary women who speak out and endeavor to write their h(er)stories. As Claire, of Marie Chauvet's *Amour*, utters, "Je crois pouvoir écrire. Je crois pouvoir penser. Je suis devenue arrogante. J'ai pris conscience de moi" [I believe I can write; I believe I can think; I have become arrogant. I have taken consciousness of myself].[3] Women authors like Chauvet, Mokeddem, Mechakra, Schwarz-Bart, and Sow Fall, as well as the heroines they have produced, are "future female subjects" who have plotted new courses to new *becomings*.[4] These women who have engaged the void of madness and lived to tell their tales "have in common the face they have earned in squaring off against an overpowering force, a horror to which each could have allowed herself to succumb." Women such as Nora, as well as the author who created her, have experienced madness in their lives, yet have lived to overcome it, never doubting that "even if they may have at one time or another given in to it, they have also discovered how to recover, how to stop submitting."[5]

This book has sought to expose the psychoanalytical, philosophical, and literary domains of modern theory that have provided the discursive framework for the contemporary francophone woman writing from (and about) Africa and the Caribbean. Liberation and, in turn, discovery for the female author writing in the francophone context has meant establishing her own rules and philosophies that extend beyond traditional well-known literary and philosophical movements, such as that of the Négritude poets of the earlier part of the twentieth century. While literary and artistic movements such as this accomplished an awareness of an original African consciousness, a *gnosis*, as V. Y. Mudimbé contends,[6] it left women not much better off in terms of sociocultural, political, and economic power than they had been before independence. Women writing in French from the Caribbean, the Maghreb, and sub-Saharan Africa were challenged to find new roads to new modes of identity that would articulate their own unique milieus. New constructions of the self would only come with writing new histories for themselves. Indeed, as Allen Thiher, quoted earlier in my work, attests, "access to a human self and to its world is largely a matter of language."[7] Once women—be they African, Caribbean, or European—infiltrated the world of the written word, they were able to appropriate a whole new language by which to define themselves. This language fostered original forms of discourse by and for women, aiding them to reevaluate their places in society and culture. The written word, as Assia Djebar, Malika Mokeddem, Aminata Sow Fall, and Hajer Djilani, among many others mentioned in this work demonstrate, is the key element in creating a feminine voice that is able to retell history in order to rectify patriarchal and masculinized renditions of it. "Woman must write woman," Hélène Cixous claims in her article "The Laugh of the Medusa." It is necessary for a woman to write because "by writing . . . from and toward women, and by taking up the challenge of speech which has been governed by the phallus . . . women will confirm a place other than that which is reserved in and by the symbolic, that is, in a place other than silence."[8]

The women authors on which this study is based have combated the symbolic and/or masculinized constructions of themselves and entered a milieu that is not silent, but rather full of noise, abjection, and madness. As the heroines who figure in this study confirm, once they assert themselves, decide to live on the margins, contest the societies and patriarchal structures which have hemmed them in, they put themselves at risk. Breaking out of confinement can be violent; a woman who throws off the bonds of servitude risks isolation, alienation, marginalization, and even death. Within the pages of these novels, women cry out through the theme of madness against the ills of the sociocultural mores and strictures that have been placed upon them and their sisters who have been relegated to muted spaces. African and Caribbean women authors, like their western Anglo-European counterparts, have created a "mad double" of themselves to express their own "raging desire to escape" the phallocratic structures that have bound them for centuries. Studying the works of nineteenth-century Anglo-Saxon women authors, literary theorists Sandra Gilbert and Susan Gubar contend:

> the explosive violence of these "moments of escape" that women writers continually imagine for themselves returns to the phenomenon of the mad double so many of these women have projected into their works. For it is, after all, through the violence of the double that the female author enacts her own raging desire to escape male houses and male texts, while at the same time it is through the double's violence that this anxious author articulates for herself the destructiveness of anger repressed until it can no longer be contained.[9]

Bouraoui's heroine, Fikria, Beyala's Tanga, Chauvet's Claire, Warner-Vieyra's Juletane, and Mariama Bâ's Mireille are the doubles par excellence for women authors of the francophone Afro-Caribbean diaspora who have no problem critiquing their societies and asking "where are we going now?" They have placed themselves on the outside, the peripheries of family, tribe, and society. They are a "Society of Outsiders," much like their earlier Anglo-European counterparts such as Virginia Woolf and Charlotte Brontë, who professed that, in order to transform the world, the female author had to exist in the margins of her society.[10] Yet, as Virginia Woolf wondered a century ago, what will be the fate of women who live outside the norm? Indeed she spent a lifetime wondering and pondering this question until her suicide.

As the postcolonial era takes on new contours in the African diaspora, women who write are asking the same questions: Now that we have broken free of the masks men have made for us, what will be our fate, where will we go? What price do we have to pay when we speak out, become one of the *Outsiders*? Has engaging a mad space been worth risking family, tribe, and culture in order to be heard? Does becoming a medusa, going against the grain, taking the lead, being bad girls in the margins who challenge the archetypes of convention achieve anything positive for us? I believe that the authors studied here would answer "yes," it has been worth it. Engaging the realm of the "unsayable," the madness that lurks in the margins of established norms of society, has been the only way to break out of the mold, to sail a boat to the other side of an unknown sea. "La femme doit agir par elle-même, et s'imposer en littérature" [a woman must act for herself and impose herself in litterature], contends Aminata Sow Fall. It is only through the strength of women and their perseverence in saying the unsayable that societies will change, dialogues be fostered, and new beginnings begun.

The women who arrive at the other side of unknown oceans and uncharted spaces discover a new womanhood, or a *womanism,* as African American author Alice Walker defines the realm of humanism in which women take active roles. This realm is that of the *Misovire*, Cameroonian playwright Werewere Liking's term for women who seek to find a new language for women. The Misovire is a woman who wants to exist out from under the tutelage of men; it's a word to "fill a void" and to describe a woman who wants to find her own self and live on her own terms.[11] In French, there are the words "misanthrope" and "misogyne," but until Liking invented the word "misovire," there was no word to describe a woman who feels that she doesn't need a man. Scholar Irène d'Almeida contends that Werewere Liking's word

> is critical in that it shows how gender ideology pervades all spheres of human endeavor, including linguistic constructions. It is precisely to counter these forms of dominant patriarchal ideologies that Liking, who is an expert at mixing categories, combines Greek and Latin components to invent misovire.[12]

A misovire is not exactly a "man-hater," Liking contests, but more a word for "une femme qui n'arrive pas à trouver un homme admirable" [A woman who cannot find an admirable man].[13] In the misovire context, the notion of an admirable man could be extended to include an admirable community, a humanity that respects women and in which women want to involve themselves. Liking's term, if expanded to also mean a woman who wishes to counter phallocratic structures and male-dominated histories, embraces the foundation of a new African feminism "that tolerates no exclusion, a humanism capable of transforming society as a whole."[14] Liking's humanism, in the same manner as Aminata Sow Falls and Simone Schwarz-Bart, "subverts women's traditional position . . . [in order to] impose their views in a way that makes them hammer out society's destiny."[15] These women not only address women's issues but also larger social topics linked to being a woman within the Afro-Caribbean diaspora. They seek the "divine spark" that will be found in all human beings. It is this spark that Werewere Liking suggests will guard the people of Africa from total corruption and lead to the continent's rebirth:

> [T]his divine spark which is in human beings, cannot submit to total corruption. Even if we have the impression at a certain moment that everything is corrupt. It is not because the diamond is covered in mud that the diamond becomes mud. I am not worried, I am sorry sometimes to live in this period where we have not attained the hour of shining in the sun . . . by ourselves. I think that work is underway. A birth is preparing to be born . . . all that we are trying to do is to bring to our little stone this rebirth.[16]

Liking and other francophone women authors know that the rebirth of their history, written in their own fashion, will be difficult to realize. There will be times when these women, like their heroines, will admit, as does Télumée in *Pluie et Vent,* that "nous n'habitons plus la terre ferme . . . nous sommes dans la haute mer et les courants" [We no longer live on solid earth . . . we're out at sea amid the currents] wondering "si [nous allons nous] noyer comme ça du premier coup" [whether (we're) going to drown outright].[17] However, for those who have seen and experienced madness and, in turn, learned to "ride the horse and not let it ride them," the paths and ways are left open.[18] And when we ask these women what they hope to do and accomplish as they plot their courses for new feminine destinies, they will most probably answer, "N'zid."

NOTES

1. Malika Mokeddem, *N'zid* (Paris: Seuil, 2001).
2. Mokeddem, *N'zid,* 160–161. My translation.
3. Chauvet, *Amour,* 10.
4. Maccannell, *Hysteric's Guide,* 265.
5. Maccannell, *Hysteric's Guide,* 265.
6. V. Y. Mudimbé, *The Invention of Africa* (Bloomington: Indiana University Press, 1988), ix.

7. Allen Thiher, *Revels in Madness*, 4.

8. Cixous, "Laugh at the Medusa," 338.

9. Gilbert and Gubar, *The Madwoman*, 85.

10. Gilbert and Gubar, *The Madwoman*, 205.

11. D'Almeida, *Francophone Writers*, 21.

12. D'Almeida, *Francophone Writers*, 20–21.

13. D'Almeida, *Francophone Writers*, 21.

14. D'Almeida, *Francophone Writers*, 21.

15. Siga Asanga et al., *Introduction to Ritual Theater: The Power of Um and A New Earth* (San Francisco: International Scholars Publications, 1996): 7–24, 7.

16. Christine Pillot, "Le Vivre vrai de Werewere Liking," *Notre Librairie* 102 (July–August 1990): 54–58, 58.

17. Schwarz-Bart, *Pluie et vent*, 145, 98.

18. Actually, the phrase from Schwarz-Bart's novel is: "But the horse mustn't ride you, you must ride it" (Bray, *The Bridge of Beyond*, 51).

Bibliography

Accad, Evelyn. *Sexuality and War: Literary Masks of the Middle East*. New York: New York University Press, 1990.

Ali-Benali, Zineb. "Dires de la folie: dires de la liberté. Discours de la folie dans la littérature des femmes en Algérie." *Bulletin of Francophone Africa* 7 (spring 1995): 9–25.

Amrane-Mine, Danièle Djamila. *Des Femmes dans la guerre d'Algérie*. Paris: Editions Karthala, 1994.

Asanga, Siga, et al., eds. and trans. *Introduction to Ritual Theater: The Power of Um and A New Earth*, by Werewere Liking. San Francisco: International Scholars Publications, 1996: 7–24.

Ashcroft, Bill, et al. *The Empire Writes Back: Theory and Practice in Post-Colonial Literatures*. New York: Routledge, 1989.

Astbury, Jill. *Crazy for You: The Making of Women's Madness*. Melbourne: Oxford University Press, 1996.

Bâ, Mariama. *Un Chant écarlate*. Dakar: Les Nouvelles Editions Africaines, 1981.

Badji, Bougoul. *La Folie en Afrique: Une rivalité pathologique*. Paris: L'Harmattan, 1993.

Bataille, Georges. *Erotism: Death and Sensuality*. San Francisco: City Lights, 1986.

Begag, Azouz, and Abdellatif Chaouite. *Ecarts d'identité*. Paris: Seuil, 1990.

Beyala, Calixthe. *Tu t'appelleras Tanga*. Paris: Editions Stock, 1986. Translated by Marjolijn de Jager under the title *Your Name Shall be Tanga*. (Portsmouth, N.H.: Heinneman, 1996).

Bhabha, Homi. *The Location of Culture*. New York: Routledge, 1994.

Boer, Inge. "The World Beyond Our Window: Nomads, Traveling Theories and the Function of Boundaries." *Parallax* 3 (September 1996): 7–26.

Bordo, Susan. *Unbearable Weight: Feminism, Western Culture, and the Body*. Berkeley: University of California Press, 1993.

Bouraoui, Nina. *La Voyeuse Interdite*. Paris: Gallimard, 1991. Translated by Melissa Marcus under the title *Forbidden Vision*. (Barrytown, N.Y.: Station Hill, 1995).

Brahimi, Denise. *Requiem pour Isabelle*. Paris: Publisud, 1983.

Braidotti, Rosi. *Nomadic Subjects.* New York: Columbia University Press, 1994.

Capécia, Mayotte. *Je suis martiniquaise.* Paris: Corrêa, 1948.

Carreteiro, Teresa C. *Exclusion sociale et construction de l'identité.* Paris: L'Harmattan, 1993.

Chauvet, Marie Vieux. *Amour, Colère, et Folie.* Paris: Gallimard, 1968.

Chesler, Phyllis. *Women and Madness.* New York: Four Walls, 1997.

Cixous, Hélène. "The Laugh of the Medusa." In *Feminisms,* ed. R. Warhol et al. Brunswick, N.J.: Rutgers University Press, 1991.

Condé, Maryse. "Language and Power." *College Language Association Journal* 39, no. 1 (September 1995): 18–25.

———. *La Parole des femmes: Essai sur des romancières des Antilles et de langue française.* Paris: L'Harmattan, 1979.

Corzani, Jack, et al. "Antilles-Guyane." In *Littératures francophones: Les Amériques: Haïti, Antilles-Guyane, Québec.* Paris: Belin-Sup, 1998.

Cottenet-Hage, Madeleine. "Violence Libératoire/Violence Mutilatoire dans Amour de Marie Chauvet." *Francophonia* 6 (spring 1984): 17–28.

D'Almeida, Irène. *Francophone African Women Writers: Destroying the Emptiness of Silence.* Gainesville: University Press of Florida, 1994.

Davies, Carole Boyce, and Anne Adams Graves. *Ngambika: Studies of Women in African Literature.* Trenton, N.J.: Africa World Press, 1986.

Delacour, Marie-Odile and Jean-René Huleu. *Yasmina et autres nouvelles algériennes d'Isabelle Eberhardt.* 5th ed. Paris: Liana Levi, 1998.

Deleuze, Gilles, and Félix Guattari. *Anti-Oedipus: Capitalism and Schizophrenia.* Minneapolis: University of Minnesota Press, 1983.

———. *The Fold: Leibniz and the Baroque.* University of Minnesota Press, 1993.

———. *A Thousand Plateaus.* University of Minnesota Press, 1987.

De Man, Paul. *"Autobiography as De-facement." MLN* 94 (1979): 925.

Djebar, Assia. *Les Enfants du nouveau monde.* Paris: Julliard, 1962.

———. *Oran, langue morte.* Paris: Actes Sud, 1997.

Djilani, Hajer. *Et pourtant le ciel était bleu. . . . Roman.* Sidi Bou Saïd, Tunisia: Editions Techniques Spécialisées, 1994.

Eberhardt, Isabelle. *Rakhil.* Paris: La Boîte à Documents, 1990.

Ebert, Teresa. *Ludic Feminism and After: Postmodernism, Desire, and Labor in Late Capitalism.* Ann Arbor: University of Michigan Press, 1996.

Fanon, Frantz. *Black Skin, White Masks.* New York: Grove Press, 1967.

———. *A Dying Colonialism.* New York: Grove Press, 1965.

———. *The Wretched of the Earth.* New York: Grove, 1963.

Felman, Shoshana. "Women and Madness." In *Feminisms,* ed. R. Warhol et al., 6–19. New Brunswick, N.J.: Rutgers University Press, 1991.

———. *Writing and Madness: Literature, Philosophy, Psychoanalysis.* Ithaca, N.Y.: Cornell University Press, 1994.

Fetzer, Glenn. "Women's Search for Voice and the Problem of Knowing." *Baltimore College Language Association Publication* 35 (September 1991): 31–41.

Foucault, Michel. *Discipline and Punish.* New York: Vintage, 1979.

———. *Histoire de la folie à l'âge classique.* Paris: Gallimard, 1972.

Freud, Sigmund. "The Ego and the Id." In *The Standard Edition of the Complete Psychological Works of Sigmund Freud.* Vol. 19. London: Hogarth, 1961.

Gilbert, Sandra, and Susan Gubar. *The Madwoman in the Attic.* New Haven, Conn.: Yale University Press, 1979.

Grosz, Elizabeth. *Volatile Bodies: Toward a Corporeal Feminism.* Bloomington: Indiana University Press, 1994.

Habermas, Jürgen. *Moral Consciousness and Communicative Action.* Cambridge, Mass.: MIT Press, 1993.

Hargreaves, Alec. *Immigration and Identity in Beur Fiction.* Oxford: Berg Press, 1997.

Hitchcott, Nicki. *Women Writers in Francophone Africa.* Oxford: Berg, 2000.

Houari, Leïla. *Zeida de nulle part.* Paris: L'Harmattan, 1985.

Jack, Belinda. *Francophone Literatures: A Survey.* Oxford: Oxford University Press, 1996.

Jay, Martin. *Downcast Eyes: The Denigration of Vision in Twentieth-Century French Thought.* Berkeley: University of California Press, 1994.

Kay, Jacqueline, and Abdelhamid Zoubir. *The Ambiguous Compromise: Language, Literature, and National Identity in Algeria and Morocco.* London: Routledge, 1990.

King, Adele. "The Personal and the Political in the Work of Mariama Bâ." *Studies in 20th Century Literature* 18, no. 2 (summer 1994): 177–88.

Kristeva, Julia. *Strangers to Ourselves.* Translated by Leon S. Roudiez. New York: Columbia University Press, 1991.

Lacascade, Suzanne. *Claire-Solange, âme africaine.* Paris: Eugène Figuière, 1924.

Lacrosil, Michèle. *Cajou.* Paris: Gallimard, 1961.

Lahens, Yanick. "L'apport de quatre romancières au roman moderne haïtien." *Notre Librairie* 33 (January–April 1998): 26–36.

Laing, Ronald. D. *The Divided Self.* New York: Pantheon, 1960.

Laronde, Michel. *Autour le roman beur.* Paris: L'Harmattan, 1993.

———. *L'Ecriture décentrée: La langue de l'Autre dans le roman contemporain.* Paris: L'Harmattan, 1996.

Larrier, Renée. *Francophone Women Writers of Africa and the Caribbean.* Gainesville: University Press of Florida, 2000.

Lazreg, Marnia. *The Eloquence of Silence: Algerian Women in Question.* New York: Routledge, 1994.

Liking, Werewere. *Elle sera de jaspe et de corail.* Paris: L'Harmattan, 1983.

Lionnet, Françoise. "Geographies of Pain: Captive Bodies and Violent Acts in the Fictions of Myriam Warner-Vieyra, Gayl Jones, and Bessie Head." *Callaloo* 16, no. 1 (1993): 132–152.

———. "Inscriptions of Exile: The Body's Knowledge and the Myth of Authenticity." *Callaloo* 15, no. 1 (1992): 30–40.

Maccannell, Juliette Flower. *The Hysteric's Guide to the Future Female Subject.* Minneapolis: University of Minnesota Press, 2000.

Makward, Christiane. "Cherchez la Franco-femme." In *Postcolonial Subjects: Francophone Women Writers,* ed. Mary Jean Green et al., 115–123. Minneapolis: University of Minnesota Press, 1996.

Mayes, Janis A. "Mind-Body-Soul: Erzulie Embodied in Marie Chauvet's Amour, Colère, Folie." *Journal of Caribbean Studies* 7, no. 1 (spring 1989): 81–89.

McClintock, Anne. *Imperial Leather: Race, Gender, and Sexuality in the Colonial Contest.* New York: Routledge, 1995.

McKinney, Kitzie. "Second Vision: Antillean Versions of the Quest in Two Novels by Simone Schwarz-Bart." *The French Review* 62, no. 4 (March 1989): 650–660.

Mechakra, Yamina. *La Grotte éclatée*. Algiers: Editions SNED, 1979.

Merleau-Ponty, Maurice. *Phenomenology of Perception*. New York: Routledge, 1996.

Mernissi, Fatima. *Beyond the Veil: Male-Female Dynamics in Modern Muslim Society*. Bloomington: Indiana University Press, 1987.

———. *Doing Daily Battle: Interviews with Moroccan Women*. New Brunswick, N.J.: Rutgers University Press, 1989.

———. *The Forgotten Queens of Islam*. Minneapolis: University of Minnesota Press, 1993.

Miller, Christopher. *Theories of Africans*. Chicago: University of Chicago Press, 1990.

Mokeddem, *L'Interdite*. Paris: Grasset, 1993.

———. Malika. *Le Siècle des sauterelles*. Paris: Ramsay, 1992.

———. *N'Zid*. Paris: Seuil, 2001.

Mortimer, Mildred. "Interview with Myriam Warner-Vieyra." *Callaloo* 16, no. 1 (1993): 108–115.

Mudimbé, V. Y. *The Invention of Africa: Gnosis, Philosophy, and the Order of Knowledge*. Bloomington: Indiana University Press, 1988.

Mudimbé-Boyi, Elisabeth. "Narrative 'Je(ux)' in *Kamouraska* and *Juletane*." In *Postcolonial Subjects: Francophone Women Writers*, ed. M. J. Green et al. Minneapolis: University of Minnesota Press, 1996.

Nfah-Abbenyi, Juliana Makuchi. "Calixthe Beyala's 'femme-fillette': Womanhood and the Politics of (M)othering." In *The Politics of (M)othering: Womanhood, Identity and Resistance in African Literature*. ed. Obioma Nnaemeka, 101–113. New York: Routledge, 1997.

———. *Gender in African Women's Writing: Identity, Sexuality, and Difference*. Bloomington: Indiana University Press, 1997.

Ngate, Jonathan. "Reading Warner-Vieyra's *Juletane*." *Callaloo* 9, no. 4 (1986): 553–563.

Noiriel, Gérard. *The French Melting Pot: Immigration, Citizenship, and National Identity*. Minneapolis: University of Minnesota Press, 1996.

O'Callaghan, Evelyn. "The Bottomless Abyss: 'Mad' Women in Some Caribbean Novels." *Bulletin of Eastern Caribbean Affairs* 11, no. 1 (March–April 1985): 45–58.

———. "Interior Schisms Dramatized: The Treatment of the 'Mad' Woman in the Work of Some Female Caribbean Novelists." *Out of Kumbla: Caribbean Women and Literature*, ed. Carole Boyce Davis et al., 89–109. Trenton, N.J.: African World Press, 1990.

Orlando, Valérie. *Nomadic Voices of Exile: Feminine Identity in Francophone Literature of the Maghreb*. Athens: Ohio University Press, 1999.

———. "Writing New H(er)stories for Francophone Women of Africa and the Caribbean." *World Literature Today* 75, no. 1 (winter 2001): 40–50.

Paravisini-Gebert, Lizabeth. "The Alienation of Power: The Woman Writer and the Planter-Heroine in Caribbean Literature." In *The Woman, The Writer and Caribbean Society*, ed. Helen Pyne-Timothy. Los Angeles: University of California Press, 1998.

Pfaff, Françoise. "Aminata Sow Fall: l'écriture au féminin." *Notre Librairie* 81 (1995): 135–38.

Pillot, Christine. *"Le Vivre vrai de Werewere Liking."* *Notre Librairie* 102 (July–August 1990): 54–58.

Ruedy, John. *Modern Algeria: The Origins and Development of a Nation.* Bloomington: Indiana University Press, 1992.

Scharfman, Ronnie. "Theorizing Terror: The Discourse of Violence in Marie Chauvet's Amour, Colère, Folie." In *Postcolonial Subjects,* ed. Mary J. Green et al. Minneapolis: University of Minnesota Press, 1996.

Schwarz-Bart, Simone. *Pluie et Vent sur Télumée Miracle.* Paris: Seuil, 1972. Translated by Barbara Bray under the title *The Bridge of Beyond.* (Portsmouth, N.H.: Heinemann, 1982).

Sharpley-Whiting, T. Denean. *Frantz Fanon: Conflicts and Feminisms.* Lanham: Rowman & Littlefield, 1998.

———. *Negritude Women.* Minneapolis: University of Minnesota Press, 2002.

———. *Sexualized Savages, Primal Fears, and Primitive Narratives in French.* Durham, N.C.: Duke University Press, 1999.

Shipper, Mineke. "Mother Africa on a Pedestal: The Male Heritage in African Literature and Criticism." *African Literature Today* 15 (1987): 35–57.

Shohat, Ella, and Robert Stam. *Unthinking Eurocentrism: Multiculturalism and the Media.* New York: Routledge, 1994.

Sow Fall, Aminata. *Douceurs du bercail.* Abidjan: Nouvelles Editions Ivoiriennes, 1998.

Spivak, Gayatri. *In Other Worlds: Essays in Culture and Politics.* New York: Routledge, 1988.

Stora, Benjamin. *La Gangrène et l'oubli: La mémoire de la guerre d'Algérie.* Paris: La Découverte, 1991.

Szasz, Thomas. *Ideology and Insanity: Essays on the Psychiatric Dehumanization of Man.* New York: Doubleday, 1970.

Tahon, Marie-Blanche. "Women Novelists and Women in the Struggle for Algeria's National Liberation (1957–1980)." *Research in African Literatures* 2 (summer 1992): 39–49.

Taylor, Charles. *Multiculturalism.* Princeton, N.J.: Princeton University Press, 1994.

Thiam, Awa. *La parole aux négresses.* Paris: Denoël, 1978.

Thiher, Allen. *Revels in Madness: Insanity in Medicine and Literature.* Ann Arbor: University of Michigan Press, 1999.

Van Den Abbeele, Georges. *Travel as Metaphor: From Montaigne to Rousseau.* Minneapolis: University of Minnesota Press, 1992.

Vergès, Françoise. *Monsters and Revolutionaries: Colonial Family Romance and Métissage.* Durham, N.C.: Duke University Press, 1999.

Walker, Keith. *Countermodernism and Francophone Literary Culture: The Game of Slipknot.* Durham, N.C.: Duke University Press, 1999.

Warner-Vieyra, Myriam. *Juletane.* Dakar: Présence Africaine, 1982.

Zimra, Clarisse. "Haitian Literature after Duvalier: An Interview with Yanick Lahens." *Callaloo* 16, no. 1 (1993): 77–93.

Index